KEYS to STUDY SKILLS

Opening Doors to Learning

Carol Carter
Joyce Bishop
Mary Bixby
Sarah Lyman Kravits

Prentice Hall
Upper Saddle River, New Jersey 07458

D1378163

Library of Congress Cataloging-in-Publication Data

Keys to study skills : opening doors to learning / Carol Carter ...
  [et al.]
    p.   cm.
  Includes bibliographical references and index.
  ISBN 0-13-917915-1 (pbk.)
    1. Study skills—United States.   2. College student orientation—
United States. I. Carter, Carol.
LB2395.K357 1999
378.1′70281—dc21   98-33550
                                     CIP

Our Mission Statement

Our mission is to give all students the tools that will help them excel in college as well as succeed in the complex world that awaits them after they complete their course of study. We aim to help students understand how they learn, hone their study skills, set and achieve their goals, manage their daily lives, take advantage of the resources and opportunities that their schools offer, and learn throughout their lives so that they continue to successfully experience the challenges and rewards that make life meaningful.

Acquisitions editor: *Sue Bierman*
Publisher: *Carol Carter*
Production editor: *Gail Gavin*
Production liaison: *Barbara Marttine Cappuccio*
Director of manufacturing and production: *Bruce Johnson*
Managing editor: *Mary Carnis*
Manufacturing buyer: *Marc Bove*
Marketing manager: *Jeff McIlroy*
Editorial assistant: *Michelle M. Williams*
Creative director: *Marianne Frasco*
Interior design: *Jill Little*
Cover design: *Liz Nemeth*
Cover illustraiton: *Paul Anderson*
Interior photos: *Sarah Lyman Kravits*
Formatting/page makeup: *The Clarinda Company*

©1999 by Prentice-Hall, Inc.
Simon & Schuster / A Viacom Company
Upper Saddle River, New Jersey 07458

Printed in the United States of America
10 9 8 7 6 5 4 3 2 1

ISBN 0-13-917915-1

Prentice-Hall International (UK) Limited, *London*
Prentice-Hall of Australia Pty. Limited, *Sydney*
Prentice-Hall Canada Inc., *Toronto*
Prentice-Hall Hispanoamericana, S.A., *Mexico*
Prentice-Hall of India Private Limited, *New Delhi*
Prentice-Hall of Japan, Inc., *Tokyo*
Simon & Schuster Asia Pte. Ltd., *Singapore*
Editora Prentice-Hall do Brasil, Ltda., *Rio de Janeiro*

CONTENTS

FOREWORD

As the student editor for *Keys to Study Skills*, it was important to me that this book really address my needs as a student. Like so many of you, my days are overflowing with classes, homework, research, part-time work, extracurricular activities—you name it. If I'm going to take a class on study skills and read a whole book on it, I need to feel that I'm getting something concrete out of the time and energy I'm putting in.

Well, I believe that this book fits the bill. In fact, although the book and the course have taken time to complete, in the long run they have actually ended up *saving* me time. Knowing how I learn best helps me tailor my studying to my learning style so that I don't waste time on methods that don't work for me. Setting specific goals helps me focus my energy instead of wasting my time wondering what path to take. Improving my study skills helps me get more studying done in less time. Working on my time management helps me decide on the most efficient way to take care of my responsibilities—while still having time for those necessary basics like dinner, time with friends, and sleep.

The authors wrote this book with the following purpose in mind: to make your study habits—and your student life—more efficient, more effective, and more focused. However, they didn't intend for you to use its ideas only while in school. The tools this book offers will serve you in the workplace as well as in your personal life. They will help you excel in whatever you do and continue to learn and grow well beyond your formal education. They are truly tools for life.

College is only the beginning of a life full of challenges and choices. Having *Keys to Study Skills* as a resource will help you make decisions that lead you to become everything you have the potential to be. This book and the course, however, are not enough—energy and dedication are crucial ingredients. Take responsibility for your success by putting your energy into your studies, both in this course and in your future. You will not regret it.

*Julie Wheeler, Student Editor,
University of Colorado at Denver*

PREFACE

Keys to Study Skills Owner and Operator's Manual

When you spend money on a coffeemaker, electric drill, television, car, tape deck, or anything else, getting your money's worth means knowing how to operate your purchase so that it delivers what you want (good coffee, perhaps, or clear channel reception, or high-speed dubbing). When you bring the item home, you generally look over the manual or pamphlet that comes with it before you do anything else, because you want to operate this appliance correctly and efficiently. The manual describes the parts, how they operate, and what should result if everything is functioning properly. With that in mind, think of this preface as your owner's manual for this book; likewise, think of this book as your owner/operator's manual to how you approach learning. Reading it will help you make the most of your reading and your work in this course.

We, your authors, have talked to and worked with students of all ages, backgrounds, and stages of life. We've learned that you are concerned about your future, you want your education to serve a purpose, you are adjusting to constant life changes, and you want honest and direct guidance on how to achieve your goals. We designed the features of *Keys to Study Skills* based on what you have told us about your needs. Knowing how to use the features in this book—and make the most from your work in this class—will help you maximize the time, effort, and money you are putting into your education.

Following are descriptions of the different pieces of this book and how to use them to your advantage.

The Contents of the Package: What's Included

We chose the topics in this book based on what you need to make the most of your edu-

cational experience. You need to understand your *learning styles* in order to discover and pursue the best course of study. You need good *reading, listening, memory, note-taking* and *math and science skills* to take in, understand, and retain what you learn both in and out of class. You need *writing* and *test-taking skills* to be able to express and show what you know and what you think. You need to know how to excel in *time management* and *goal-setting* so that you can weather life's shifts and feel comfortable in this ever-changing world. *Keys to Study Skills* can guide you in all of these areas and more.

The Parts: Useful Features

The features (distinguishing characteristics and sections) of this book are designed to make your life easier by helping you take in and understand the material you read.

Lifelong Learning. If what you study in this course only helped you read textbooks and pass tests, its usefulness would end at graduation, and you would have to start all over to learn how to deal with the real world. The ideas and strategies you learn that will help you succeed in school are the same ones that will bring you success in your career and in your personal life. Therefore, this book focuses on study success strategies for *in-school* purposes and then goes on to apply them to *work* and *personal life* as well.

Thinking Skills. Being able to remember facts and figures won't do you much good, at school or beyond, unless you can put that information to work through clear and competent thinking. This book has a chapter on *critical thinking* that will help you explore your mind's seven primary actions—the building blocks to competent thinking. You will also see how to combine those actions in order to perform thinking processes such as problem solving, decision making, and strategic planning.

Skill-building Exercises. Today's graduates need to be effective thinkers, team players, writers, and strategic planners. The exercises at the end of the chapters will encourage you to develop these valuable career skills and to apply thinking processes to any topic or situation.

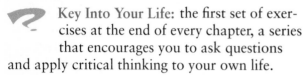 **Key Into Your Life:** the first set of exercises at the end of every chapter, a series that encourages you to ask questions and apply critical thinking to your own life.

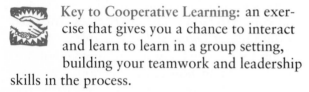 **Key to Cooperative Learning:** an exercise that gives you a chance to interact and learn to learn in a group setting, building your teamwork and leadership skills in the process.

Key to Self-Expression: a journal-writing exercise that provides an opportunity for you to express your thoughts, discover more about yourself, and develop your writing ability.

Key to Your Personal Portfolio: an exercise that enables you to gather and organize concrete evidence of your learning, through the writing of an essay that unites what you have learned in the chapter with your own personal thoughts, needs, and experience.

Diversity of Voice. The world is becoming increasingly diverse in ethnicities, perspectives, cultures, lifestyles, races, choices, abilities, needs, and more. Every student, instructor, course, and school is unique. One point of view can't possibly apply to everyone. Therefore, many voices will speak to you from these pages. What you read will speak to your needs, offer ideas, and treat you with respect.

➤ *Real World Perspectives,* a question-and-answer feature, will appear once per chapter. In it, one person will present a question about an issue in his or her life, and another person who has had similar experiences will give advice in response.

➤ *Examples* throughout the text deal with the different situations that different students face—working while in school, parenting,

dealing with different financial needs, supporting various lifestyles and schedules, and so on.

➤ The *exercises* throughout the book recognize and reinforce your uniqueness; they are designed so that you apply what you learn to the particulars of your own life.

Using the Parts: Helpful Hints for Operation

We've worked to make this book as user-friendly as possible. The following features will make your life easier in small but significant ways.

➤ **Book length.** There's always more to say, but we've tried to say it in as few words as possible. We know you only have so much reading time in your life.

➤ **Perforations.** Each page of this book is perforated so you can tear out exercises to hand in, should your instructor ask you to do so. You can also tear out sections if you like, perhaps to take with you somewhere or to keep in your datebook as a reference.

➤ **Exercises.** The exercises are together at the ends of the chapters. If you want to hand them all in you can do so without removing any of the text. There is a space at the beginning of the exercises for you to write your name.

➤ **Definitions.** Selected words are defined in the margins of the text. If you don't know these words, the definitions save you a trip to the dictionary; if you do know them, the definitions offer a quick and easy refresher.

➤ **Long-term usefulness.** Yes, most people sell back some of the textbooks they use. If you take a good look at the material in *Keys to Study Skills,* however, you may want to keep this book around. We know that you are concerned about the competitiveness of the job market, your future careers, and your quality of life. *Keys to Study Skills* is a reference that you can return to over and over again as you work toward your goals.

Take Action: Read

You are responsible for your education, your growth, your knowledge, and your future. If you know yourself, choose the right paths, and follow them with determination, you will earn the success that you deserve in school, the workplace, and your personal life. The best we can do is offer some great tools—suggestions, strategies, ideas, and structures—that can help. Ultimately, however, it's up to you to use them. So take whatever tools fit your personality with all of your particular situations, needs, and wants, and make them your own. You've made a terrific start by choosing to pursue an education—now take advantage of all that it can give you. Good luck!

ACKNOWLEDGMENTS

No co-author team is an island. Many people have contributed their time, energy, and hard work to this book, and we would like to take this opportunity to recognize them. Our heartfelt appreciation to:

- Doug Clark, math guy extraordinaire from the University of Missouri-Columbia Learning Center, for his great math, science, and computer materials.

- Dr. Dorothy Watson, award-winning professor from MU, whom Mary credits with helping her find her "teacher-self."

- The faculty, staff, and students who have been involved with the adventure known as "Learning Strategies for College Students" for the past ten years at old "Mizzou."

- The students at Golden State who have allowed Joyce, as their professor, the privilege of sharing part of their journey through college.

- Sue Bierman, our acquisitions editor, for her tireless commitment, keen insights, and unflappable good humor.

- Jeff McIlroy, our marketing manager, for his stellar efforts on the web site and in the field.

- Our student editor, Julie Wheeler, for her hard work, advice, and the foreword.

- Our fabulous production team, especially Barbara Cappuccio, Mary Carnis, Marianne Frasco, Marc Bove, Ed O'Dougherty, and Gail Gavin and the folks at Clarinda, whose expertise and thoroughness have made this book happen.

- Sabrina Friedman for naming and helping the "Learning Doctor."

- Scott Halvorson and Mike Kagan for their assistance with the photo program.

- Dr. Frank T. Lyman, Jr., for being a constant source of ideas, advice, and support.

Much of the material in this book is derived from the first edition of *Keys to Effective Learning*. In recognition of their role in *Keys to Effective Learning*, we thank:

- Student reviewers Sandi Armitage, Marisa Connell, Jennifer Moe, and Alex Toth for their insightful comments.

- Our reviewers, for their advice and excellent guidance: Glenda Belote—Florida International University; John Bennett, Jr.—University of Connecticut; Ann Bingham-Newman—California State University-LA; Barbara Blandford—Education Enhancement Center at Lawrenceville, NJ; Jerry Bouchie—St. Cloud State University; Mona Casady—SW Missouri State University; Janet Cutshall—Sussex County Community College, NJ; Valerie DeAngelis—Miami-Dade Community College; Rita Delude—NH Community Technical College; Judy Elsley—Weber State University in Utah; Sue Halter—Delgado Community College in Louisiana, Suzy Hampton—University of Montana; Maureen Hurley—University of Missouri-Kansas City; Karen Iversen—Heald Colleges; Kathryn K. Kelly—St. Cloud State University; Nancy Kosmicke—Mesa State College in Colorado; Frank T. Lyman, Jr.—University of Maryland; Barnette Miller Moore—Indian River Community College in Florida; Rebecca Munro—Gonzaga University in Washington; Virginia Phares—DeVry of

Atlanta; Brenda Prinzavalli—Beloit College in Wisconsin; Jacqueline Simon—Education Enhancement Center at Lawrenceville, NJ; Carolyn Smith—University of Southern Indiana; Joan Stottlemeyer—Carroll College in Montana; Thomas Tyson—SUNY Stony Brook, NY; Rose Wassman—DeAnza College in California; Michelle G. Wolf—Florida Southern College.

➤ The folks at Baltimore City Community College, Liberty Campus—College President Dr. Jim Tschechtelin, Co-ordinator Jim Coleman, and the PRE 100 instructors, especially Rita Lenkin Hawkins, Sonia Lynch, Jack Taylor, and Peggy Winfield. Many thanks also to Alice Barr, the Prentice Hall representative who so comprehensively serves BCCC.

➤ The instructors at DeVry, especially Susan Chin and Carol Ozee, for their support and suggestions.

➤ The instructors at Suffolk Community College, and Prentice Hall representative Carol Abolafia, for their helpful comments.

➤ Our editorial consultant, Rich Bucher, professor of sociology at Baltimore City Community College, who provided important advice and consultation on diversity.

➤ Dr. Frank T. Lyman, Jr., for his generous permission to use and adapt his his Think-trix system.

➤ Professor Barbara Soloman for again granting the use of her Learning Styles Inventory.

➤ The generous people who contributed their stories for *Real World Perspectives:* Clacy Albert, Kathleen Cole, Erica Epstein, Norma Espina, Jeff Felardeau, Edith Hall, Jacque Hall, Mike Jackson, Mirium Kapner, Karin Lounsbury, Matt Millard, Todd Montalbo, Giuseppe Morella, Chelsea Phillips, Patti Reed-Zweiger, Raymond Reyes, Jason Schierkolk, Carlos Vela Shimano, Tom Smith, Litzka Stark, Julie Wheeler, and Shirley Williamson.

➤ The multitalented Kathleen Cole, assistant and student reviewer extraordinaire, for innumerable contributions.

➤ Jackie Fitzgerald, whose commitment is unfaltering.

➤ Beth Bollinger, Jennifer Collins, Amy Diehl, Frank Mortimer, Byron Smith, and Robin Diamond for their contributions.

➤ Judy Block, whose research and work on the study skills material, as well as editing suggestions on the text as a whole, were essential and invaluable.

➤ The Prentice Hall representatives and the management team, led by Gary June, who have shown tremendous support for the success of students of all ages.

➤ Our families and friends, who have encouraged us and put up with our near-constant working.

We offer our most heartfelt thanks to our editor, Todd Rossell, who has moved on to a new position at Prentice Hall. The legacy of his insights, ability to take action, and constant support will live on in this and future editions of *Keys to Study Skills.*

Finally, for their ideas, opinions, and stories, we would like to thank all of the students and professors with whom we work. We appreciate that, through reading this book, you give us the opportunity to learn and discover with you—in your classroom, in your home, on the bus, and wherever else learning takes place.

SUPPLEMENTS

Adopter's Resource Kit. This complete instructor's manual contains everything a teacher needs to successfully teach study skills and includes transparency masters for each class.

Study Skills Video. This video discusses the secrets of successful note-taking, reading, writing, test-taking, and critical thinking and can be used as a class teaching supplement.

Themes of the Times. This **The New York Times** New York Times Student Success Supplement features articles pertinent to college freshmen. It can be used as a reader to help students become comfortable reading the newspaper and keeping up with current events.

Packaging Options

Student Planner. This free supplement, which can be packaged with the text, allows students to plan effectively for class, work, and life.

Student Reflection Journal for Student Success. This supplement can be packaged for free with the text and provides a way for students to enhance their writing skills on a daily basis.

Packaging Options for Additional Charge

Graduating Into the Nineties
(0-13-323957-8)

Majoring in the Rest of Your Life: Career Secrets for College Students
(0-13-098351-9)

The Seven Habits of Highly Effective People audiotape (0-13-098377-2)

ABOUT THE AUTHORS

Carol Carter is Vice President, College Division, Publisher for Student Success and Career Development at Prentice Hall. She has written *Majoring in the Rest of Your Life: Career Secrets for College Students* and *Majoring in High School*. She has also co-authored *Graduating into the Nineties, The Career Tool Kit, Keys to Career Success, Keys to Effective Learning,* and *Keys to Success*. In 1992 Carol and other businesspeople co-founded a nonprofit organization called LifeSkills, Inc., to help high school students explore their goals, their career options, and the real world through part-time employment and internships. LifeSkills is now part of the Tucson Unified School District and is featured in seventeen high schools in Tucson, Arizona.

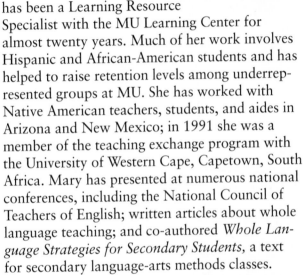

Mary K. Bixby, EdD, is an Assistant Professor of Education at the University of Missouri-Columbia. For over ten years she has been the director of MU's First-Year Experience Program. An expert on reading, writing, and learning, she has been a Learning Resource Specialist with the MU Learning Center for almost twenty years. Much of her work involves Hispanic and African-American students and has helped to raise retention levels among underrepresented groups at MU. She has worked with Native American teachers, students, and aides in Arizona and New Mexico; in 1991 she was a member of the teaching exchange program with the University of Western Cape, Capetown, South Africa. Mary has presented at numerous national conferences, including the National Council of Teachers of English; written articles about whole language teaching; and co-authored *Whole Language Strategies for Secondary Students,* a text for secondary language-arts methods classes.

Joyce Bishop holds a Ph.D. in psychology and has taught for more than twenty years, receiving a number of honors, including Teacher of the Year. For the past four years she has been voted "favorite teacher" by the student body and Honor Society at Golden West College, Huntington Beach, California, where she has taught since 1986 and is a tenured professor. She is currently working with a federal grant to establish Learning Communities and Workplace Learning in her district, and has developed workshops and trained faculty in cooperative learning, active learning, multiple intelligences, workplace relevancy, learning styles, authentic assessment, team building, and the development of learning communities. She also co-authored *Keys to Success*.

Sarah Lyman Kravits comes from a family of educators and has long cultivated an interest in educational development. She co-authored *The Career Tool Kit, Keys to Effective Learning,* and *Keys to Success,* and has served as program director for LifeSkills, Inc., a nonprofit organization that aims to further the career and personal development of high school students. In that capacity she helped to formulate both curricular and organizational elements of the program, working closely with instructors as well as with members of the business community. Sarah holds a B.A. in English and drama from the University of Virginia, where she was a Jefferson Scholar, and an M.F.A. from Catholic University.

OTHER BOOKS BY CAROL CARTER

KEYS to STUDY SKILLS

EXPLORE

LEARNING STYLES:

Knowing Who You Are and How You Learn

In this chapter, you will explore answers to the following questions:

Is there one best way to learn?

How can you discover your learning styles?

What are the benefits of knowing your learning styles?

How can you start thinking about choosing a major?

The branches of the tree of knowledge reach beyond the recall of facts. Learning is a complex process that involves taking in information, interpreting it, and associating it with information you already know. With so much involved in learning, it follows that styles of learning vary widely from person to person. A group of different students can hear the same information and come up with different notes, interpretations, and levels of retention.

For success both in class and during study time, exploring learning style is essential. The more you know about how you take in information, the more you will be able to adjust to different instructors' styles. The more you know about how you retain information, the more you will be able to choose study techniques that suit your needs. The two learning-style assessments in this chapter will help you discover your own particular style of climbing the tree of knowledge. You will also explore how to begin thinking about choosing a major.

IS THERE ONE BEST WAY TO LEARN?

Your mind is the most powerful tool you will ever possess. You are accomplished at many skills and can process all kinds of information. When you have trouble accomplishing a particular task, however, you may become convinced that you can't learn how to do anything new. You may feel that those who can do what you can't have the "right" kind of ability. Not only is this perception incorrect, it can also damage your belief in yourself.

Every individual is highly developed in some abilities and underdeveloped in others. Many famously successful people were brilliant in one area but functioned poorly in other areas. Winston Churchill failed the sixth grade. Abraham Lincoln was demoted to a private in the Black Hawk War. Louis Pasteur was a poor student in chemistry. Walt Disney was fired from a job and told he had no good ideas. What some might interpret as a deficiency or disability may be simply a different method of learning.

Learning style,
A particular way in which the mind receives and processes information.

There is no one "best" way to learn. Instead, there are many different **learning styles**, and different styles are suited to different people and/or situations. Your particular learning style, or styles, are simply the ways in which your mind best processes and retains information. Your learning styles influence your level of learning success. For example, you have probably experienced both sides of the learning curve—sometimes new information just doesn't seem to want to go into the brain, while at other times you catch on to something immediately. When you have difficulty learning something you are probably processing the information outside your learning style, whereas when you understand the material quickly, you are most likely using one of your preferred learning styles.

Your individual learning profile is made up of a combination of learning styles. Each person's profile is a unique part of his or her characteristics. Knowing how you learn is an important step in discovering who you are. This kind of self-knowledge will help you in both areas of strength and areas of difficulty. On one hand it can help you discover, and focus on, the topics and kinds of learning that come easily to you. On the other hand it can also help you find strategies to understand topics or styles of teaching that fall outside your preferred learning styles.

HOW CAN YOU DISCOVER YOUR LEARNING STYLES?

Following are two different assessments—the Learning Styles Inventory and the Pathways to Learning inventory (based on the Multiple Intelligences Theory). Each of these assessments evaluates your mind's abilities in a different way, although they often have related ideas. Your results will combine to form your learning-styles profile, consisting of the styles and types that best fit the ways that you learn and interact with others. After you complete the inventories, you will read about study strategies that can help you make the most of your particular styles and types. Your learning-styles profile will help you to improve your understanding of yourself and how you learn.

Learning Styles Inventory

One of the first instruments to measure psychological types, the Myers-Briggs Type Inventory (MBTI), was designed by Katharine Briggs and her daughter, Isabel Briggs Myers. Later, David Keirsey and Marilyn Bates combined the sixteen Myers-Briggs types into four temperaments. Barbara Soloman, Associate Director of the University Undesignated Student Program at North Carolina State University, has developed the following learning-styles inventory based on these theories and on her work with thousands of students.[1]

"Students learn in many ways," says Professor Soloman. "Mismatches often exist between common learning styles and standard teaching styles. Therefore, students often do poorly and get discouraged. Some students doubt themselves and doubt their ability to succeed in the curriculum of their choice. Some settle for low grades and even leave school. If students understand how they learn most effectively, they can tailor their studying to their own needs."

"Learning effectively" and "tailoring studying" to your own needs mean choosing study techniques that help you learn. For example, if a student responds more to visual images than to words, he or she may want to construct notes in a more visual way. Or, if a student learns better when talking to people than when studying alone, he or she may want to study primarily in pairs or groups.

> " To be what we are, and to become what we are capable of becoming, is the only end of life"
> Robert Louis Stevenson

LEARNING STYLES INVENTORY

This inventory has four "dimensions," within each of which are two opposing styles. At the end of the inventory, you will have two scores in each of the four dimensions. The difference between your two scores in any dimension tells you which of the two styles in that dimension is dominant for you. A few people will score right in between the two styles, indicating that they have almost equal parts of both. Following are brief descriptions of the four dimensions. You will learn more about them after you complete both assessments.

Active/Reflective.   Active learners learn best by experiencing knowledge through their own actions. Reflective learners understand information best when they have had time to reflect on it on their own.

Factual/Theoretical.   Factual learners learn best through specific facts, data, and detailed experimentation. Theoretical learners are more comfortable with big-picture ideas, symbols, and new concepts.

Visual/Verbal.   Visual learners remember best what they see: diagrams, flowcharts, time lines, films, and demonstrations. Verbal learners gain the most learning from reading, hearing spoken words, participating in discussion, and explaining things to others.

Holistic,
Relating to the wholes of complete systems rather than the analysis of parts.

Linear/Holistic. Linear learners find it easiest to learn material presented step by step in a logical, ordered progression. Holistic learners progress in fits and starts, perhaps feeling lost for a while, but eventually seeing the big picture in a clear and creative way.

> Please complete this inventory by circling a or b to indicate your answer to each question. Answer every question; choose only one answer for each question. If both answers seem to apply to you, choose the answer that applies more often.

1. I study best
   a. in a study group.
   b. alone or with a partner.

2. I would rather be considered
   a. realistic.
   b. imaginative.

3. When I recall what I did yesterday, I am most likely to think in terms of
   a. pictures/images.
   b. words/verbal descriptions.

4. I usually think new material is
   a. easier at the beginning and then harder as it gets more complicated.
   b. often confusing at the beginning but easier as I start to understand what the whole subject is about.

5. When given a new activity to learn, I would rather first
   a. try it out.
   b. think about how I'm going to do it.

6. If I were an instructor, I would rather teach a course
   a. that deals with real-life situations and what to do about them.
   b. that deals with ideas and encourages students to think about them.

7. I prefer to receive new information in the form of
   a. pictures, diagrams, graphs, or maps.
   b. written directions or verbal information.

8. I learn
   a. at a fairly regular pace. If I study hard I'll "get it" and then move on.
   b. in fits and starts. I might be totally confused and then suddenly it all "clicks."

9. I understand something better after
   a. I attempt to do it myself.
   b. I give myself time to think about how it works.

10. I find it easier
    a. to learn facts.
    b. to learn ideas/concepts.

11. In a book with lots of pictures and charts, I am likely to
    a. look over the pictures and charts carefully.
    b. focus on the written text.

12. It's easier for me to memorize facts from
    a. a list.
    b. a whole story/essay with the facts embedded in it.

13. I will more easily remember
    a. something I have done myself.
    b. something I have thought or read about.

14. I am usually
    a. aware of my surroundings. I remember people and places and usually recall where I put things.
    b. unaware of my surroundings. I forget people and places. I frequently misplace things.

15. I like instructors
    a. who put a lot of diagrams on the board.
    b. who spend a lot of time explaining.

16. Once I understand
    a. all the parts, I understand the whole thing.
    b. the whole thing, I see how the parts fit.

17. When I am learning something new, I would rather
    a. talk about it.
    b. think about it.

18. I am good at
    a. being careful about the details of my work.
    b. having creative ideas about how to do my work.

19. I remember best
    a. what I see.
    b. what I hear.

20. When I solve problems that involve some math, I usually
    a. work my way to the solutions one step at a time.
    b. see the solutions but then have to struggle to figure out the steps to get to them.

21. In a lecture class, I would prefer occasional in-class
    a. discussions or group problem-solving sessions.
    b. pauses that give opportunities to think or write about ideas presented in the lecture.

22. On a multiple-choice test, I am more likely to
    a. run out of time.
    b. lose points because of not reading carefully or making careless errors.

23. When I get directions to a new place, I prefer
    a. a map.
    b. written instructions.

24. When I'm thinking about something I've read,
    a. I remember the incidents and try to put them together to figure out the themes.
    b. I just know what the themes are when I finish reading and then I have to back up and find the incidents that demonstrate them.

25. When I get a new computer or VCR, I tend to
    a. plug it in and start punching buttons.
    b. read the manual and follow instructions.

26. In reading for pleasure, I prefer
    a. something that teaches me new facts or tells me how to do something.
    b. something that gives me new ideas to think about.

27. When I see a diagram or sketch in class, I am most likely to remember
    a. the picture.
    b. what the instructor said about it.

28. It is more important to me that an instructor
    a. lay out the material in clear, sequential steps.
    b. give me an overall picture and relate the material to other subjects.

SCORING SHEET: Use Table 1–1 to enter your scores.

1. Put 1's in the appropriate boxes in the table (e.g., if you answered **a** to Question 3, put a 1 in Column **a** by Question 3).
2. Total the 1's in the columns and write the totals in the indicated spaces at the base of the columns.
3. For each of the four dimensions, circle your two scores on the bar scale and then fill in the bar between the scores. For example, if under "ACTV/REFL" you had 2 **a** and 5 **b** responses, you would fill in the bar between those two scores, as this sample shows:

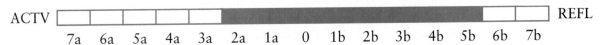

ACTV   REFL
        7a   6a   5a   4a   3a   2a   1a   0   1b   2b   3b   4b   5b   6b   7b

TABLE 2-1 LEARNING STYLES INVENTORY SCORES

ACTV/REFL			FACT/THEO			VISL/VRBL			LINR/HOLS		
Q#	a	b	Q#	a	b	Q#	a	b	Q#	a	b
1			2			3			4		
5			6			7			8		
9			10			11			12		
13			14			15			16		
17			18			19			20		
21			22			23			24		
25			26			27			28		

Write totals for each column in the spaces below.

LEARNING-STYLES SCALES

ACTV [   ] REFL
     7a 6a 5a 4a 3a 2a 1a 0 1b 2b 3b 4b 5b 6b 7b

FACT [   ] THEO
     7a 6a 5a 4a 3a 2a 1a 0 1b 2b 3b 4b 5b 6b 7b

VISL [   ] VRBL
     7a 6a 5a 4a 3a 2a 1a 0 1b 2b 3b 4b 5b 6b 7b

LINR [   ] HOLS
     7a 6a 5a 4a 3a 2a 1a 0 1b 2b 3b 4b 5b 6b 7b

If your bar has the 0 close to the center, you are well balanced on the two dimensions of that scale. If your bar is drawn mainly to one side, you have a strong preference for that one dimension and may have difficulty learning in the other dimension.

Continue on to the next assessment. After you complete it, the next section of the chapter will help you understand and make use of your results from each assessment.

Multiple Intelligences Theory

Howard Gardner, a Harvard University professor, has developed a theory called Multiple Intelligences. He believes there are at least eight distinct intelligences possessed by all people, and that every person has developed some intelligences more fully than others. Most people have experienced a time when they learned something quickly and comfortably. Most have also had the opposite experience—when no matter how hard they tried, something they wanted to learn just would not sink in. According to the Multiple Intelligences theory, when you find a task or subject easy, you are probably using a more fully developed intelligence; when you have more trouble, you may be using a less developed intelligence.[2]

Following are brief descriptions of the focus of each of the intelligences. Study skills that reinforce each intelligence will be described later in the chapter.

> Verbal-Linguistic Intelligence—ability to communicate through language (listening, reading, writing, speaking)

> Logical-Mathematical Intelligence—ability to understand logical reasoning and problem solving (math, science, patterns, sequences)

> Bodily-Kinesthetic Intelligence—ability to use the physical body skillfully and to take in knowledge through bodily sensation (coordination, working with hands)

> Visual-Spatial Intelligence—ability to understand spatial relationships and to perceive and create images (visual art, graphic design, charts and maps)

> Interpersonal Intelligence—ability to relate to others, noticing their moods, motivations, and feelings (social activity, cooperative learning, teamwork)

> Intrapersonal Intelligence—ability to understand one's own behavior and feelings (independence, time spent alone)

> Musical Intelligence—ability to comprehend and create meaningful sound (music, sensitivity to sound)

> Naturalistic Intelligence—ability to understand features of the environment (interest in nature, environmental balance, ecosystem, stress relief brought by natural environments)

Intelligence,
As defined by H. Gardner, an ability to solve problems or fashion products that are useful in a particular cultural setting or community.

Kinesthetic,
Coming from physical sensation caused by body movements and tensions.

Please complete the following assessment of your Multiple Intelligences, called Pathways to Learning, developed by Joyce Bishop. It will help you determine which of your intelligences are most fully developed. Don't be concerned if some of your scores are low. That is true of most people, even your instructors and your authors!

PATHWAYS TO LEARNING[3]

Directions: Rate each statement as follows: 1 = rarely; 2 = sometimes; 3 = usually; 4 = always. Write the number of your response (1–4) on the line next to the statement and total each set of six questions.

1. ____ I enjoy physical activities.
2. ____ I am uncomfortable sitting still.
3. ____ I prefer to learn through doing.
4. ____ When sitting, I move my legs or hands.
5. ____ I enjoy working with my hands.
6. ____ I like to pace when I'm thinking or studying.

____ **TOTAL for Bodily-Kinesthetic**

7. ____ I use maps easily.
8. ____ I draw pictures/diagrams when explaining ideas.
9. ____ I can assemble items easily from diagrams.
10. ____ I enjoy drawing or photography.
11. ____ I do not like to read long paragraphs.
12. ____ I prefer a drawn map over written directions.

____ **TOTAL for Visual-Spatial**

13. ____ I enjoy telling stories.
14. ____ I like to write.
15. ____ I like to read.
16. ____ I express myself clearly.
17. ____ I am good at negotiating.
18. ____ I like to discuss topics that interest me.

____ **TOTAL for Verbal-Linguistic**

19. ____ I liked math in high school.
20. ____ I like science.
21. ____ I problem-solve well.
22. ____ I question how things work.
23. ____ I enjoy planning or designing something new.
24. ____ I am able to fix things.

____ **TOTAL for Logical-Mathematical**

25. ____ I listen to music.
26. ____ I move my fingers or feet when I hear music.
27. ____ I have good rhythm.
28. ____ I like to sing along with music.
29. ____ People have said I have musical talent.
30. ____ I like to express my ideas through music.

____ **TOTAL for Musical**

31. ____ I like doing a project with other people.
32. ____ People come to me to help settle conflicts.
33. ____ I like to spend time with friends.
34. ____ I am good at understanding people.
35. ____ I am good at making people feel comfortable.
36. ____ I enjoy helping others.

____ **TOTAL for Interpersonal**

37. ____ I need quiet time to think.
38. ____ I think about issues before I want to talk.
39. ____ I am interested in self-improvement.
40. ____ I understand my thoughts and feelings.
41. ____ I know what I want out of life.
42. ____ I prefer to work on projects alone.

____ **TOTAL for Intrapersonal**

43. ____ I enjoy nature whenever possible.
44. ____ I think about having a career involving nature.
45. ____ I enjoy studying plants, animals, or oceans.
46. ____ I avoid being indoors except when I sleep.
47. ____ As a child I played with bugs and leaves.
48. ____ When I feel stressed I want to be out in nature.

____ **TOTAL for Naturalistic**

Write each of your eight intelligences in the column where it fits below. For each, choose the column that corresponds with your total in that intelligence.

SCORES OF **20–24** HIGHLY DEVELOPED		SCORES OF **14–19** MODERATELY DEVELOPED		SCORES BELOW **14** UNDERDEVELOPED	
Scores	Intelligences	Scores	Intelligences	Scores	Intelligences

Learning styles and multiple intelligences are gauges to help you understand yourself. Instead of labeling yourself narrowly using one category or another, learn as much as you can about your preferences and how you can maximize your learning. Most people are a blend of styles and preferences, with one or two being dominant. In addition, you may change preferences depending on the situation. For example, a student might find it easy to take notes in outline style when the instructor lectures in an organized way. However, if another instructor jumps from topic to topic, the student might choose to use the Cornell system or a think link (Chapter 6 goes into detail about note-taking styles).

WHAT ARE THE BENEFITS OF KNOWING YOUR LEARNING STYLES?

Determining your learning-styles profile takes work and self-exploration. For it to be worth your while, you need to understand what knowing your profile can do for you. Following are benefits specific to study skills.

Study Benefits

Most students aim to maximize learning while minimizing frustration and time spent studying. If you know your particular learning style, you can use techniques that complement it. Such techniques take advantage of your highly developed areas while helping you through your less developed ones. For example, say you perform better in smaller, discussion-based classes. When you have the opportunity, you might choose a course section that is smaller or that is taught by an instructor who prefers group discussion. You might also apply specific strategies to improve your retention in a lecture situation.

Following are techniques that tend to complement the strengths and shortcomings of each style. Many of these techniques come from students in Professor Soloman's program who made suggestions according to what worked for their own styles. Concepts from different assessments that benefit from similar strategies are grouped together. In Figure 1-1, you can see which styles tend to be dominant among students.

Remember that you may have characteristics from many different styles, even though some are dominant. Therefore, you may see suggestions for styles other than your dominant ones that may apply to you. What's important is that you use what works. Note the boxes next to the names of each style or type. In order to spot your best suggestions quickly, mark your most dominant styles or types by making check marks in the appropriate boxes.

Are You Active or Reflective?

<u>Active learners</u> ☐ include <u>Bodily-Kinesthetic</u> ☐ and <u>Interpersonal</u> ☐ learners.   They like to apply the information to the real world, experience it in their own actions, or discuss or explain to others what they have learned.

Student-suggested strategies for active learners:

> ➢ Study in a group in which members take turns explaining topics to each other and then discussing them.

> ➢ Think of practical uses of the course material.

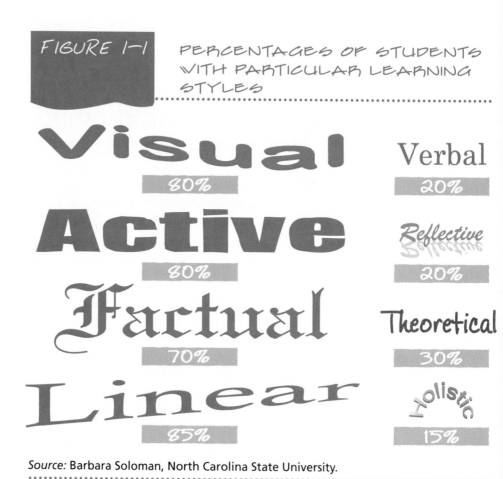

FIGURE 1-1   PERCENTAGES OF STUDENTS WITH PARTICULAR LEARNING STYLES

Visual 80%   Verbal 20%

Active 80%   Reflective 20%

Factual 70%   Theoretical 30%

Linear 85%   Holistic 15%

Source: Barbara Soloman, North Carolina State University.

➤ Pace and recite while you learn.

➤ Act out material or design games.

➤ Use flashcards with other people.

➤ Teach the material to someone else.

Reflective learners ☐ include Intrapersonal ☐ and Logical/mathematical ☐ learners.   They retain and understand information better after they have taken time to think about it.

   Student-suggested strategies for reflective learners:

➤ Study in a quiet setting.

➤ When you are reading, stop periodically to think about what you have read.

➤ Don't just memorize material; think about why it is important and what it relates to, considering the causes and effects involved.

➤ Write short summaries of what the material means to you.

Are You Factual or Theoretical?

Factual learners ☐ prefer concrete and specific facts, data, and detailed experimentation.   They like to solve problems with standard methods and are patient with details. They don't respond well to surprises and unique complications that upset normal procedure. They are good at memorizing facts.

   Student-suggested strategies for the factual learner:

➤ Ask the instructor how ideas and concepts apply in practice.

➤ Ask for specific examples of the ideas and concepts.

➤ Brainstorm specific examples with classmates or by yourself.

➤ Think about how theories make specific connections with the real world.

Theoretical learners ☐ are often also logical/mathematical and prefer innovation and theories.   They are good at grasping new concepts and big-picture ideas. They dislike repetition and fact-based learning. They are comfortable with symbols and abstractions, often connecting them with prior knowledge and experience. Most classes are aimed at theoretical learners.

   Student-suggested strategies for the theoretical learners:

➤ If a class deals primarily with factual information, try to think of concepts, interpretations, or theories that link the facts together.

➤ Because you become impatient with details, you may be prone to careless mistakes on tests. Read directions and entire questions before answering, and be sure to check your work.

➤ Look for systems and patterns that arrange facts in a way that makes sense to you.

➤ Spend time analyzing the material.

Are You Visual/Spatial or Verbal/Linguistic?

<u>Visual/spatial learners</u> □ remember best what they see: diagrams, flow-charts, time lines, films, and demonstrations. They tend to forget spoken words and ideas. Classes generally don't include that much visual information. Note that although words written on paper or shown via an overhead projector are something you see, visual learners learn most easily from visual cues that don't involve words.

Student-suggested strategies for the visual/spatial learner:

➤ Add diagrams to your notes whenever possible. Dates can be drawn on a time line; math functions can be graphed; percentages can be drawn in a pie chart.

➤ Organize your notes so you can clearly see main points and supporting facts and how things are connected. You will learn more about different styles of note-taking in Chapter 6.

➤ Connect related facts in your notes by drawing arrows.

➤ Color-code your notes with highlighters so that everything relating to a topic is the same color.

<u>Verbal/linguistic learners</u> □ (often also interpersonal) remember much of what they hear and more of what they hear and then say. They benefit from discussion, prefer verbal explanation to visual demonstration, and learn effectively by explaining things to others. Because written words are processed as verbal information, verbal learners learn well through reading. The majority of classes, since they present material through the written word, lecture, or discussion, are geared to verbal learners.

Student-suggested strategies for the verbal learner:

➤ Talk about what you learn. Work in study groups so that you have an opportunity to explain and discuss what you are learning.

➤ Read the textbook and highlight no more than 10 percent.

➤ Rewrite your notes.

➤ Outline chapters.

➤ Recite information or write scripts and debates.

Are You Linear or Holistic?

<u>Linear learners</u> ☐ find it easiest to learn material presented a logical, ordered progression.   They solve problems in a step-by-step manner. They can work with sections of material without yet fully understanding the whole picture. They tend to be stronger when looking at the parts, or discrete details, of a whole rather than understanding the whole and then dividing it up into parts. They learn best when taking in material in a progression from easiest to more complex to most difficult. Many courses are taught in a linear fashion.

> "Education is not preparation for life; education is life itself."
> John Dewey

Student-suggested strategies for the linear learner:

> ➤ If you have an instructor who jumps around from topic to topic, spend time outside of class with the instructor or a class-mate who can help you fill the gaps in your notes.

> ➤ If class notes are random, rewrite the material according to whatever logic helps you understand it best.

> ➤ Outline the material.

<u>Holistic learners</u> ☐ learn in fits and starts.   They may feel lost for days or weeks, unable to solve even the simplest problems or show the most basic understanding, until they suddenly "get it." They may feel discouraged when struggling with material that many other students seem to learn easily. Once they understand, though, they tend to see the big picture to an extent that others rarely achieve. They are often highly creative.

Student-suggested strategies for the holistic learner:

> ➤ Recognize that you are not slow or stupid. Don't lose faith in yourself. You will get it!

> ➤ Look for the big picture before trying to focus on details. You need to understand where the details fit into the main idea before you can understand and retain them well.

> ➤ Before reading a chapter, preview it by reading all the subhead-ings, summaries, and any margin glossary terms. The chapter may also start with an outline and overview of the entire chapter.

> ➤ Instead of spending a short time on every subject every night, try setting aside evenings for specific subjects; immerse yourself in just one subject at a time.

> ➤ Try taking difficult subjects in summer school when you are handling fewer courses.

> ➤ Try to relate subjects to other things you already know. Keep asking yourself how you could apply the material.

Study Techniques for Additional Multiple Intelligences

People who score high in the <u>Musical/Rhythmic</u> ☐ intelligence have strong memories for rhymes and can be energized by music.   They often have a song running through their mind and find themselves tapping a foot or their fingers when they hear music.

Student-suggested strategies for musical/rhythmic people:

➢ Create rhymes out of vocabulary words.

➢ Beat out rhythms when studying.

➢ Play instrumental music while studying if it does not distract you, but first determine what type of music most improves your concentration.

➢ Take study breaks and listen to music.

➢ Write a rap about your topic.

<u>Naturalistic learners</u> ☐ feel energized when they are connected to nature. Their career choices and hobbies reflect their love of nature.

Student-suggested strategies for naturalistic people:

➢ Study outside whenever practical, but only if it is not distracting.

➢ Explore subject areas that reflect your love for nature. Learning is much easier when you have a passion for it.

➢ Relate abstract information to something concrete in nature.

➢ Take breaks to do something you love related to nature—take a walk or watch your fish or a nature video. Use nature as a reward for getting other work done.

These study tips will go far toward helping you make the most of your study time. The benefits of being aware of learning styles, however, extend into your classroom time, work time, and personal life.

Classroom Benefits

Knowing your learning styles does more than help you adjust to different kinds of material. It can also help you make the most of the teaching styles of your instructors. Your particular learning styles may work much better with the way some instructors teach, and may be a mismatch with other instructors. The first step is to understand the various teaching styles you encounter (remember that an instructor's teaching style often reflects his or her preferred learning styles). The next step is to make adjustments so that you can maximize your learning.

After perhaps two class meetings, you can make a pretty good assessment of any instructor's teaching styles (instructors may exhibit more than one). Some common styles include:

> Lecture: Instructor speaks to the class for the entire class period; there is little to no class interaction.

> Group Discussion: Instructor presents material but encourages class discussion throughout.

> Small Groups: Instructor presents material and then breaks class into small groups for discussion or project work.

> Visual Focus: Instructor uses visual elements such as diagrams, photographs, drawings, transparencies.

> Verbal Focus: Instructor relies primarily on words, either spoken or written on the board or overhead projector.

> Sequential Presentation: Instructor organizes material in a logical sequence, such as by time or importance.

> Global Presentation: Instructor tackles topics in no particular order, jumps around a lot, or digresses.

After you have an idea of what you're working with, you can assess how well your own styles match up with the teaching styles. If your styles mesh well with an instructor's teaching styles, you're in luck. If not, you have a number of options.

You can bring extra focus to your weaker learning-style areas.   Although it's not easy, working on your weaker points can help you break new ground in your learning. For example, if you're a verbal person in a math- and logic-oriented class, you can try to increase your focus and concentration during class so that you get as much as you can from the presentation. Then you can spend extra study time on the material, make a point to ask others from your class to help you, and search for additional supplemental materials and exercises that might reinforce your knowledge.

You can ask your instructor for additional help.   For example, if you are a visual person, you might ask your instructor if he or she can recommend any visuals to look at that would help to illustrate the points made in class. If the class breaks into smaller groups, you might ask the instructor to divide those groups roughly according to learning style so the visual students can help each other understand the material.

You can "convert" class material during study time.   For example, an interpersonal and factual learner takes a class with an instructor who presents big-picture information in lecture format. This student might organize study groups and, in those groups, focus on filling in the factual gaps using reading materials assigned for that class. Likewise, a visual student might rewrite notes in different colors to add a visual

" The greatest discovery of any generation is that human beings can alter their lives by altering their attitudes of mind"
Albert Schweitzer

element—for example, assigning a different color to each main point or topic, or using one color for central ideas, another for supporting examples.

Your instructors are as individual as the students. Spending some time to focus on their teaching styles, and on how you can make adjustments, will help you learn more effectively and avoid frustration. Don't forget to take advantage of your instructor's office hours when you have a learning-styles issue that is causing you difficulty.

General Benefits

Although schools have traditionally favored verbal/linguistic students, there is no general advantage to one style over another. The only advantage is in discovering your profile, whatever it may be, by analyzing yourself accurately and honestly. Following are three general benefits of knowing your learning styles.

1. **You will have a better chance of avoiding problematic situations.** If you don't explore what works best for you, you risk forcing yourself into situations that stifle your creativity, development, and happiness. Knowing how you learn and how you relate to the world can help you make smarter choices—of courses, instructors, curriculum, jobs, careers, and relationships.

2. **You will be more successful on the job.** Your learning style is essentially your working style. If you know how you learn, you will be able to look for an environment that suits you the best and you'll be able to work effectively on work teams. This will prepare you for successful employment in the twenty-first century.

3. **You will be more able to target areas that need improvement.** The more you know about your learning styles, the more you will be able to pinpoint the areas that are more difficult for you. That offers two advantages: One, you can begin to work on difficult areas, step by step. Two, when a task comes up requiring a skill that is tough for you, you can either take special care with it or suggest someone else whose style may be better suited to it.

Your learning-style profile is an important part of self-knowledge that will help you as you explore choosing a major.

HOW CAN YOU START THINKING ABOUT CHOOSING A MAJOR?

While many students come to college knowing what they want to study, many do not. That's completely normal. College is a perfect time to begin exploring your different interests. In the process, you may discover talents and strengths you never realized you had. For example, taking an environ-

How can I adjust my learning style to my instructor's teaching styles?

Patti Reed-Zweiger, Non-traditional Student, South Puget Sound Community College, Tacoma, Washington

This last year I took a class in math that left me extremely stressed and exhausted. The way the teacher presented the material just didn't work for me. He threw out way too much information in a short period of time with little or no tools for completing the tasks. I really think he was unprepared. When he'd get to class, he'd fumble through his book for a while until he latched

onto something to share. Sometimes he'd spend the whole class answering a question or two about the previous homework and then, at the very last minute, give us a new assignment for the next class. We'd leave without any understanding of what we were to accomplish. It seems to me this teacher did very little teaching.

I'm a state trooper, so I'm used to handling enormous pressure, but in this case nothing seemed to work. I'd leave in tears, class after class. This is frustrating for me. I'm forty years old and very confident and yet in this class I felt like I was back in grade school again. I felt inadequate, foolish, and out of control—so much so that I would become nauseous and sick to my stomach. I wouldn't wish this experience on my worst enemy. What can I do to succeed in math and still maintain my self-esteem? At this point, I'm ready to drop it altogether.

Jacque Hall, Non-traditional Student, University of Georgia, Terry College of Business

You're not alone. Math is frightening to most people. When I began taking math classes, I felt like a total failure. In fact, I dropped out of my math 102 class. I just couldn't handle it. That's the first thing I'd recommend to you. Get out of the class if the teacher is not what you need. But make sure you talk with the teacher first and see if

there's something the two of you can do to make the class successful for you. If you feel that it just won't work, let it go and try to find a better situation for yourself. Math is hard enough without subjecting yourself to inadequate teaching. I found that networking with other students on what classes and instructors to take really helped. The younger students always seem to know who the best teachers are.

If you can afford the additional time, I recommend you audit a class. If that isn't an option, hire a math tutor or take advantage of the math lab on a regular basis. Most importantly, remember that you are not a failure. And you're also not alone. I have felt a great deal of despair over math myself. I have seen people cry in class and others leave in total frustration. At some time or other, every student is going to run into a teacher or a classroom situation that leaves them feeling dissatisfied. Do your part by communicating with the teacher. If that doesn't work, move on. I'm glad I did.

mental class may teach you that you have a passion for finding solutions to pollution problems. You may discover a talent for public speaking and decide to explore on-camera journalism.

While some of your explorations may take you down paths that don't resonate with your personality and interests, each experience will help to clarify who you really are and what you want to do with your life. Thinking about choosing a major involves exploring potential majors, being open to changing majors, and linking majors to career areas.

Exploring Potential Majors

Here are some steps to help you explore majors that may interest you.

Take a variety of classes. Although you will generally have core requirements to fulfill, use your electives to branch out. Try to take at least one class in each area that sparks your interest.

Don't rule out subject areas that aren't classified as "safe." Friends or parents may have warned you against pursuing certain careers, encouraging you to stay with "safe" careers that pay well. Even though financial stability is important, following your heart's dreams and desires is equally important. Deciding between the "safe" path and the path of the heart can be challenging. Only you can decide which is the best for you.

Spend time getting to know yourself, your interests, and your abilities. The more you know about yourself, the more ability you will have to focus on areas that make the most of who you are and what you can do. Pay close attention to which areas inspire you to greater heights and which areas seem to deaden your initiative.

Work closely with your advisor. Begin discussing your major early on with your advisor, even if you don't intend to declare a major right away. For any given major, your advisor may be able to advise you about both the corresponding department at your school and the possibilities in related career areas. You may also discuss with your advisor the possibility of double majoring (completing the requirements for two different majors) or designing your own major, if your school offers an opportunity to do so.

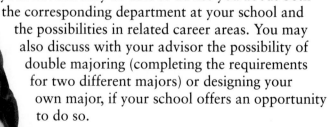

Take advantage of other resources. Seek opinions from instructors, friends, and family members. Talk to students who have declared majors that interest you. Explore the course materials your college gives you in order to see what majors your college offers.

Develop your critical-thinking skills.   Working toward any major will help you develop your most important skill—knowing how to use your mind. Critical thinking is the most crucial ingredient in any recipe for school and career success. Your future career and employer will depend on your ability to think clearly, effectively, creatively, and wisely, and to contribute to the workplace by truly making a difference.

Changing Majors

Some people may change their minds several times before honing in on a major that fits. Although this may add to the time you spend in college, being happy with your decision is important. For example, an education major may begin student teaching only to discover that he really didn't feel comfortable in front of students. Or a student may have declared English as a major only to realize that her passion was in religion.

If this happens to you, don't be discouraged. You're certainly not alone. Changing a major is much like changing a job. As many skills and experiences from one job will assist you in your next position, so may some of the courses from your first major apply—or even transfer as credits—to your next major. Talk with your academic advisor about any desire to change majors. Sometimes an advisor can speak to department heads in order to get the maximum number of credits transferred to your new major.

Whatever you decide, realize that you do have the right to change your mind. Continual self-discovery is part of the journey. No matter how many detours you make, each interesting class you take along the way helps to point you toward a major that feels like home.

Linking Majors to Career Areas

The point of declaring and pursuing a major is to help you reach a significant level of knowledge in one subject, often in preparation for a particular career area. Before you discard a major as not practical enough, consider where it might be able to take you. Thinking through the possibilities may open doors that you never knew existed. Besides finding an exciting path, you may discover something highly marketable and beneficial to humankind as well.

For each major there are many career options that aren't immediately obvious. For example, a student working toward a teaching certification doesn't have to teach in public school. This student could develop curriculum, act as a consultant for businesses, develop an on-line education service, teach overseas for the Peace Corps, or create a public television program. The sky's the limit.

Explore the educational requirements of any career area that interests you. Your choice of major may be more or less crucial depending on the career area. For example, pursuing a career in medicine almost always requires a major in some area of the biological sciences, while aspiring lawyers may have majored in anything from political science to philosophy.

Many employers are more interested in your ability to think than in your specific knowledge; therefore, they may not pay as much attention to your major as they do to your critical-thinking skills. Ask advisors or people in your areas of interest what educational background is necessary or helpful to someone pursuing a career in that area.

Sabiduría

In Spanish, the term *sabiduría* represents the two sides of learning—knowledge and wisdom. Knowledge—building what you know about how the world works—is the first part. Wisdom—deriving meaning and significance from knowledge, and deciding how to use that knowledge—is the second. As you continually learn and experience new things, the *sabiduría* you build will help you make knowledgeable and wise choices about how to lead your life.

Think of this concept as you discover more about how you learn and receive knowledge in all aspects of your life—in school, work, and personal situations. As you learn how your unique mind works and how to use it, you can more confidently assert yourself. As you expand your ability to use your mind in different ways, you can create lifelong advantages for yourself.

Chapter 1: Applications

Name _____   Date _____

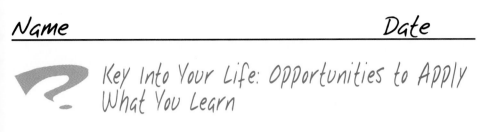 Key Into Your Life: Opportunities to Apply What You Learn

Exercise 1: How Do You Learn Best?

Start by writing your scores next to each term.

LEARNING-STYLE INVENTORY	PATHWAYS TO LEARNING
Active	Bodily-Kinesthetic
Reflective	Visual-Spatial
Factual	Verbal-Linguistic
Theoretical	Logical-Mathematical
Visual	Musical
Verbal	Interpersonal
Linear	Intrapersonal
Holistic	Naturalist

Circle your highest preferences (largest numbers) for each assessment. What positive experiences have you had at school and work that you can link to the strengths you circled? _____

_____

_____

_____

What negative experiences have you had that may be related to your least-developed learning styles or intelligences? _____

_____

_____

_____

Exercise 2: Making School More Enjoyable

List three required classes that you are not necessarily looking forward to taking. For each, name one or more parts of your learning-style profile that may be related to your lack of enthusiasm. Finally, name learning-styles-related study techniques that may help you get the most out of the class and enjoy it more.

CLASS	REASON FOR LACK OF ENTHUSIASM	LEARNING OR STUDY TECHNIQUES
1.		
2.		
3.		

Exercise 3: Interests, Majors, and Careers

Start by listing activities and subjects you like.

1. _____

2. _____

3. _____

4. _____

5. _____

Name three majors that might relate to your interests and help you achieve your career goals.

1. _____

2. _____

3. _____

For each major, name a corresponding career area you may want to explore.

1. _____

2. _____

3. _____

Keep these majors and career areas in mind as you gradually narrow your course choices in the time before you declare a major.

KEY TO COOPERATIVE LEARNING: BUILDING TEAMWORK SKILLS

Multiple Intelligences   Divide the class into eight areas, one for each of the Multiple Intelligences. Then choose an area that is one of your strongest intelligences. Try to even yourselves out so that no group has fewer than three students (if your group is too large, you might move to a smaller group that corresponds to another of your strongest intelligences). In your groups, complete the following chart on notebook paper or on a large flip chart, if available.

INTELLIGENCE		EXAMPLE FOR AN INTERPERSONAL	
Strengths	**Struggles**	**Strengths**	**Struggles**
1.	1.	1. Working with others	1. Self-inspiration
2.	2.	2.	2.
3.	3.		
4.	4.		
5.	5.		
Stressors	**Careers**	**Stressors**	**Careers**
1.	1.	1. Solo work	1. Human resources
2.	2.	2.	2.
3.	3.		
4.	4.		
5.	5.		

You may want to present this information to the entire class to enable everyone to have a better understanding and acceptance of each other's intelligences. You might also brainstorm strategies for dealing with the struggles and stressors of your intelligence, and present those ideas to the class as well.

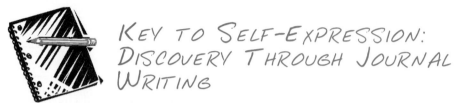

KEY TO SELF-EXPRESSION: DISCOVERY THROUGH JOURNAL WRITING

To record your thoughts, use the lined pages preceding the next chapter or a separate journal.

Learning Style Profile   Discuss the insights you have gained, through exploring your learning-style profile, about your strengths and struggles at school. What new strengths have come to your attention? What struggles have you become aware of that you couldn't explain before? Talk about how your insights may have changed the way you see yourself.

KEY TO YOUR PERSONAL PORTFOLIO: YOUR PAPER TRAIL TO SUCCESS

End-of-Chapter Cumulative Essay   Synthesize everything you have been exploring into one comprehensive "self-portrait" of yourself as a student. As a way of mapping out your essay, design a self-portrait in think-link style, using words and visual shapes to describe your learning-style profile.

A think link is a visual construction of related ideas, similar to a map or web, that represents your thought process. Ideas are written inside geometric shapes, often boxes or circles, and related ideas and facts are attached to those ideas by lines drawn connecting the shapes. You will learn more about think links in the note-taking section in Chapter 6.

Use the style shown in the example in Figure 1-2, or create your own. For example, in this exercise you may want to create a "wheel" of ideas (learning styles) coming off your central shape entitled "Myself." Then, spreading out from each of those ideas, you would draw lines connecting all of the thoughts that go along with that idea. Connected to "Linear," for example, might be "good memory," "planning skills," "math skills." You don't have to use the wheel image. You might want to design a treelike think link, or a line of boxes with connecting thoughts written below the boxes, or anything else you like. Let your design reflect who you are just as the think link itself does.

After you complete your think link, use it as a plan for your self-portrait essay. Use the first part of the essay to describe yourself, based on what you put in the think link. Then, in the final section of the essay, analyze

FIGURE 1-2　SAMPLE SELF-PORTRAIT THINK LINK

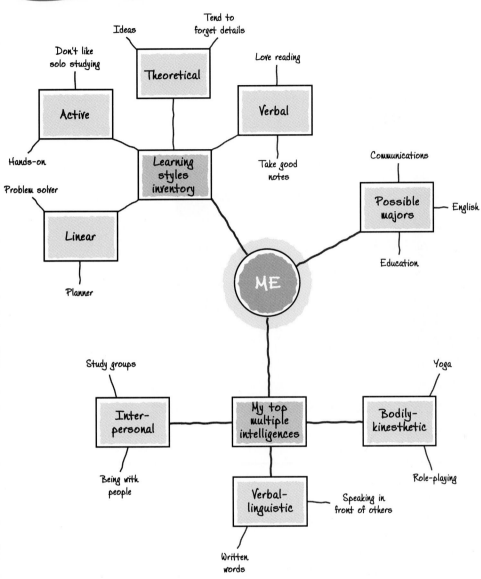

that information. What does it tell you about yourself and your goals? Based on what you have described about yourself, what conclusions can you draw about potential educational and career paths to follow? Let yourself learn something new from the information you have gathered, and use that information to become a more efficient and proficient learner.

Journal Entry

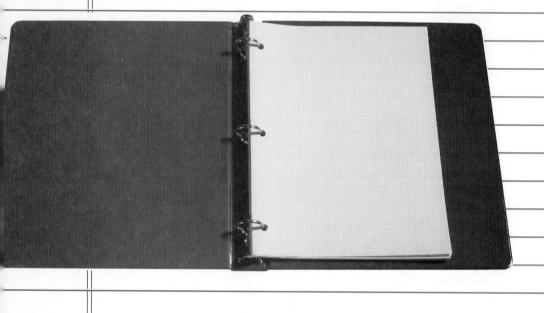

Prentice Hall

Name _____ Date _____

Journal Entry

ASPIRE

GOALS AND TIME MANAGEMENT:

Taking Responsibility for Your Time

In this chapter, you will explore answers to the following questions:

How do you set and achieve goals?

What are your priorities?

How can you manage your time?

People dream of what they want to get out of being in school, but not everyone knows how to turn dreams into reality. Often dreams seem far off in time, too difficult, or completely unreachable. It may seem that graduation or a particular career is at the end of a long race and you are at the starting line. You can make your way along the course by identifying the steps you need to take, one by one, to arrive at the finish-line tape. The steps are goals. When you set goals, prioritize, and manage your time effectively, you increase your ability to take those steps to achieve your long-term goals.

This chapter shows how the pursuit of goals gives meaning to your educational experience and helps you turn your dreams into reality. You will discover how to set long-term and short-term goals, and how exploring your values and setting priorities can help you work toward your goals more efficiently. The section on time management will discuss how to translate those goals into daily, weekly, monthly, and yearly steps, while avoiding the dangers of procrastination.

HOW DO YOU SET AND ACHIEVE GOALS?

Goal,
An end toward which effort is directed; an aim or intention.

A **goal** can be something as concrete as passing a course or as abstract as working to control your temper in class. When you set goals and work to achieve them, you engage your intelligence, abilities, time, and energy in order to move ahead. From major life decisions to the tiniest day-to-day activities, setting goals will help you define how you want to live and what you want to achieve.

Paul Timm, a best-selling author and teacher who is an expert in self-management, feels that focus is a key ingredient in setting and achieving goals. "Focus adds power to our actions. If somebody threw a bucket of water on you, you'd get wet, and probably get mad. But if water was shot at you through a high-pressure nozzle, you might get injured. The only difference is focus."[1] Each part of this section will explain ways to focus your energy through goal-setting. You can set and achieve goals through placing your goals in long-term and short-term time frames, evaluating goals in terms of your values, and linking academic goals to career goals.

Placing Goals in Time

Everyone has the same twenty-four hours in a day, but it often doesn't feel like enough. Have you ever had a busy day flash by so quickly that it seems you accomplished nothing? Have you ever felt that way about a longer period of time, like a month or even a year? Your commitments can overwhelm you unless you decide how to use time to plan your steps toward goal achievement.

" You must first be who you really are, then, do what you need to do, in order to <u>have</u> what you want."
Margaret Young

Placing your goals within particular time frames allows you to bring individual areas of that picture into the foreground. It's a rare goal that is reached overnight. Lay out the plan by breaking a long-term goal into stages of what you will accomplish in one day, one week, one month, six months, one year, five years, ten years, even twenty years. Planning your progress step by step will help you maintain your efforts over the extended time period often needed to accomplish a goal. Goals fall into two categories: long-term and short-term.

Setting Long-Term Goals

Establish first the goals that have the largest scope, the *long-term goals* that you aim to attain over a lengthy period of time, up to a few years or more. As a student, you know what long-term goals are all about. You have set yourself a goal to attend school and earn a degree or certificate. Getting an education is an admirable goal that takes a good number of years to reach.

Some long-term goals are lifelong, such as a goal to continually learn more about yourself and the world around you. Others have a more definite end, such as a goal to complete a course successfully. To determine your long-term goals, think about what you want out of your professional, educational, and personal life. Here is Carol Carter's long-term goal statement.

> Carol's Goals: To write books, give seminars, and create programs to effect opportunities for students to learn and develop. To create a personal, professional, and family environment that allows me to manifest my abilities and duly tend to each of my responsibilities.

You may establish long-term goals such as these:

> ➤ I will graduate from school and know that I have learned all that I could, whether my grade point average shows it or not.

> ➤ I will use my current and future job experience to develop practical skills that will help me later in life.

> ➤ I will build my leadership and teamwork skills by forming positive, productive relationships with classmates, instructors, and co-workers.

Long-term goals don't have to be lifelong goals. Think about your long-term goals for the coming year. Considering what you want to accomplish in a year's time will give you clarity, focus, and a sense of what needs to take place right away. When Carol thought about her long-term goals for the coming year, she came up with the following list:

1. Develop programs to provide internships, scholarships, and other quality initiatives for students.

2. Write a book for students emphasizing an interactive, highly visual approach to learning.

3. Allow time in my personal life to eat well, run five days a week, and spend quality time with family and friends. Allow time daily for quiet reflection and spiritual devotion.

In the same way Carol's goals are tailored to her personality and interests, your goals should reflect who you are. Personal goals are as unique as each individual. Among the long-term goals that a student might adopt for the coming year are the following:

> ➤ I will earn passing grades in all my classes.

> ➤ I will look for a part-time job with a local newspaper or newsroom.

> ➤ I will join two clubs and make an effort to take leadership roles in each.

Setting Short-Term Goals

When you divide your long-term goals into smaller, manageable goals that you hope to accomplish within a relatively short time, you are setting *short-term goals*. Short-term goals narrow your focus, helping you to maintain your progress toward your long-term goals. They are the steps that take you where you want to go. Say you have set the three long-term goals you just read in the previous section. To stay on track toward those goals, you may want to accomplish these short-term goals in the next six months:

> ➢ I will pass Business Writing I so that I can move on to Business Writing II.

> ➢ I will make an effort to ask my co-workers for advice on how to get into the news business.

> ➢ I will attend four of the monthly meetings of the Journalism Club.

These same goals can be broken down into even smaller parts, such as one month.

> ➢ I will complete five of the ten essays for Business Writing.

> ➢ I will have lunch with my office mate at work so that I can talk with her about her work experience.

> ➢ I will write an article for next month's Journalism Club newsletter.

In addition to monthly goals, you may have short-term goals for a week, a day, or even a couple of hours in a given day. Take as an example the article you have planned to write for the next month's Journalism Club newsletter. Such short-term goals may include the following:

> ➢ Three weeks from now: Have a final draft ready. Submit it to the editor of the newsletter.

> ➢ Two weeks from now: Have a second draft ready, and give it to one more person to review.

> ➢ One week from now: Have a first draft ready. Ask my writing instructor if he will review it.

> ➢ Today by the end of the day: Freewrite about the subject of the article, and narrow down to a specific topic.

> ➢ By 3 P.M. today: Brainstorm ideas and subjects for the article (more on brainstorming and freewriting in Chapter 7).

As you consider your long-term and short-term goals, notice how all of your goals are linked to one another. As Figure 2-1 shows, your long-term goals establish a context for the short-term goals. In turn, your short-term goals make the long-term goals seem clearer and more reachable. The whole system works together to keep you on track.

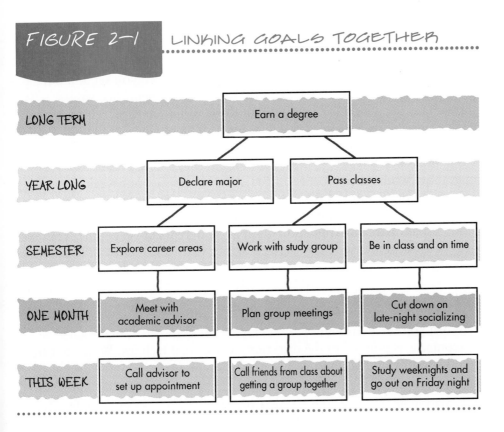

FIGURE 2–1 LINKING GOALS TOGETHER

LONG TERM	Earn a degree	
YEAR LONG	Declare major	Pass classes
SEMESTER	Explore career areas · Work with study group · Be in class and on time	
ONE MONTH	Meet with academic advisor · Plan group meetings · Cut down on late-night socializing	
THIS WEEK	Call advisor to set up appointment · Call friends from class about getting a group together · Study weeknights and go out on Friday night	

Linking Goals With Values

If you are not sure how to start establishing goals, look to your **values** to guide you. Define your goals based on what is important to you.

Values in Your Life

Your personal values are the beliefs that guide your choices. Examples of values include a good education, family togetherness, caring for others, and worthwhile employment. The sum total of all your values is your value system. You demonstrate your particular value system in your educational and career choices, the priorities you set, how you communicate with others, and your personal life.

Each individual value system is unique, even if many values come from other sources such as parents, school, religious systems, or the media. Your value system is yours alone. Your responsibility is to make sure your values are your own choice, not the choice of others. Examine your values carefully to see if they make sense to you. Make value choices for yourself based on what feels right for you, for your life, and for those who are touched by your life.

The Relationship Between Values and Goals

Understanding your values will help you set goals, because ideal goals help you achieve what you value. If you value getting to know your instructors, for example, related goals may include taking advantage of instructor office

Values,
Principles or qualities that one considers important, right, or good.

hours, looking for situations in which you can volunteer to help with courses, or living near the school where it's convenient to stay on campus during non-class time.

Goals enable you to put values into practice. When you set and pursue goals that are based on values, you demonstrate and reinforce values through taking action. The strength of those values, in turn, reinforces your goals. You will experience a much stronger drive to achieve if you build goals around what is most important to you.

If you value physical fitness, your long-term goal might be to run a marathon, while your short-term goals might involve your weekly exercise and eating plan. Similarly, if you value a close family, your long-term goals might involve finding a job that allows for family time or living in a town close to your parents. Your short-term goals may focus on helping your son learn a musical instrument or having dinner with your family at least twice a week.

Current and Personal Values Mean Appropriate Goals

When you use your values as a compass for your goals, make sure the compass is pointed in the direction of your real feelings. Watch out for the following two pitfalls:

Setting goals according to other people's values. Friends or family may encourage you to strive for what they think you should value. If you follow their advice without believing in it, you may have a harder time sticking to your path. For example, someone who attends school primarily because a parent or spouse thought it was right may have less motivation than someone who made an independent decision to become a student. If you look hard at what you really want, and why you want it, you will be more able to make decisions that are right for you.

Setting goals that reflect values you held in the past. What you felt yesterday may no longer apply, because life changes can alter your values. The best goals reflect what you believe today. For example, a person who has been through a near-fatal car accident may experience a dramatic increase in how he or she values time with friends and family, and a drop in how he or she values material possessions. Someone who survives a serious illness may value healthy living above all else. Keep in touch with your life's changes so your goals can reflect who you are.

Setting and working toward goals can be frightening and difficult at times. Like learning a new physical task, it takes a lot of practice and repeated efforts. As long as you do all that you can to achieve a goal, you haven't failed, even if you don't achieve it completely or in the time frame you want. Even one step in the right direction is an achievement. For example, if you wanted to raise your course grade to a B from a D, and you ended up with a C, you have still accomplished something important. Achieving your goals becomes easier when you are realistic about what is and isn't possible. Setting priorities will help you to make that distinction.

WHAT ARE YOUR PRIORITIES?

When you set a **priority**, you identify what's important at any given moment. Prioritizing helps you focus on your most important goals, even when they are difficult to achieve. If you were to pursue your goals in no particular order, you might tackle the easy ones first and leave the tough ones for later, perhaps never addressing goals that are important to your success.

To explore your priorities, look at your current goals. At this stage in your life, which two or three goals are most critical? How would you prioritize your goals from most important to least important?

You are a unique individual, and your priorities are yours alone. What may be top priority to someone else may not mean that much to you, and vice versa. You can see this in Figure 2-2, which compares the priorities of two very different students. Each student's priorities are listed in order, with the first priority at the top and the lowest priority at the bottom.

First and foremost, your priorities should reflect your personal goals. In addition, they should reflect your relationships with others. For example, if you are a parent, your children's needs will probably be high on the priority list. You may decide to go back to school so you can get a better job, earn more money, and give them a better life. If you are in a committed relationship, you may consider the needs of your partner. You may schedule your classes so that you and your partner are home together as often as possible. Even as you consider the needs of others, though, never lose sight of your

Priority,
An action or intention that takes precedence in time, attention, or position.

FIGURE 2-2   TWO STUDENTS COMPARE PRIORITIES

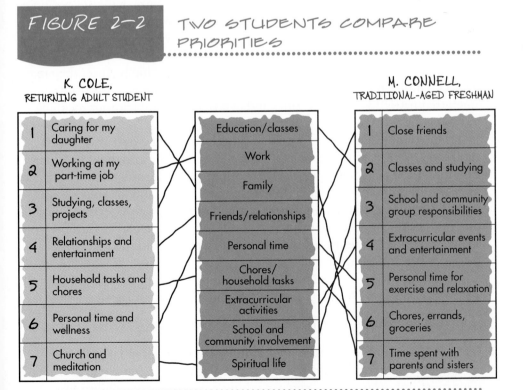

K. COLE,
RETURNING ADULT STUDENT

1	Caring for my daughter
2	Working at my part-time job
3	Studying, classes, projects
4	Relationships and entertainment
5	Household tasks and chores
6	Personal time and wellness
7	Church and meditation

Education/classes
Work
Family
Friends/relationships
Personal time
Chores/household tasks
Extracurricular activities
School and community involvement
Spiritual life

M. CONNELL,
TRADITIONAL-AGED FRESHMAN

1	Close friends
2	Classes and studying
3	School and community group responsibilities
4	Extracurricular events and entertainment
5	Personal time for exercise and relaxation
6	Chores, errands, groceries
7	Time spent with parents and sisters

personal goals. Be true to your goals and priorities so that you can make the most of who you are.

Setting priorities moves you closer to accomplishing specific goals. It also helps you begin to plan to achieve your goals within specific time frames. Being able to achieve your goals is directly linked to effective time management.

HOW CAN YOU MANAGE YOUR TIME?

Time is one of your most valuable and precious resources. Unlike money, or opportunity, or connections, time doesn't discriminate—everyone has the same twenty-four hours in a day, every day. You cannot manipulate or change how time passes, but you can learn to manage how you spend it, in a way that helps you achieve your goals step by step.

Make no mistake—time management is one of the biggest problems college students face. Juggling all of your tasks, and managing the constant changes that your schedule undergoes, is extremely challenging. The only answer to the challenge is your own energy and responsibility. You and you alone are responsible for making decisions about how you manage each hour of your day. Your potential for success—or failure—lies in your ability to make choices that help you accomplish the most in the time you have. Remember that while not all choices are ideal, any deliberate choice about how to spend your time is better than no choice at all.

People have a variety of different approaches to time management. Your learning style can help you identify how you currently use your time. For example, factual and linear learners tend to organize activities within a framework of time. Because they stay aware of how long it takes them to do something or travel somewhere, they are usually prompt. Theoretical and holistic learners tend to miss the passing of time while they are busy thinking of something else. Because they focus on the big picture, they may neglect details such as structuring their activities within available time. They frequently lose track of time and can often be late without meaning to be.

Time management, like physical fitness, is a lifelong pursuit. No one can plan a perfect schedule or build a terrific physique and then be "done." You'll work at time management throughout your life, and it can be tiring. Your ability to manage your time will vary with your mood, your stress level, how busy you are, and other factors. Don't expect perfection—just do your best. Time management involves taking responsibility for how you spend your time, building a schedule, and making your schedule work through lists and other strategies.

Taking Responsibility for How You Spend Your Time

Being in control of how you manage your time is an essential part of responsibility. When you plan your activities with an eye toward achieving your most important goals, you are taking personal responsibility for

how you live. Staying responsible, however, isn't always easy. Life changes and the judgments of others are among the factors that can affect your situation.

Life Changes

Life's sudden changes and circumstances often make you feel out of control. One minute you seem to be on track, and the next minute chaos hits: Your car breaks down, your relationship falls apart, you fail a class, you get laid off at work. Coping with all of these changes can cause stress. As your stress level rises, your sense of control dwindles.

Although you cannot always choose your circumstances, you might be able to choose how to *handle* them. Dr. Stephen Covey, author of the bestseller *The Seven Habits of Highly Effective People,* says that language is important in trying to take action. Using language like "I have to" and "They made me" robs you of personal power. For example, saying that you "have to" go to school or move out of your parents' house can make you feel that others control your life. However, language like "I have decided to" and "I prefer" helps energize your power to choose. Then you can turn "I have to go to school" into "I prefer to go to school rather than work in a dead-end job."

Judgments of Others

The judgments of others can also intimidate you into not taking responsibility for your time. A student who feels her instructor is prejudiced against her might not study for that instructor's course. A student who feels no one will hire him because of his weight may not search for jobs. Try not to let these barriers rob you of your control of your time.

Instead of giving in to judgments, try to choose actions that improve your circumstances. If you lose a job, spending an hour a day investigating other job opportunities is a better use of your time than sitting around watching TV. If you have trouble with an instructor, you can address the problem with that instructor directly and try to make the most of your time in the course. If that didn't work, you could drop the course, spend that time in other important pursuits, and retake the course in summer school while working part time. Try to find an option that will allow you to be in control of your time.

Time can be your ally if you make smart choices about how to use it. Building a schedule can help you to decide when to accomplish the activities you choose.

Judgments, Considered opinions, assessments, or evaluations.

Building a Schedule

Just as a road map helps you travel from place to place, a schedule is a time-and-activity map that helps you get from the beginning of the day (or week or month) to the end as smoothly as possible. *For almost every student, some kind of written schedule is essential for recording and keeping track of time-management choices.* Schedules have two major advantages: They allocate segments of time for the fulfillment of your daily, weekly, monthly, and longer-term goals, and they serve as a concrete reminder of tasks, events, due

dates, responsibilities, and deadlines. Few moments are more stressful than when you suddenly realize you have forgotten to pick up a prescription, take a test, or be on duty at work. Scheduling can help you avoid events like these.

Keep a Date Book

Gather the tools of the trade: a pen or pencil and a *date book* (sometimes called a planner). Some of you already have date books and may have used them for years. Others may have had no luck with them or have never tried to use them. Even if you don't feel you are the type of person who would use one, give it a try. A date book is indispensable for keeping track of your time. Paul Timm says, "Most time management experts agree that rule number one in a thoughtful planning process is: Use some form of a planner where you can write things down."

There are two major types of date books. The *day-at-a-glance* version devotes a page to each day. While it gives you ample space to write the day's activities, this version makes it difficult to see what's ahead. The *week-at-a-glance* book gives you a view of the week's plans, but has less room to write per day. If you write out your daily plans in detail, you might like the day-at-a-glance version. If you prefer to remind yourself of plans ahead of time, try the book that shows a week's schedule all at once. Some date books contain additional sections that allow you to note plans and goals for the year as a whole and for each month.

Another option to consider is an electronic planner. These are compact mini-computers that can hold a large amount of information. You can use them to schedule your days and weeks, make to-do lists, and create and store an address book. Electronic planners are powerful, convenient, and often fun. On the other hand, they certainly cost more than the paper version, and you can lose a lot of important data if something goes wrong with the mechanism. Evaluate your options and decide what you like best.

Set Daily and Weekly Goals

The most ideal time management starts with the smallest tasks and builds to bigger ones. Setting short-term goals that tie in to your long-term goals lends the following benefits:

> ➤ Increased meaning for your daily activities

> ➤ Shaping your path toward the achievement of your long-term goals

> ➤ A sense of order and progress

For both college students and working people, the week is often the easiest unit of time to consider at one shot. Weekly goal-setting and planning allows you to keep track of day-to-day activities while giving you the larger perspective of what is coming up during the week. Take some time before each week starts to remind yourself of your long-term goals. Keeping long-term goals in mind will help you determine related short-term goals you can accomplish during the week to come.

Figure 2-3 shows parts of a daily schedule and a weekly schedule.

Link Daily and Weekly Goals With Long-Term Goals

After you evaluate what you need to accomplish in the coming year, semester, month, week, and day in order to reach your long-term goals, use your schedule to get those steps down on paper. Write down the short-term goals that will enable you to stay on track. Here is how a student might map out two different goals over a year's time.

This year: Complete enough courses to graduate.
                      Improve my physical fitness.

This semester: Complete my accounting class with a B average or higher.
                      Lose 10 pounds and exercise regularly.

This month: Set up study-group schedule to coincide with quizzes.
                      Begin walking and weight lifting.

This week: Meet with study group; go over material for Friday's quiz.
                      Go for a fitness walk three times; go to weight room twice.

Today: Go over Chapter 3 in accounting text.
                      Walk for 40 minutes.

Prioritize Goals

Prioritizing enables you to use your date book with maximum efficiency. On any given day, your goals will have varying degrees of importance. Record your goals first, and then label them according to level of importance, using these categories: Priority 1, Priority 2, and Priority 3. Identify these categories using any code that makes sense to you. Some people use numbers, as above. Some use letters (A, B, C). Some write activities in different colors according to priority level. Some use symbols (*, +, −).

Priority 1.   Activities are the most important things in your life. They may include attending class, picking up a child from day care, putting gas in the car, and paying bills.

Priority 2.   Activities are part of your routine. Examples include grocery shopping, working out, participating in a school organization, or cleaning. Priority 2 tasks are important but more flexible than priority 1 activities.

Priority 3.   Activities are those you would like to do but can reschedule without much sacrifice. Examples might be a trip to the mall, a visit to a friend, a social phone call, a sports event, a movie, or a hair appointment.

FIGURE 2-3 DAILY AND WEEKLY SCHEDULES

MONDAY, MARCH 24		1997
		PRIORITY
TIME	**TASKS**	
7:00 AM		☆
8:00	Up at 8am — finish homework	
9:00		
10:00	Business Administration	☆
11:00	Renew driver's license @ DMV	
12:00 PM		
1:00	Lunch	☆
2:00	Writing Seminar (peer editing today)	
3:00	↓	
4:00	check on Ms. Schwartz's office hrs.	
5:00	5:30 work out	
6:00	↳6:30	
7:00	Dinner	
8:00	Read two chapters for Business Admin.	
9:00	↓	
10:00		
11:00		

Monday, March 24

8			
9	BIO 212	CALL: Maggie Blair	1
10		Financial Aid Office	
11	CHEM 203	EMS 262 ☆ Paramedic role-play ☆	2
12			3
Evening 6pm yoga class			4

Tuesday, March 25

8	Finish reading assignment!		5
9		Work @ library	
10	ENG 112		1
11	↓		
12		(study for quiz)	2
Evening			3
			4

Wednesday, March 26

8		↓ until 7pm	5
9	BIO 212	Meet w/advisor	
10			1
11	CHEM 203 ☆ QUIZ ☆	EMS 262	2
12			3
Evening 6pm Aerobics	☆ Pick up photos		4
			5

As much as you would like to accomplish them, you don't consider them urgent. Many people don't enter priority 3 tasks in their date books until they know that they have time to get them done.

Prioritizing your activities is essential for two reasons. First, some activities are more important than others, and effective time management requires that you focus most of your energy on priority 1 items. Second, looking at all your priorities helps you plan when you can get things done. Often it's not possible to get all your priority 1 activities done early in the day, especially if these activities involve scheduled classes or meetings. Prioritizing helps you set priority 1 items and then schedule priority 2 and 3 items around them as they fit.

Keep Track of Events

Your date book also enables you to schedule *events*. Rather than thinking of events as separate from goals, tie them to your long-term goals just as you would your other tasks. For example, attending a wedding in a few months contributes to your commitment to spending time with your family. Quiz dates, due dates for assignments, and meeting dates aid your goals to achieve in school and become involved.

Note events in your date book so that you can stay aware of them ahead of time. Write them in daily, weekly, monthly, or even yearly sections, where a quick look will remind you that they are coming up. Writing them down will also help you see where they fit in the context of all your other activities. For example, if you have three big tests and a presentation all in one week, you'll want to take time in the weeks before to prepare for them all.

Following are some kinds of events worth noting in your date book:

> ➤ Due dates for papers, projects, presentations, and tests

> ➤ Important meetings, medical appointments, or due dates for bill payments

> ➤ Birthdays, anniversaries, social events, holidays, and other special occasions

> ➤ Benchmarks for steps toward a goal, such as due dates for sections of a project, or a deadline for losing five pounds on your way to twenty

"Even if you're on the right track, you'll get run over if you just sit there."
Will Rogers

Time-Management Strategies

Managing your time is essential and critical to your study success. The following important strategies will help you accomplish your time-management goals.

1. Plan your schedule each week. Before each week starts, note events, goals, and priorities. Look at the map of your week to decide where to fit activities like studying and priority 3 items. For example, if you have a test on Thursday, you can plan study sessions on the days up until then. If you have more free time on Tuesday and Friday than other days, you can plan workouts or priority 3 activities at those times.

2. Make and use to-do lists. Use a to-do list to record the things you want to accomplish. If you generate a daily or weekly to-do list on a separate piece of paper, you can look at all tasks and goals at once. This will help you consider time frames and

FIGURE 2-4   SAMPLE MONTHLY CALENDAR

APRIL
1997

Sunday	Monday	Tuesday	Wednesday	Thursday
		1 Turn in English paper topic	2 Dentist 2pm	3
6 Frank's Birthday	7 9am PSYCH TEST ____ WORK	8 6:30pm Meeting @ Student Ctr.	9	
13	(14) ENGLISH PAPER DUE! ____ WORK	15		
20	21			
27				

priorities. You might want to prioritize your tasks and transfer them to appropriate places in your date book. Some people create daily to-do lists right on their date book pages. You can tailor a to-do list to an important event such as exam week or an especially busy day when you have a family gathering or a presentation to make. This kind of specific to-do list can help you prioritize and accomplish an unusually large task load.

3. Post monthly and yearly calendars at home. Keeping a calendar on the wall will help you stay aware of important events. You can purchase one or draw it yourself, month by month, on plain paper. Use a yearly or a monthly version (Figure 2-4 shows part of a monthly calendar) and keep it where you can refer to it often. If you live with family or friends, make the calendar a group project so that you stay aware of each other's plans. Knowing each other's schedules can also help you avoid scheduling problems such as two people needing the car at the same time or one partner scheduling a get-together when the other has to work.

4. Schedule down time. When you're wiped out from too much activity, you don't have the energy to accomplish much with your time. A little **down time** will refresh you and improve your attitude. Even half an hour a day will help. Fill the time with whatever relaxes you—having a snack, reading, watching TV, playing a game or sport, walking, writing, or just doing nothing at all. Make down time a priority.

Down time,
Quiet time set aside for relaxation and low-key activity.

Fighting Procrastination

No matter how well you schedule your time, you will have moments when it's hard to stay in control. Knowing how to identify and avoid procrastination and other time traps will help you get back on track.

Procrastination occurs when you postpone unpleasant or burdensome tasks. People procrastinate for different reasons. Having trouble with goal-setting is one reason. People may project goals too far into the future, set unrealistic goals that are too frustrating to reach, or have no goals at all. People also procrastinate because they don't believe in their ability to complete a task or don't believe in themselves in general. If continued over a

Procrastination,
The act of putting something off that needs to be done.

period of time, procrastination can develop into a harmful habit. Following are some ways to face your tendencies to procrastinate and *just do it!*

Weigh the benefits to you and others of completing the task versus the effects of procrastinating. What rewards lie ahead if you get it done? A burden off your shoulders? Some free time? Career advancement? What will be the effects if you continue to put it off? Which situation has better effects? Chances are you will benefit more in the long term from facing the task head-on.

Set reasonable goals. Plan your goals carefully, allowing enough time to complete them. Unreasonable goals can be so intimidating that you do nothing at all. "Pay off the credit card bill next month" could throw you. However, "Pay off the credit card bill in six months" might inspire you to take action.

Get started. Going from doing nothing to doing something is often the hardest part of avoiding procrastination. Once you start, you may find it easier to continue.

> " The right time is any time that one is still so lucky as to have . . . Live!"
> Henry James

Break the task into smaller parts. If it seems overwhelming, look at the task in terms of its parts. How can you approach it step by step? If you can concentrate on achieving one small goal at a time, the task may become less of a burden.

Ask for help with tasks and projects. You don't always have to go it alone. Instructors, supervisors, and family members can lend support, helping you to complete a dreaded task. For example, if you have put off an intimidating assignment, ask your instructor for guidance. If you avoid a project because you dislike the employee with whom you have to work, talk to your supervisor about adjusting the assignment of tasks or personnel. If you need accommodations due to a disability, don't assume that others know about it. Once you identify what's holding you up, see who can help you face it.

Don't expect perfection. No one is perfect. Being able to do something flawlessly is not a requirement for trying. Most people learn by starting at the beginning and wading through plenty of mistakes and confusion. It's better to try your best than to do nothing at all.

Consider how you would operate if you were looking forward to something you really want to do. You might not be late if you were headed to the train station on your way to a weekend at the beach! See if you can transfer that behavior to a task that isn't quite as much fun.

Procrastination is natural, but it can cause you problems if you let it get the best of you. When it does happen, take some time to think about the causes. What is it about this situation that frightens you or puts you off? Answering that question can help you address the causes that underlie the procrastination. These causes might indicate a deeper problem that needs to be solved.

How can I stay focused on my goals?

Karin Lounsbury, Non-traditional Student–Gonzaga University, Spokane, Washington, Bachelor of General Studies in Human Resources

I decided to return to school when I had just turned forty. I didn't like feeling dependent on my husband for my financial security so I thought that I'd do something about it. I also did it for my two children. My marriage had been shaky for quite a few years and I was scared to death that I wouldn't be able to provide for them on my own. Even though I'd worked in the busi-  ness world for a long time, the salary was never very good. I was overexperienced and underpaid. I thought that by completing my education, I could find a great job that allowed me to support my family. Although I knew that college would be challenging, I wasn't concerned with the work load—I'm used to carrying a lot of responsibilities. In fact, probably more than most people. Besides my two young children, I'm married to a man who lost both his legs in the Vietnam War. He's in a wheelchair, which means a lot of extra work falls on my shoulders.

These last few months everything seems to be falling apart. My husband and I decided to get a divorce; my son has been struggling at school; my mother was just diagnosed with cancer; and I feel like I can hardly keep my head above water. All of this is taking a toll on my grades. I'm usually so emotionally and physically exhausted by the end of the day, I just don't have the energy to put into my work. And when I'm at school, I'm distracted thinking about the future. I don't want to drop out of school but I also don't want my kids to suffer when they need me so badly. How can I get through this difficult time and still accomplish my educational goals?

Shirley Williamson, Student at the University of Georgia

To begin with, I want to encourage you to hold onto your dream of finishing your education. Even though there are probably going to be some very cloudy days ahead, don't give up. The long-term rewards are worth all the extra effort it's going to take for a while. If you could lighten your academic load in any way, I think it would  be wise to do so. It might take you a little longer to graduate, but you and your children will appreciate the extra time you get with one another. Right now, maintaining your family life is extremely important. It's healthy for children to learn that you have goals and that they may have to make compromises sometimes, but they should never suffer at the expense of those goals. If that means putting off your studies until after they're in bed, then that's what you should do. You might even try studying at the same time they are doing their homework. Make it a family activity. Whatever you do, try to keep your family structure consistent.

My heart goes out to you. You really have a lot on your plate right now. I would also suggest you find some time to care for yourself. I think the greatest stress reducer is exercise. It gets your adrenaline going and keeps your body and mind healthy. You may have to get up a little earlier or work out on your lunch hour like I do, but it's worth the extra effort.

חי

In Hebrew, the word *chai* means "life," representing all aspects of life—spiritual, emotional, family, educational, and career. The Hebrew character for *chai,* shown here, is often worn as a good-luck charm. As you plan your goals, think about your view of luck. Many people feel that someone can create his or her own luck by pursuing goals persistently and staying open to possibilities and opportunities. Canadian novelist Robertson Davies once said, "What we call luck is the inner man externalized. We make things happen to us."

Consider that your vision of life may largely determine how you live. You can prepare the way for luck by establishing a personal mission and forging ahead toward your goals. If you believe that the life you want awaits you, you will be able to recognize and make the most of luck when it comes around. *L'Chaim*—to life, and good luck.

Chapter 2: Applications

Name _____ Date _____

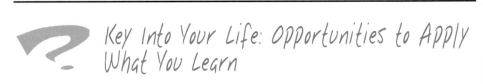 Key Into Your Life: Opportunities to Apply What You Learn

Exercise 1: Establishing and Tracking Long-Term Goals

Name two important long-term goals for your own life. Then imagine that you will begin working toward each goal. Indicate the steps you will take to achieve your goals on a short-term and long-term basis. Write what you hope to accomplish in the next year, the next six months, the next month, the next week, and the next day.

YOUR GOAL	ONE YEAR	SIX MONTHS	MONTH	WEEK	DAY
Example: I want to develop a better relationship with my father.	Instead of moving, I will complete my course of study at a school near my parents' home.	I will work to understand our relationship by talking with a counselor at school.	I will see my counselor every two weeks and make sure that I see my father at least once.	I will see if my father needs help with anything around the house this weekend.	I will call my dad after the basketball game because I know he'll be watching.

Exercise 2: Discover How You Spend Your Time

In the chart below, estimate the total time you think you spend per week on each listed activity. Then add the hours together. If your number is over 168 (the number of hours in a week), rethink your original estimates and recalculate the total so that it equals or is below 168.

ACTIVITY	ESTIMATED TIME SPENT
Class	
Work	
Studying	
Sleeping	
Eating	
Family time/child care	
Commuting/traveling	
Chores and personal business	
Friends and important relationships	
Telephone time	
Leisure/entertainment	
Spiritual life	
TOTAL	

When your estimate is at or below 168, subtract that number (the total number of hours you estimate you spend on these activities) from 168. Whatever is left over is your estimate of hours that you spend in unscheduled activities.

168

Minus total _____

Unscheduled time _____

Now, spend a week recording exactly how you spend your time. The following chart has blocks showing half-hour increments. As you go through the week, write in what you do each hour, indicating when you started and when you stopped. Don't forget activities that don't feel like "activities," such as sleeping, relaxing, and watching TV. Also, beware of recording how you *want* to spend your time or how you think you *should* have spent your time; be perfectly honest about your schedule. There are no wrong answers.

| MONDAY | | TUESDAY | | WEDNESDAY | | THURSDAY | |
Time	Activity	Time	Activity	Time	Activity	Time	Activity
5:00 AM		5:00AM		5:00 AM		5:00 AM	
5:30 AM		5:30 AM		5:30 AM		5:30 AM	
6:00 AM		6:00 AM		6:00 AM		6:00 AM	
6:30 AM		6:30 AM		6:30 AM		6:30 AM	
7:00 AM		7:00 AM		7:00 AM		7:00 AM	
7:30 AM		7:30 AM		7:30 AM		7:30 AM	
8:00 AM		8:00 AM		8:00 AM		8:00 AM	
8:30AM		8:30 AM		8:30 AM		8:30 AM	
9:00 AM		9:00 AM		9:00 AM		9:00 AM	
9:30 AM		9:30 AM		9:30 AM		9:30 AM	
10:00 AM		10:00 AM		10:00 AM		10:00 AM	
10:30 AM		10:30 AM		10:30 AM		10:30 AM	
11:00 AM		11:00 AM		11:00 AM		11:00 AM	
11:30 AM		11:30 AM		11:30 AM		11:30 AM	
12:00 PM		12:00 PM		12:00 PM		12:00 PM	
12:30 PM		12:30 PM		12:30 PM		12:30 PM	
1:00 PM		1:00 PM		1:00 PM		1:00 PM	
1:30 PM		1:30 PM		1:30 PM		1:30 PM	
2:00 PM		2:00 PM		2:00 PM		2:00 PM	
2:30 PM		2:30 PM		2:30 PM		2:30 PM	
3:00 PM		3:00 PM		3:00 PM		3:00 PM	
3:30 PM		3:30 PM		3:30 PM		3:30 PM	
4:00 PM		4:00 PM		4:00 PM		4:00 PM	
4:30 PM		4:30 PM		4:30 PM		4:30 PM	
5:00 PM		5:00 PM		5:00 PM		5:00 PM	
5:30 PM		5:30 PM		5:30 PM		5:30 PM	
6:00 PM		6:00 PM		6:00 PM		6:00 PM	
6:30 PM		6:30 PM		6:30 PM		6:30 PM	
7:00 PM		7:00 PM		7:00 PM		7:00 PM	
7:30 PM		7:30 PM		7:30 PM		7:30 PM	
8:00 PM		8:00 PM		8:00 PM		8:00 PM	
8:30 PM		8:30 PM		8:30 PM		8:30 PM	
9:00 PM		9:00 PM		9:00 PM		9:00 PM	
9:30 PM		9:30 PM		9:30 PM		9:30 PM	
10:00 PM		10:00 PM		10:00 PM		10:00 PM	
10:30 PM		10:30 PM		10:30 PM		10:30 PM	
11:00 PM		11:00 PM		11:00 PM		11:00 PM	
11:30 PM		11:30 PM		11:30 PM		11:30 PM	

FRIDAY		SATURDAY		SUNDAY	
TIME	ACTIVITY	TIME	ACTIVITY	TIME	ACTIVITY
5:00 AM		5:00 AM		5:00 AM	
5:30 AM		5:30 AM		5:30 AM	
6:00 AM		6:00 AM		6:00 AM	
6:30 AM		6:30 AM		6:30 AM	
7:00 AM		7:00 AM		7:00 AM	
7:30 AM		7:30 AM		7:30 AM	
8:00 AM		8:00 AM		8:00 AM	
8:30 AM		8:30 AM		8:30 AM	
9:00 AM		9:00 AM		9:00 AM	
9:30 AM		9:30 AM		9:30 AM	
10:00 AM		10:00 AM		10:00 AM	
10:30 AM		10:30 AM		10:30 AM	
11:00 AM		11:00 AM		11:00 AM	
11:30 AM		11:30 AM		11:30 AM	
12:00 PM		12:00 PM		12:00 PM	
12:30 PM		12:30 PM		12:30 PM	
1:00 PM		1:00 PM		1:00 PM	
1:30 PM		1:30 PM		1:30 PM	
2:00 PM		2:00 PM		2:00 PM	
2:30 PM		2:30 PM		2:30 PM	
3:00 PM		3:00 PM		3:00 PM	
3:30 PM		3:30 PM		3:30 PM	
4:00 PM		4:00 PM		4:00 PM	
4:30 PM		4:30 PM		4:30 PM	
5:00 PM		5:00 PM		5:00 PM	
5:30 PM		5:30 PM		5:30 PM	
6:00 PM		6:00 PM		6:00 PM	
6:30 PM		6:30 PM		6:30 PM	
7:00 PM		7:00 PM		7:00 PM	
7:30 PM		7:30 PM		7:30 PM	
8:00 PM		8:00 PM		8:00 PM	
8:30 PM		8:30 PM		8:30 PM	
9:00 PM		9:00 PM		9:00 PM	
9:30 PM		9:30 PM		9:30 PM	
10:00 PM		10:00 PM		10:00 PM	
10:30 PM		10:30 PM		10:30 PM	
11:00 PM		11:00 PM		11:00 PM	
11:30 PM		11:30 PM		11:30 PM	

Now, go through this chart and look at how many hours you actually spent on the activities for which you estimated your hours before. Tally the hours in the boxes in the following table using straight tally marks; round off to half-hours and use a short tally mark for a half-hour spent. At the far right of the table, total the hours for each activity.

ACTIVITY	TIME TALLIED OVER A PERIOD OF ONE WEEK	TOTAL TIME IN HOURS
Example: Class	~~HHt~~ ~~HHtHHt~~ ll	16.5
Class		
Work		
Studying		
Sleeping		
Eating		
Family time/child care		
Commuting/traveling		
Chores and personal business		
Friends and important relationships		
Telephone time		
Leisure/entertainment		
Spiritual life		

Add the totals on the right to find your GRAND TOTAL: _____

Compare your grand total to your estimated grand total, and your actual activity-hour totals to your estimated activity-hour totals. What matches and what doesn't? Describe the similarities and differences.

_____

_____

_____

_____

_____

What is the one biggest surprise about how you spend your time?

_____

_____

Name one change you would like to make in how you spend your time.

_____

_____

_____

Exercise 3: To-Do Lists

Make a to-do list for what you have to do tomorrow. Include all tasks—priority 1, 2, and 3—and events.

TOMORROW'S DATE: _____

1. _____

2. _____

3. _____

4. _____

5. _____

6. _____

7. _____

8. _____

9. _____

10. _____

11. _____

12. _____

Use a coding system of your choice to indicate the priority level of both tasks and events. Place a check by the items that are important enough to note in your date book. Use this list to make your schedule for tomorrow in the date book, making a separate list for priority 3 items. At the end of the day, evaluate this system. Did the to-do list help you? How did it make a difference? If you liked it, use this exercise as a guide for using to-do lists regularly.

KEY TO COOPERATIVE LEARNING: BUILDING TEAMWORK SKILLS

Individual Priorities   In a group of three or four people, brainstorm a list of long-term goals (for the year ahead or longer) and have one member of the group write them down. From that list, pick out ten that everyone can relate to most. Each group member should then take five minutes alone to evaluate the relative importance of the ten goals and rank them in the order that he or she prefers, using a 1 to 10 scale, with 1 being the highest priority and 10 the lowest.

Display the rankings of each group member side by side. How many different orders are there? Discuss why each person has a different set of priorities, and be open to different views. What factors in different people's lives have caused them to select particular rankings? If you have time, discuss how priorities have changed for each group member over the course of a year, perhaps by having each person re-rank the goals according to his or her needs a year ago.

KEY TO SELF-EXPRESSION: DISCOVERY THROUGH JOURNAL WRITING

To record your thoughts, use the lined pages preceding the next chapter or a separate journal.

Your Reasons for Pursuing an Education   Why did you decide to enroll in school? Many people have more than one answer. Discuss your reasons, noting which are most important to you and why. Discuss also if you dislike any of your reasons for attending college; if so, why. Then, based on your evaluation of your reasons, note your primary educational goals.

KEY TO YOUR PERSONAL PORTFOLIO: YOUR PAPER TRAIL TO SUCCESS

End-of-Chapter Cumulative Essay   Finding a time-management plan that works for you is essential to your success in school and beyond. For this essay, you will describe and justify your own time-management plan. First, map out the details. What equipment will you use? When will you use it? What strategies from the chapter do you think will be most helpful to you, and why?

After you have your data, plan and write your essay. Start by describing your schedule and its particular demands. Then explain your time-management strategies, how you will use them, and why you think they will work for you. Be sure to consider your learning styles and what kinds of time-management strategies would work best with them. If you have evidence about how certain strategies have worked or not worked in the past, include it in your discussion.

Journal Entry

Name _____ Date _____

Journal Entry

CREATE

CRITICAL THINKING:

Tapping the Power of Your Mind

In this chapter, you will explore answers to the following questions:

What is critical thinking?

How does your mind work?

How does critical thinking help you solve problems and make decisions?

How do you construct an effective argument?

How do you establish truth?

Why shift your perspective?

Why plan strategically?

Your mind's powers show in everything you do, from the smallest chores (comparing prices on books at the bookstore) to more complex situations (evaluating the results of a scientific experiment). Your mind is able to process, store, and create with the facts and ideas it encounters. Critical thinking is what enables those skills to come alive. Whether you are constructing an essay assignment or a plan for your chosen course of study, critical thinking can help you open the window of your mind, let knowledge in, and use that knowledge toward the achievement of your goals.

Understanding how your mind works is the first step toward critical thinking. When you have that understanding, you can perform the essential critical thinking task: asking important questions about ideas and information. This chapter will show you both the mind's basic actions and the thinking processes that use those actions. You will explore what it means to be an open-minded critical thinker, able to ask and understand questions that promote your success in college and beyond.

WHAT IS CRITICAL THINKING?

Critical thinking is thinking that goes beyond the basic recall of information. If the word "critical" sounds negative to you, consider that the dictionary defines its meaning as "indispensable" and "important." Critical thinking is important thinking that involves asking questions. Using critical thinking, you question established ideas, create new ideas, turn information into tools to solve problems and make decisions, and take the long-term as well as the day-to-day view.

A critical thinker asks as many kinds of questions as possible about a given piece of information. The following are examples of possible questions: *Where did it come from? What could explain it? In what ways is it true or false, and what examples could prove or disprove it? How do I feel about it, and why? How is this information similar to or different from what I already know? Is it good or bad? What causes led to it, and what effects does it have?* Critical thinkers also ask themselves whether the information can help them solve a problem, make a decision, learn or create something new, or anticipate the future. Such questions help the critical thinker learn, grow, and create.

Not thinking critically means not asking questions about information or ideas. A person who does not think critically tends to accept or reject information or ideas without examining them. Table 3-1 compares how a critical thinker and a noncritical thinker might respond to particular situations.

Asking questions (the focus of this chart), considering without judgment as many responses as you can, and choosing responses that are as complete and accurate as possible are some primary ingredients that make up critical thinking.

Anyone can develop the ability to think critically. Critical thinking is a *skill* that can be taught to students at all different levels of ability. One of the most crucial components of this skill is learning information. For instance, part of the skill of critical thinking is comparing new information with what you already know. Your prior knowledge provides a framework within which to evaluate new information. Without that knowledge, critical thinking is harder to achieve. For example, thinking critically about the statement "Shakespeare's character King Richard III is like an early version of Adolf Hitler" is impossible without basic knowledge of both World War II and Shakespeare's play *Richard III*.

The skill of critical thinking focuses on generating questions about statements and information. To examine potential critical-thinking responses in more depth, explore the different questions that a critical thinker may have about one particular statement.

		NON-QUESTIONING RESPONSE	QUESTIONING RESPONSE
YOUR ROLE	SITUATION		
STUDENT	Instructor is lecturing on the causes of the Vietnam War.	You assume that everything your instructor tells you is true.	You consider what the instructor says, write down questions about issues you want to clarify, and initiate discussion with the professor or other classmates.
SPOUSE/PARTNER	Your partner feels that he or she no longer has quality time with you.	You think he or she is wrong and defend yourself.	You ask how long he/she has felt this way, ask your partner and yourself why this is happening, and explore how you can improve the situation.
EMPLOYEE	Your supervisor is angry at you.	You ignore or avoid your supervisor, or you deny responsibility for what the supervisor is angry about.	You are willing to discuss the situation in order to determine what the perception about you is and what you might do about that perception.
NEIGHBOR	People different from you move in next door.	You ignore or avoid them; you think their way of living is weird.	You introduce yourself; you offer to help if they need it; you respectfully explore what's different about them.
CONSUMER	You want to buy a car.	You decide on a brand-new car and don't think through how you will handle the payments.	You consider the different effects of buying a new car vs. buying a used car; you examine your money situation to see what kind of payment you can handle each month.

TABLE 3-1   NOT THINKING CRITICALLY VS. THINKING CRITICALLY

A Critical-Thinking Response to a Statement

Consider the following statement of opinion:

"My obstacles are keeping me from succeeding in school. Other people make it through school because they don't have to deal with the obstacles that I have."

Nonquestioning thinkers may accept an opinion such as this as an absolute truth. As a result, on the road to achieving their goals they may lose motivation to overcome those obstacles. In contrast, critical thinkers would examine the opinion through a series of questions. Here are some examples of questions they might ask (the type of each question is indicated in parentheses after the question):

"What exactly are my obstacles? Examples of my obstacles are a heavy work schedule, single parenting, being in debt, and returning to school after ten years out." (**recall**)

"Are there other cases different from mine? I do have one friend who is going through problems worse than mine, and she's getting by. I also know another guy who doesn't have too much to deal with that I can tell, and he's struggling just like I am." (**difference**)

"Who has problems similar to mine? Well, if I consider my obstacles specifically, my statement might mean that single parents and returning adult students will all have trouble in school. That is not necessarily true. People who have trouble in school may still become successful." (**similarity**)

"What is an example of someone who has had success despite obstacles? What about Oseola McCarty, the cleaning woman who saved money all her life and raised $150,000 to create a scholarship at the University of Southern Mississippi? She didn't have what anyone would call advantages, such as a high-paying job or a college education." (**idea to example**)

"What conclusion can I draw from my questions? From thinking about my friend and about Oseola McCarty, I would say that people can successfully overcome their obstacles by working hard, focusing on their abilities, and concentrating on their goals." (**example to idea**)

"Why do I think this? Maybe I am scared of returning to school and adjusting to a new environment. Maybe I am afraid to challenge myself, because I haven't done that in a long time. Whatever the cause, the effect is that I feel bad about myself and don't work to the best of my abilities, and that can hurt both me and my family, who depend on me." (**cause and effect**)

"How do I evaluate the effects of this statement? I think it's harmful. When we say that obstacles equal difficulty, we can damage our desire to try to overcome those obstacles. When we say that successful people don't have obstacles, we might overlook that some very successful people have to deal with hidden disadvantages such as learning disabilities or abusive families." (**evaluation**)

Remember these types of questions. When you explore the seven mind actions later in the chapter, refer to these questions to see how they illustrate the different actions your mind performs.

The Value of Critical Thinking

Critical thinking has many important advantages. Following are some of the positive effects, or benefits, of putting energy into critical thinking.

You will increase your ability to perform thinking processes that help you reach your goals.   Critical thinking is a learned skill, just like shooting a basketball or using a word-processing program on the computer. As with any other skill, the more you use it, the better you become at it. The more you ask questions, the better you think. The better you think, the more effective you will be when completing schoolwork, managing your personal life, and performing on the job.

You can produce knowledge, rather than just reproduce it.   The interaction of newly learned information with what you already know creates new knowledge. The usefulness of such knowledge can be judged by how you apply it to new situations. For instance, it won't mean much for an early childhood education student to quote the stages of child development on an exam unless he or she can make judgments about children's needs when on the job.

You can be a valuable employee.   You won't be a failure in the workplace if you follow directions. However, you will be even more valuable if you ask strategic questions about how to make improvements, large or small. Questions could range from "Is there a better way to deliver messages?" to "How can we increase business?" An employee who shows the initiative to think critically will be more likely to earn responsibility and promotions.

You can increase your creativity.   You cannot be a successful critical thinker without being able to come up with new and different questions to ask, possibilities to explore, and ideas to try. Creativity is essential in producing what is new. Being creative generally improves your outlook, your sense of humor, and your perspective as you cope with problems.

What your mind does when thinking and asking important questions can be broken down into seven basic actions. These actions are the basic blocks you will use to build the critical-thinking processes that you will explore later in the chapter.

> " We do not live to think, but, on the contrary, we think in order that we may succeed in surviving."
> José Ortega y Gasset

HOW DOES YOUR MIND WORK?

Critical thinking depends on a thorough understanding of the workings of the mind. Your mind has some basic moves, or actions, that it performs in order to understand relationships among ideas and concepts. Sometimes it uses one action by itself, but most often it uses two or more in combination.

Mind Actions: The Thinktrix

You can identify your mind's actions using a system called the Thinktrix, originally conceived by educators Frank Lyman, Arlene Mindus, and Charlene Lopez[1] and developed by numerous other instructors. They studied how students think and named seven mind actions that are the basic building blocks of thought. These actions are not new to you, although some of their names may be. They represent the ways you think all the time.

Through exploring these actions, you can go beyond just thinking and learn *how* you think. This will help you take charge of your own thinking. The more you know about how your mind works, the more control you will have over thinking processes such as problem solving and decision making.

Following are explanations of each of the mind actions. Each explanation names the action, defines it, and explains it with examples. As you read, write your own examples in the blank spaces provided. Each action is also represented by a picture or *icon* that helps you visualize and remember it.

Recall: Facts, sequence, and description. This is the simplest action. When you **recall** you name or describe facts, objects, or events, or put them into sequence. *Examples:*

> ➤ Naming the steps of a geometry proof, in order

> ➤ Remembering your instructors' names and office locations

Your example: Recall two important in-class events this month.

_____

_____

The icon: A string tied around a finger is a familiar image of recall, or remembering.

Similarity: Analogy, likeness, comparison. This action examines what is **similar** about one or more things. You might compare situations, ideas, people, stories, events, or objects. *Examples:*

> ➤ Comparing notes with another student to see what facts and ideas you have both considered important

> ➤ Analyzing the arguments you've had with an instructor this month and seeing how they all seem to be about the same problem

Your example: Tell what is similar about two of your favorite instructors.

_____

_____

The icon: Two alike objects, in this case triangles, indicate similarity.

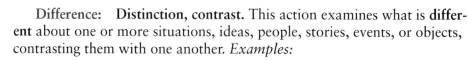

Difference: Distinction, contrast. This action examines what is **different** about one or more situations, ideas, people, stories, events, or objects, contrasting them with one another. *Examples:*

> ➤ Seeing how two instructors differ in style—one divides the class into groups and encourages discussion, and the other keeps desks in straight lines and lectures for most of the class

> ➤ Contrasting a weekday where you work a half day and go to school a half day with a weekday when you attend class and then have the rest of the day to study

Your example: Explain how your response to a course you like differs from your response to a course you don't like as much.

_____

_____

The icon: Two differing objects, in this case a triangle and a square, indicate difference.

Cause and effect: **Reasons, consequences, prediction.** Using this action, you look at what has **caused** a fact, situation, or event, and/or what **effects,** or consequences, come from it. In other words, you examine what led up to something and/or what will follow because of it. *Examples:*

> ➤ You see how staying up late at night causes you to oversleep, which has the effect of your being late to class. This causes you to miss some of the material, which has a further effect of your having problems on the test.

> ➤ When you pay your tuition bills on time, the effects are an uninterrupted ability to attend school, a better credit rating, and a favorable relationship with your college's financial office.

Your example: List what causes you to like your favorite class, and the effects that liking the class has on you.

_____

_____

The icon: The water droplets making ripples indicate causes and their resulting effects.

Example to idea: **Generalization, classification, conceptualization.** From one or more **examples** (facts or events), you develop a general **idea** or ideas. Grouping facts or events into patterns may allow you to make a general statement about several of them at once. Classifying a fact or event helps you build knowledge. This mind action moves from the specific to the general. *Examples:*

> ➤ You have had trouble finding a baby sitter who can match your schedule. A classmate even brought her child to class once. Your brother has had to drop off his daughter at your mom's and doesn't like being unable to see her all day. From these examples, you derive the idea that your school needs an on-campus day-care program.

> You read a novel for English class and you decide it is mostly about pride.

Your example: Name activities you enjoy; from them, come up with an idea of a major you would like to explore.

_____

_____

The icon: The arrow and "Ex" pointing to a light bulb on their right indicate how an example or examples lead to the idea or ideas (the light bulb, lit up).

Idea to example: **Categorization, substantiation, proof.** In a reverse of the previous action, you take an **idea** or ideas and think of **examples** (events or facts) that support or prove that idea. This mind action moves from the general to the specific. *Examples:*

> When writing a paper for a composition class, you start with a thesis statement, which is your idea: "Men are favored over women in the modern workplace." Then you gather examples to back up that idea: Men make more money on average than women in the same jobs; there are more men in upper management positions than women; women can be denied advancement when they make their families a priority; etc.

> You talk to your instructor about the idea of changing your major, giving examples that support your idea: You have worked in the field you want to change to, you have fulfilled some of the requirements for that major already, and you are unhappy with your current course of study.

Your example: Name someone whom you consider to be a successful student. Give three examples that show how this person is successful.

_____

_____

The icon: In a reverse of the previous icon, this one starts with the light bulb and has an arrow pointing to "Ex." This indicates that you start with the idea, the lit bulb, and then branch into the example or examples that support the idea.

Evaluation: **Value, judgment, rating.** Here you **judge** whether something is useful or not useful, important or unimportant, good or bad, or right or wrong by identifying and weighing its positive and negative effects (pros and cons). Be sure to consider the specific situation at hand (a cold drink might be good on the beach in August, not so good in the snowdrifts in January). With the facts you have gathered, you determine the value of something in terms of both predicted effects and your own needs. Cause-and-effect analysis always accompanies evaluation. *Examples:*

> ➤ You decide to try taking later classes for a semester. You schedule classes in the afternoons and spend nights working. You find that instead of getting up early to study, you tend to sleep in and then get up not too long before you have to be at school. From those harmful effects, you evaluate that this system doesn't work for you. You decide to schedule earlier classes next time.

> ➤ Someone offers you a chance to cheat on a test. You evaluate the potential effects if you are caught. You also evaluate the long-term effects on you of not learning the material and of doing something ethically wrong. You decide that it isn't right or worthwhile to cheat.

Your example: Evaluate your mode of transportation to school.

_____

_____

The icon: A set of scales out of balance indicates how you weigh positive and negative effects to arrive at an evaluation.

You may want to use a *mnemonic device*—a memory tool, explained in more detail in Chapter 5—to remember the seven mind actions. Try recalling them using the word "DECRIES"—each letter is the first letter of a mind action. You can also make a sentence of words that each start with a mind action's first letter. Here's an example: "Really Smart Dogs Cook Eggs In Enchiladas" (the first letter of each word stands for one of the mind actions).

How Mind Actions Build Thinking Processes

The seven mind actions that your mind uses every day are the fundamental building blocks, indicating the relationships among ideas and concepts. Note that you will rarely use them one at a time in a step-by-step process, as they are presented here. You will usually combine them, overlap them, and repeat them more than once, using different actions for different situations. For example, when you want to say something nice at the end of a date, you might consider past comments that had an effect *similar* to what you want now. When a test question asks you to explain what prejudice is, you might name similar *examples* that show your *idea* of what prejudice means.

When you combine mind actions in working toward a specific goal, you are performing a thinking process. Following are explorations of six of the most important critical-thinking processes: solving problems, making decisions, constructing effective arguments, establishing truth, shifting your perspective, and planning strategically. Each thinking process helps you succeed by directing your critical thinking toward the achievement of your goals. Figure 3-3, appearing later in the chapter, shows all of the mind actions and thinking processes together and reminds you that the mind actions form the core of the thinking processes.

HOW DOES CRITICAL THINKING HELP YOU SOLVE PROBLEMS AND MAKE DECISIONS?

Problem solving and decision making are probably the two most crucial and common thinking processes. Each requires various mind actions. They overlap somewhat, because every problem that needs solving requires you to make a decision; however, not every decision requires that you solve a problem (for example, not many people would say that deciding what to have for lunch is a problem). Each process will be considered separately here. You will notice similarities in the steps involved in each.

Although both of these processes have multiple steps, you will not always have to work your way through each step. As you become more comfortable with solving problems and making decisions, your mind will click more easily through the steps whenever you encounter a problem or decision. Also, you will become more able to evaluate which problems and decisions need serious consideration and which can be taken care of more quickly and simply. Critical thinking enhances proficient learning.

> *« Progress, not perfection, is what we should be asking of ourselves."*
> Julia Cameron
> *Source:* Reprinted by permission of Jeremy Tarcher, Inc., a division of The Putnam Publishing Group from the ARTIST'S WAY by Julia Cameron. Copyright © 1992 by Julia Cameron.)

Problem Solving

Life constantly presents problems to be solved, ranging from average daily problems (how to manage study time or learn not to misplace your keys) to life-altering situations (how to adjust to a debilitating injury or design a custody plan during a divorce). Choosing a solution without thinking critically may have negative effects. If you use the steps of the following problem-solving process, however, you have the best chance of coming up with a favorable solution.

You can apply this problem-solving plan to any problem. Using the following steps will maximize the number of possible solutions you generate and will allow you to explore each one as fully as possible.

1. State the problem clearly. What are the facts? *Recall* the details of the situation. Be sure to name the problem specifically, without focusing on causes or effects. For example, a student might state this as a problem: "I'm not understanding the class material." However, that may be a *cause* of the actual problem at hand: "I'm failing my economics quizzes."

2. Analyze the problem. What is happening that, in your opinion, needs to change? In other words, what *effects* does the situation have that cause a problem for you? What *causes* these effects? Are there hidden causes? Look at the *causes* and *effects* that surround the problem. Continuing the example of the economics student, if some effects of failing quizzes include poor grades in the course and disinterest, some causes may include poor study habits, poor test-taking skills, lack of sleep, or not understanding the material.

3. Brainstorm possible solutions. **Brainstorming** will help you think of examples of how you solved similar problems, consider what is different about this problem, and see if you can find new possible solutions. You are brainstorming when you approach a problem by letting your mind free-associate and come up with as many possible ideas, examples, or solutions as you can, without immediately evaluating them as good or bad. Rules for successful brainstorming include:[2]

> *Don't evaluate or criticize an idea right away.* Write down your ideas so that you remember them. Evaluate later, after you have had a chance to think about them.

> *Focus on quantity and worry about quality later.* Try to generate as many ideas as you can. The more thoughts you generate, the better the chance that one may be useful.

> *Let yourself consider wild and wacky ideas.* Sometimes the craziest ideas end up being the most productive, positive, workable solutions around.

*To get to the heart of a problem you must base possible solutions upon **causes** (the most important, or weighted, causes) rather than putting a bandage on the **effects.*** If the economics student were to aim for better assignment grades to offset low quiz grades, that might raise his GPA but wouldn't address the cause of not understanding the material. Looking at this cause, on the other hand, might lead him to work on study habits or seek help from his instructor, a study group, or a tutor.

4. Explore each solution. Why might your solution work, or not? Might a solution work partially, or in a certain situation? *Evaluate* ahead of time the pros and cons (positive and negative effects) of each plan. Create a chain of causes and effects in your head, as far into the future as you can, to see where this solution might lead. The economics student might consider the effects of improved study habits, more sleep, tutoring, or dropping the class.

5. Choose and execute the solution you decide is best. Decide how you will put your solution to work. Then, execute your solution. The economics student could decide on a combination of improved study habits and tutoring.

6. Evaluate the solution that you acted upon, looking at its *effects*. What are the positive and negative effects of what you did? In terms of your needs, was it a useful solution or not? Could the solution use any adjustments in order to be more useful? Would you do the same again or not? In evaluating, you are collecting data. Evaluating his choice, the economics student may decide that the effects are good but that his fatigue still causes a problem.

Brainstorming, The spontaneous, rapid generation of ideas or solutions, undertaken by a group or an individual, often as part of a problem-solving process.

7. **Continue to refine the solution.** Problem solving is always a process. You may have opportunities to apply the same solution over and over again. Evaluate repeatedly, making changes that you decide make the solution better (meaning, more reflective of the causes of the problem). The economics student may decide to study more regularly but, after a few weeks of tutoring, could opt to trade the tutoring time for some extra sleep. He may decide to take what he has learned from the tutor and apply it to his increased study efforts.

Using this process will enable you to solve personal, educational, and workplace problems in a thoughtful, comprehensive way. Figure 3-1 is a think link that demonstrates a way to visualize the flow of problem solving. Figure 3-2 contains a sample of how one person used this plan to solve a problem. Figure 3-2 represents the same plan as 3-1 but gives room to write so that it can be used in the problem-solving process.

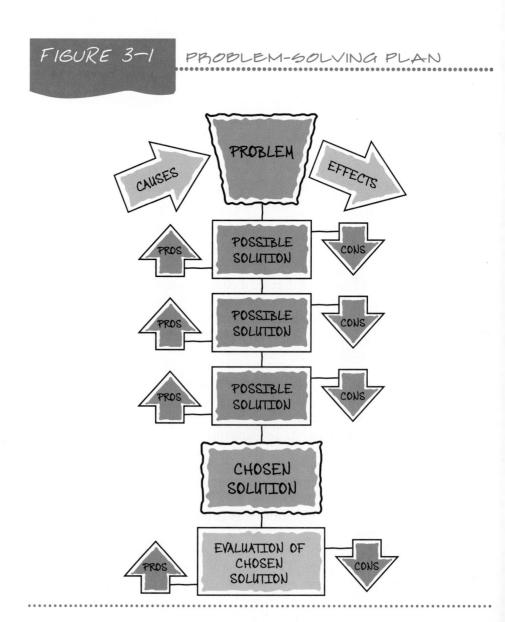

FIGURE 3-1   PROBLEM-SOLVING PLAN

FIGURE 3–2 HOW ONE STUDENT WORKED THROUGH A PROBLEM

LIST CAUSES OF PROBLEM:

Must go to school to take classes

Can't have child with me in class

No one else at home to watch child

STATE PROBLEM HERE:

Need some way to provide child-care while I'm at school

LIST EFFECTS OF PROBLEM:

Missed exams and classes sometimes

Logistics take extra time, transport

Stress created for me and child

Lack of routine & comfort

List potential POSITIVE effects for each solution:

Care is consistent

Reliable and familiar setting

Doesn't matter if child is sick

Use boxes below to list possible solutions:

SOLUTION #1

Have a nanny at home

List potential NEGATIVE effects for each solution:

Expensive

Hard to find someone to trust

Person must follow my schedule

Meet parents like myself

Child has playmates

Inexpensive

SOLUTION #2

Join child-care co-op

Must trust other parents

Sick child might get others sick

Close by to classes

Reliable care

No extra transport time

SOLUTION #3

Get school to provide child-care on campus

Costs school money

Need to find space and create facility

Restrictions & waiting lists

Now choose the solution you think is best—and try it.

CHOSEN SOLUTION

Join child-care co-op

List the actual POSITIVE effects of the solution:

Met some helpful people who understand me

My child likes the other three children

Low cost helps my budget

List the actual NEGATIVE effects of the solution:

When it's my turn, I have to care for four children

Sometimes our schedules clash

Can't let a sick child participate

FINAL EVALUATION: was it a good or bad choice?

All in all, I think this is the best I could do on my budget. There are times when I have to stay home with a sick child, but I'm mostly able to stay committed to both parenting and school.

Source: Adapted from a heuristic developed by Frank T. Lyman Jr., Ph.D., University of Maryland, 1983.

Decision Making

Although every problem-solving process involves making a decision—when you decide which solution to try—not all decisions involve solving problems. Decisions are choices. Making a choice, or decision, requires thinking critically through all of the possible choices and evaluating which will work best for you and for the situation. Decisions large and small come up daily, hourly, even every few minutes. Do you drop a course? Do you call your landlord when the heat doesn't come on? Should you stay in a relationship? Can you work part time without interfering with school?

Before you begin the decision-making process, evaluate the level of the decision you are making. Do you have to decide what books to bring to class (usually a minor issue), or whether to quit a good job (often a major life change)? Some decisions are little, day-to-day considerations that you can take care of quickly on your own. Others require thoughtful evaluation, time, and perhaps the input of others you trust. The following is a list of steps to take in order to think critically through a decision.

1. Decide on a goal. Why is this decision necessary? In other words, what result do you want from this decision, and what is its value? Considering the *effects* you want can help you formulate your goal. For example, say a student currently attends a small private college. Her goal is to become a physical therapist. The school has a good program, but her financial situation has changed and has made this school too expensive for her.

2. Establish needs. *Recall* the needs of everyone (or everything) involved in the decision. She needs a school with a full physical therapy program; she and her parents need to cut costs (her father changed jobs and her family cannot continue to afford the current school); she needs to be able to transfer credits.

3. Name, investigate, and evaluate available options. Brainstorm possible choices, and then look at the facts surrounding each. *Evaluate* the good and bad effects of each possibility. Weigh these effects and judge which is the best course of action. Here are some possibilities that the student in the college example might consider:

   ➤ *Continue at the current college.* **Positive effects:** I wouldn't have to adjust to a new place or people. I could continue my course work as planned. **Negative effects:** I would have to find a way to finance most of my tuition and costs on my own, whether through loans, grants, or work. I'm not sure I could find time to work as much as I would need to, and I don't think I would qualify for as much aid as I now need.

   ➤ *Transfer to the state college.* **Positive effects:** I could reconnect there with people I know from high school. Tuition and room costs would be cheaper than at my current school. I could transfer credits. **Negative effects:** I would still have to work some or find minimal financial aid. The physical therapy program is small and not very strong.

> *Transfer to the community college.* **Positive effects:** They have many of the courses I need to continue with the physical therapy curriculum. The school is twenty minutes from my parents' house so I could live at home and avoid paying housing costs. Credits will transfer. The tuition is extremely reasonable. **Negative effects:** I don't know anyone there. I would be less independent. The school doesn't offer a bachelor's degree.

4. Decide on a plan of action and pursue it. Make a choice based on your evaluation, and act on your choice. In this case the student might decide to go to the community college for two years and then transfer back to a four-year school to earn a bachelor's degree in physical therapy. Although she might lose some independence and contact with friends, the positive effects are money saved, opportunity to spend time on studies rather than working to earn tuition money, and the availability of classes that match the physical therapy program requirements.

5. Evaluate the result. Was it useful? Not useful? Some of both? Weigh the positive and negative effects. If the student decides to transfer, she may find that it can be hard being back home, although her parents are adjusting to her independence and she is trying to respect their concerns. Fewer social distractions result in her getting more work done. The financial situation is more favorable. All things considered, she evaluates that this decision was the best one.

Making important decisions can take time. Think through your decision thoroughly, considering your own ideas as well as those of others you trust, but don't hesitate to act once you have your plan. You cannot benefit from your decision until you act upon it and follow through.

HOW DO YOU CONSTRUCT AN EFFECTIVE ARGUMENT?

In this case, "argument" does not refer to a fight you would have with someone; it is a persuasive case that you make to prove or disprove a point. You will often encounter situations in which your success depends on your being able to **persuade** someone, either verbally or in writing, to agree with you. You may need to write a paper persuading the reader that a particular historical event changed the world, for example, or you may need to convince an instructor that you deserve a second chance on an assignment.

When you come to crossroads in your life, much may be at stake—a grade, a degree, a job, and more. Thinking critically will allow you to build

Persuade,

To convince someone through argument or reasoning to adopt a belief, position, or course of action.

How can I find a satisfactory solution to my problem?

Chelsea Phillips, Hampshire College, Massachusetts, Environmental Science Major

I attend Hampshire College in Massachusetts. This year I'm involved in a field study program called Earth Lands. The college gives me credits but the program is not affiliated with Hampshire. I live and work in a sustainable community and study ecological issues. There are nine of us that live together. All of us are environmental activists and we agree to live by certain princi-  ples. The lodge we live in is run by solar power. We use kerosene and flashlights, too. Our food is entirely vegan, which means we not only don't eat meat, we also don't eat other foods that come from animals, like milk and butter.

Five of the participants in the program, including myself, are here as paying students. The other members are brought in to live with us and support us as we learn about the environment and community living. When we got involved, we believed the program was an entirely collaborative effort—at least that's what the brochure said. We're coming to find out there is a subtle power structure that exists between the five of us and the group called the "centering team." We don't have as much input as we'd like into the schedule or decisions that need to be made. Because we're learning how to build community and resolve problems, I'd like to find a way to resolve this feeling of separation between the two groups. I'd like to see much more dialogue and collaboration so that we're all equal participants. What process could I initiate that would address this problem and allow for more equality within our community?

Raymond Reyes, Community and Organizational Consultant

There seems to be a "tale of two cities" where there are two distinct groups of people. I would recommend that you revisit and "reclaim" the core principles that you have said were agreed upon by everyone in the community. There is an obvious gap between what has been said and reality. As a community, you need to journey into the gap, or what Plato called "the fertile void." You may  want to give serious consideration to identifying and inviting an individual who can guide you through a process to establish a greater level of trust and authenticity and to do some team building.

Communities and other "learning organizations" need to address what I often refer to as the "other three R's" of education: relationship, relevance, and respect. First, address the need for honest and healthy relationships by specifically identifying and working through the trust and power issues. Secondly, make the core principles upon which your community is based more relevant so that the members truly "own" them, whether they are paying students or part of the "centering team." Lastly, your community needs to establish a social culture that has wake-up calls that remind everyone to practice respect. Just as you are practicing respect for our Earth Mother, your community needs to have the daily fellowship behaviors which are likewise respectful.

a persuasive argument that can help you achieve what you want. Put the mind actions to work, using the following steps:

Establish the goal—what's at stake.   No argument provides an absolute guarantee of achieving a goal, but a persuasive argument will give you your best shot. Ask yourself what you want. As an example, imagine that you want a raise and promotion to a new position at work.

Gather examples that support your idea.   What will support your request? In this case, your examples may be that you have worked at this company for a year and a half, you have gotten good reviews from your supervisor, and you have ideas for the position you want. These examples argue that your promotion will have positive effects for the company.

Anticipate questions.   What will the other person or people ask you to explain? In the promotion example, they could ask you about your prior track record, what you have achieved in your current position, what you know about the position you want to take, whether you know the people you would be working with, and what new and creative ideas you have.

Anticipate points against you.   What might someone bring up that argues against your position? Whatever you think of, decide what you will say to oppose it. If your supervisor says that you can't handle the longer hours the new position would require, you may have looked into adjusting your school schedule. If the supervisor says that you don't have the necessary experience, you may have studied the job or talked with people who do that type of work.

Be flexible.   You never know what will happen as you present your argument. You might not even need to push; on the other hand, it may turn out to be much tougher than you thought. By rehearsing your response to questions beforehand, you will be as prepared as possible to handle any twists and turns that the conversation may take.

HOW DO YOU ESTABLISH TRUTH?

Investigating the truth and accuracy of information, rather than automatically accepting it as true, is an important critical-thinking process. In order to seek truth through critical thinking, you question the validity of statements or information. Critical-thinking experts Sylvan Barnet and Hugo Bedau state that when you test for the truth of a statement, you "determine whether what it asserts corresponds with reality; if it does, then it is true, and if it doesn't, then it is false."[3] In order to determine to what degree a statement "corresponds with reality," ask questions based on the mind actions. The search for truth takes two primary forms: distinguishing fact from opinion and challenging assumptions.

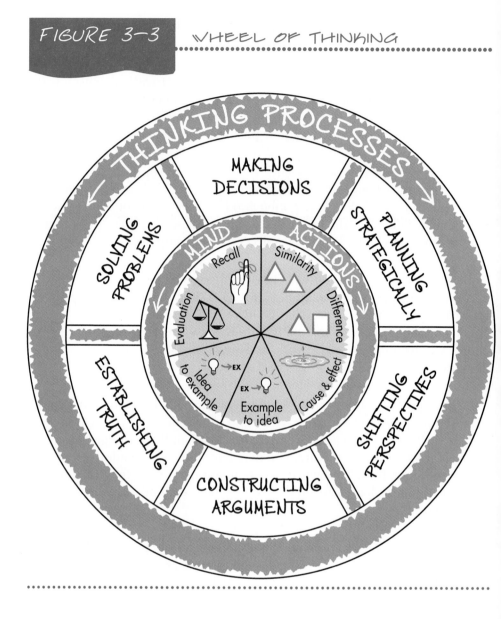

FIGURE 3-3 · · · · · WHEEL OF THINKING ·

Distinguishing Fact From Opinion

Fact, according to the dictionary, is information presented as objectively real. *Opinion* is defined as a belief, conclusion, or judgment. Whether you are studying for a test or doing research for a paper, being able to evaluate reading material to distinguish fact from opinion is crucial to your understanding of the material. Fact and opinion generate different reactions in a reader. If you decide that a statement is opinion, you may focus on whether you agree with that opinion based on how it is explained and supported. If you decide that a statement is fact, you have agreed to accept it as true, and your focus moves to evaluating how that fact is used to support other ideas or opinions.

There is a degree of overlap to fact and opinion. Opinions can be proved to be partially or completely factual after investigation. Statements that seem factual may emerge as opinions if any part of them is proven wrong through questioning. Qualifiers, such as *all, none, never, often, sometimes,* and *many,* will frequently mean the difference between fact and opinion. Absolute quali-fiers such as *all* and *none* indicate an opinion more often than a fact, while in-definite qualifiers such as *some* and *many* may make a fact out of what seems to be an opinion. For example, "All college students need to take math" is an opinion, whereas "Some college students need to take math" is a fact.

Both facts and opinions require investigation through questioning. Even though opinions would seem to require more examination than facts, some opinions masquerade as facts and are revealed only through examination. For example, an article may state, "Twenty to thirty minutes of vigorous exercise three to five times a week is essential for good health." That may sound like a fact. When you examine it through questioning, however, you may reveal it as the opinion of the author. To be safe, consider all statements opinions until proven otherwise. Questions you may ask include the following:

➤ What facts or examples provide evidence of truth?

➤ How does the maker of the statement know this to be true?

➤ Is there another fact that disproves this statement or informa-tion, or shows it to be an opinion?

➤ How reliable are the sources of information?

➤ What about this statement is similar to or different from other information I consider to be fact?

➤ How could I test the validity of this statement or information?

Even though you may find a truth in and agree with the statement after examining how the author supports it, the statement remains an opinion. The observation that some healthy people exist who do not exercise in this way proves that the statement is not completely factual.

Take a different statement as another example. It has been stated as a fact that the economically poor take unfair advantage of the welfare

TABLE 3–2 EXAMPLES OF FACTS AND OPINIONS

SUBJECT	FACTUAL STATEMENT	STATEMENT OF OPINION
Animal speed	The cheetah has been clocked at speeds that prove it to be the world's fastest animal.	No animal can ever escape the speed of the cheetah.
Weather	It's raining outside.	This is the worst rainstorm in recent history.
Fats in foods	Two slices of stuffed-crust pizza have more fat than a Big Mac.	Diners will have more luck avoiding fat at a burger joint than at a pizza place.

system. A critical thinker who questions this statement may find that the statement is actually an opinion with some degree of truth. Some poor citizens may try to cheat the welfare system, while others may have an honest claim to their welfare checks and may try hard to find work. See Table 3-2 for some more examples of factual statements versus statements of opinion.

Another crucial step in determining the truth is to question the assumptions that you and others hold, and which are the underlying force in shaping opinions.

Challenging Assumptions

Assumption,
An idea or statement accepted as true without examination or proof.

"If it's more expensive, it's better." "It's best to start your day before 8 A.M." "You should study in a library." These statements reveal **assumptions**—evaluations or generalizations based on observing cause and effect—that often hide within seemingly truthful assertions. Assumptions can influence educational choices: You may assume that you should attend a particular kind of school, earn a certain degree, study in a particular manner, or attend school during the day rather than at night. Many people don't question whether their assumptions make sense, nor do they challenge the assumptions of others.

Assumptions come from sources such as parents or relatives, TV and other media, friends, and your personal experiences. As much as you think such assumptions work for you, it's just as possible that they don't. Assumptions can close your mind to opportunities and even harm people. For example, the old false assumption that people who speak with a regional or foreign accent are somehow less intelligent or less qualified has caused a great deal of harm through the years.

Think critically to uncover and investigate assumptions. Ask these questions:

1. Is the truth of this statement supported with fact, or does it hide an assumption?

2. In what cases is this assumption true or not true? What examples prove or disprove it?

3. Has making this assumption benefited me or others? Has it hurt me or others? In what ways?

4. If someone taught me this assumption, why? Did that person think it over or just accept it?

5. What harm could be done by always taking this assumption as fact?

For example, here's how you might use these questions to investigate the following statement: "The most productive schedule involves getting started early in the day."

1. This statement *hides* an assumption that the morning is when all people feel most energetic and are able to get lots of things done.

2. The assumption may be generally *true* for people who enjoy early morning hours and have good energy during that part of the day. But the assumption may be *not true* for people who work best in the afternoon or evening hours.

3. Society's basic standard of daytime classes and 8 A.M. to 5 P.M. working hours supports this assumption. Therefore, the assumption may *work* for people who have early jobs and classes. It may *not work*, however, for people who work late shifts or who take classes in the evening.

4. Maybe people who believe this assumption were raised in a household where people started their days early. Or perhaps they just go along with what seems to be the standard. Still, there are plenty of people who operate on a different schedule and still enjoy successful, productive lives.

5. Taking this assumption as fact could hurt people who don't operate at their peak in the earlier hours. For example, if a "night owl" tries to conform to an early schedule of classes, he or she may experience concentration and focus problems that would not necessarily occur during later classes. In situations that favor their particular characteristics—later classes or jobs that start in the afternoon or evening—such people have just as much potential to succeed as anyone else.

Be careful to look for and question all assumptions, not just those that seem problematic from the start. Because assumptions may work differently in different situations, a seemingly good assumption may cause problems under particular circumstances. Here is one such assumption: "We should keep finding new uses for computers." Computers have improved industry and communication. However, many have lost their jobs because what they used to do by hand is now being performed by a computer. Some people may become addicted to computers and neglect other important activities. You also may miss talking to a real person when you get a computer answering system on the phone—"Press '7' if you want . . ." Rather than automatically agreeing with an assumption, investigate the positive and negative effects of the situation to form your opinion.

WHY SHIFT YOUR PERSPECTIVE?

Seeing the world only from your own perspective, or point of view, is inflexible, limiting, and frustrating to both you and others. You probably know how hard it can be to relate to someone who cannot understand where you are coming from—an instructor who doesn't like that you leave early on Thursdays for physical therapy, a parent who doesn't see why you can't take a study break to visit, a friend who can't understand why you would date someone of a different race. Seeing beyond one's own perspective can be difficult, especially when life problems and fatigue take their toll.

Perspective,
A mental point of view or outlook, based on a cluster of related assumptions, incorporating values, interests, and knowledge.

On the other hand, when you shift your own perspective to consider someone else's, you open the lines of communication. Trying to understand what other people feel, need, and want makes you more responsive to them and builds mutual respect. For example, if you want to add or drop a course and your advisor says it's impossible, not listening to your request, you might not feel much like explaining. On the other hand, if your advisor asks to hear your point of view, you may sense that your needs are respected. Feeling respected may encourage you to respond, or even to change your mind.

Every time you shift your perspective, you can also learn something new. There are worlds of knowledge and possibilities outside your individual existence. You may learn that what you eat daily may be against someone else's religious beliefs. You may discover people who don't fit a stereotype. You may find different and equally valid ways of getting an education, living as a family, relating to one another, having a spiritual life, or spending free time. Above all else, you may see that each person is entitled to his or her own perspective, no matter how foreign it may be to you.

Asking questions like these will help you maintain flexibility and openness in your perspective.

> What is similar and different about this person/belief/method and me/my beliefs/my methods?

> What positive and negative effects come from this different way of being/acting/believing? Even if this perspective seems to have negative effects for me, how might it have positive effects for others, and therefore have value?

> What can I learn from this different perspective? Is there anything I could adopt for my own life— something that would help me improve who I am or what I do? Is there anything that I wouldn't do myself but that I can still respect and learn from?

Shifting your perspective is at the heart of all successful communication. Each person is unique. Even within a group of people similar to yourself, there will be a variety of perspectives. Each one you consider helps you increase your knowledge and respect others. Being able to shift perspective and communicate more effectively may mean the difference between success and failure in today's diverse world.

WHY PLAN STRATEGICALLY?

If you've ever played a game of chess or checkers, participated in a wrestling or martial arts match, or had a drawn-out argument, you have had experience with strategy . In those situations and many others, you continually have to think through and anticipate the moves the other person is about to make. Often you have to think ahead about how you would respond to several possible options held by the other person.

Strategy,
A plan of action designed to accomplish a specific goal.

Strategy is the plan of action, the method, the "how" behind any goal you want to achieve. Specifically, strategic planning means having a plan for the future, whether you are looking at the next week, month, year, ten years, or fifty years. It means exploring the future positive and negative effects of the choices you make and actions you take today. You are planning strategically right now just by being in school. You made a decision that making the effort to attend college is a legitimate price to pay for the skills, contacts, and opportunities that will help you in the future.

You don't have to compete against someone else in order to be strategic. You can be strategic on your own or even in a cooperative situation. For example, as a student, you are challenging yourself to achieve. You are learning to set goals for the future, analyze what you want in the long term, and increase your career options. Being strategic with yourself means challenging yourself as you would challenge a competitor, demanding that you work to achieve your goals with conviction and determination. It means being versatile, having options, and making choices for best accomplishing tasks.

What are some benefits, or positive effects, of strategic planning?

Strategy is an essential skill at school and at work. A student who wants to ace a course needs to plan study and research sessions ahead of time in order to complete assignments when they are due. A lawyer needs to anticipate how to respond to any allegation the opposing side will bring up in court. Strategic planning creates a vision into the future that allows the planner to anticipate all kinds of possibilities and, most importantly, to have the versatility to be prepared for them.

Strategic planning powers your short-term and long-term goal setting. Once you have set goals, you need to plan the steps that will help you achieve those goals over time. For example, a strategic student who wants to pay for his own tuition might drive a used car, cut out luxuries, and maintain a part-time job. In class, a strategic planner will think critically about the material presented, knowing that information is most useful later on if it is clearly understood.

Strategic planning helps you keep up with technology.   As technology develops more and more quickly, jobs become obsolete. It's possible to spend years in school training for a career area that will be drying up when you are ready to enter the work force. When you plan strategically, you can take a broader range of courses or choose a major and career in an area that is expanding. This will make it more likely that your skills will be in demand when you graduate.

Effective critical thinking is essential to strategic planning. If you aim for a certain goal, what steps will move you toward that goal? What positive effects do you anticipate these steps will have? What can you learn from previous experiences in order to take different steps today? Critical thinking runs like a thread through all of your strategic planning.

Here are some tips for becoming a strategic planner:

Develop an appropriate plan.   What approach will best achieve your goal? What steps toward your goal will you need to take one year from now, five years, ten years, twenty years?

Anticipate all possible outcomes of your actions.   What are the positive and negative effects that may occur?

Ask the question "how."   How do you achieve your goals? How do you learn effectively and remember what you learn? How do you develop a productive idea on the job? How do you distinguish yourself at school and at work?

Experiment with strategies.   Try different plans, and evaluate their positive and negative effects to see what works best for you. For example, you might try two different kinds of date books to help you plan your semester, eventually deciding that one works better than the other.

Use human resources.   Talk to people who are where you want to be, whether professionally or personally. What caused them to get there? Ask them what they believe are the important steps to take, degrees to have, training to experience, knowledge to gain.

"I have always thought that one man of tolerable abilities may work great changes, and accomplish great affairs among mankind, if he first forms a good plan."
Benjamin Franklin

Be prepared to take the risk to change.   Know that the strategies you are accustomed to might not be the best ones for you. If you discover that you need to make a change, be willing to take the risk and know that you are on the road to important learning.

In each thinking process, you use your creativity to come up with ideas, examples, causes, effects, and solutions. You have a capacity to be creative, whether you are aware of it or not. Open up your mind and awaken your creativity. It will enhance your critical thinking and make life more enjoyable.

You use critical-thinking mind actions throughout everything you do in school and in your daily life. In this chapter and in some of the other study skills chapters, you will notice mind-action icons placed where they can help you to label your thinking.

Κρινειν

The word "critical" is derived from the Greek word *krinein,* which means "to separate in order to choose or select." To be a mindful, aware critical thinker, you need to be able to separate, evaluate, and select ideas, facts, and thoughts.

Think of this concept as you apply critical thinking to your reading, writing, and interaction with others. Be aware of the information you take in and of your thoughts, and be selective as you process them. Critical thinking gives you the power to make sense of life by deliberately selecting how to respond to the information, people, and events you encounter.

Chapter 3: Applications

Name _____ Date _____

 Key Into Your Life: Opportunities to Apply What You Learn

Exercise 1: Making a Decision

In this series of exercises you will make a personal decision using the seven mind actions and the decision-making steps described in this chapter. Before you proceed through each of the steps, write here an important personal decision you have to make. Choose a decision that you want to act on and will be able to address soon.

_____

_____

Step 1   Name Your Goal

Be specific: What goal, or desired effects, do you seek from this decision? For example, if your decision is a choice between two jobs, desired effects may be financial security, convenience, or experience. It could also be a combination of these effects. Write down three effects that you hope to gain. Note priorities by writing the effects in order of importance.

1. _____

2. _____

3. _____

Step 2   Establish Needs

Who and what will be affected by your decision? If you are deciding how to finance your education and you have a family to support, you must take into consideration their financial needs as well as your own when exploring options.

List here the people/things/situations that may be affected by your decision and indicate how your decision will affect them.

_____

_____

_____

_____

_____

 **EX**

Step 3   Check Out Your Options

Look at all the options you can imagine. Consider options even if they seem impossible or unlikely—you can evaluate them later. Some decisions have only two options (to move to a new apartment or not, to get a new roommate or not); others have a wider selection of choices. For example, a full-time student and parent needs to coordinate class schedules with his or her child's needs. Options may include: (1) day care, (2) having a relative care for the child, (3) full-time nanny, or (4) sharing duties with another parent.

List three possible options for your decision. Evaluate the good and bad effects of each.

Option 1 _____

Positive effects _____

Negative effects _____

Option 2 _____

Positive effects _____

Negative effects _____

Option 3 _____

Positive effects _____

Negative effects _____

Have you or someone else ever made a decision similar to the one you are about to make? What can you learn from that decision that may help you?

_____

_____

Step 4   Make Your Decision and Pursue It to the Goal

Taking your entire analysis into account, decide what to do. Write your decision here.

_____

_____

Next is perhaps the most important step: *Act on your decision.*

Step 5   Evaluate the Result

After you have acted on your decision, evaluate how everything turned out. Did you achieve the effects you wanted to achieve? What were the effects on you? On others? On the situation? To what extent were they positive, negative, or some of both?

List two effects here. Name each effect, circle *Positive* or *Negative,* and explain that evaluation.

Effect _____

      Positive   *Negative*

Why? _____

Effect _____

      Positive   *Negative*

Why? _____

Final evaluation: Write one statement in reaction to the decision you made. Indicate whether you feel the decision was useful or not useful, and why. Indicate any adjustments that could have made the effects of your decision more positive.

_____

_____

_____

Exercise 2: Constructing an Argument About Assumptions and Perspectives

Name an assumption that you know is common, or that you have made yourself. It can be about anything—people, lifestyles, education, differences, money, relationships, and so on. Write it here:

_____

_____

Now you will construct two arguments: one that supports the assumption and one that disputes it. Use your mind actions to ask important questions as you construct your arguments. Think of cases or examples that fit and don't fit the assumption, positive and negative effects of believing the assumption, similar and different assumptions, and what experiences might cause the assumption.

Argument supporting _____

_____

_____

_____

Argument disputing _____

_____

_____

_____

Analyze each argument. Which perspective seems more open-minded? Which works better for situations in your life? Which perspective is closer to your own? Can you learn anything from the perspective that is more different from your own?

_____

_____

_____

_____

KEY TO COOPERATIVE LEARNING: BUILDING TEAMWORK SKILLS

Group Problem Solving As a class, brainstorm a list of school-related problems. Write the problems on the board or on a large piece of paper on an easel. Include any problems you feel comfortable discussing with others. Problems can be in the categories of learning styles, in-school or personal relationships, study techniques, time management, outside stresses such as work or parenting, procrastination, and anything else that directly or indirectly affects your performance in school. Divide into groups of two to four. Each group will choose or be assigned one problem to work on. Use the empty problem-solving flowchart to fill in your work.

1. Identify the problem. As a group, state your problem specifically, without causes ("I'm not attending all of my classes" is better than "lack of motivation"). Then, look at the causes and effects that surround it. Record the effects that the problem has on your lives. List what causes the problem. Remember to look for "hidden" causes (you may perceive that traffic makes you late to school, but the hidden cause might be that you don't get up early enough to have adequate commuting time in the morning).

2. Brainstorm possible solutions. Determine the most likely causes of the problem; from those causes, derive possible solutions. Record all of the ideas that group members offer. After ten minutes or so, each group member should choose one possible solution to explore independently.

3. Explore each solution. In thinking independently through the assigned solution, each group member should (a) weigh the positive and negative effects, (b) consider similar problems, (c) determine whether the problem requires a different strategy from other problems like it, and (d) describe how the solution affects the causes of the problem. Evaluate your assigned solution. Is it a good one? Will it work?

4. Choose your top solution(s). Come together again as a group. Take turns sharing your observations and recommendations; then take a vote. Which solution is the best? You may have a tie or may combine two different solutions. Either way is fine. Different solutions suit different people and situations. Although it's not always possible to reach agreement, try to find the solution that works for most of the group.

5. Evaluate the solution you decide is best. When you decide on your top solution or solutions, discuss what would happen if you went through with it. What do you predict would be the positive and negative effects of what you would do? Would it turn out to truly be a good solution for everyone?

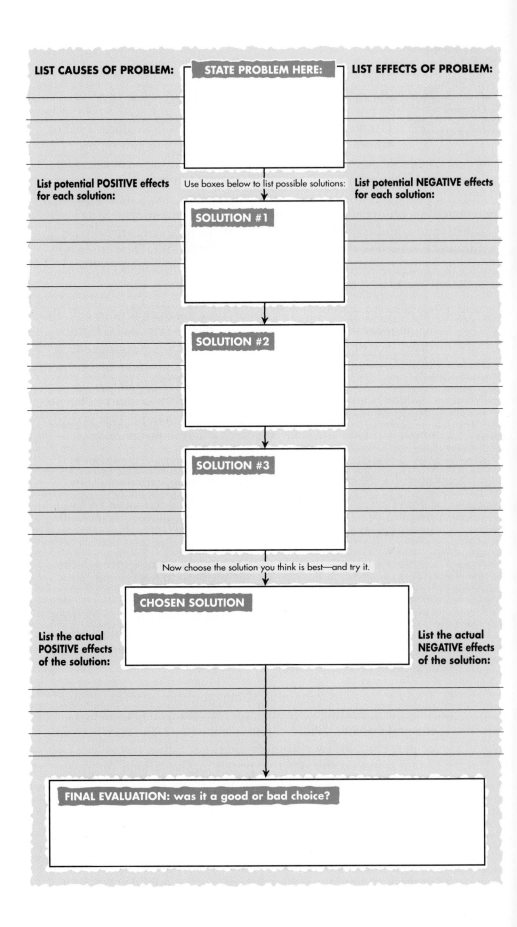

KEY TO SELF-EXPRESSION: DISCOVERY THROUGH JOURNAL WRITING

To record your thoughts, use the lined page preceding the next chapter or a separate journal.

Strategic Planning   Discuss how you feel about long-term goals. Do you tend to plan ahead of time? Why or why not? What do you like and dislike about strategically planning ahead? Discuss a long-term educational goal in terms of what you want in one semester, one year, and by graduation. How do you plan to accomplish this goal?

KEY TO YOUR PERSONAL PORTFOLIO: YOUR PAPER TRAIL TO SUCCESS

End-of-Chapter Cumulative Essay   Evaluate your study habits using your critical thinking skills. Decide what changes you want to make. Use the following questions and tasks to create and map out information for your essay.

Recall your habits. Be sure to include habits that don't relate directly to studying but do affect it—i.e., time-management habits, eating habits, habits of how you communicate with instructors or fellow students, and so on. Don't censor; make a list of good and bad habits alike.

Rewrite your list. Divide the habits into two columns: Helpful (good) and Harmful (bad).

Evaluate your habits. Rank each habit according to how strong a hold it has on you. In terms of their effects, which do you feel are the two most helpful and two most harmful? Circle them.

Start a new page for each of the four habits you circled. For each, answer these questions:

> ➤ What circumstances caused this habit?

> ➤ What effects, positive or negative, does this habit have? In other words, what rewards or negative consequences come about because of it?

> ➤ Do you want to keep or to change/stop this habit?

Use your problem-solving skills. For each habit you want to change, build a habit-altering solution to the problems the habit causes. Create a problem-solving flowchart or think link. You may want to include a plan for developing a new habit in its place.

Using the material you have generated, write your essay, focusing on your two worst habits and two best habits. Be sure to conclude your essay with ideas about what your habits say about you and how you plan to improve the habits that cause trouble for you.

Habits take consistent effort to change. You may find that your will to change fades in and out, depending on your circumstances. Don't criticize yourself if you slip. Just ask yourself questions about why it happened, and work to get back on track. Given the chance, your mind has the power to bring powerful and positive changes to your life.

Journal Entry

UNDERSTAND

READING AND STUDYING:

Your Keys to Constructing Knowledge

In this chapter, you will explore answers to the following questions:

How are you affected by your reading background?

What new challenges does college reading present?

Why and how do you define your purposes for reading?

How can PQ3R help you own what you read?

How can you respond critically to what you read?

The society you live in revolves around the written word. Although the growth of computer technology may seem to have made technical knowledge more important than reading, the focus on word processing and computer handling of documents has actually *increased* the need for employees who function at a high level of literacy. As the *Condition of Education 1996* report states, "In recent years, literacy has been viewed . . . as the ability to understand and use printed information in daily activities, at home, at work, and in the community." [1]

Two crucial keys to your college success are reading and studying, both of which are active processes that construct knowledge. The aim of both reading and studying is understanding. If you read effectively and understand what you read, and if you use writing as a reading strategy, you can improve your capacity to learn and understand. In this chapter you will learn to implement the process necessary for effective college reading, how to overcome possible past barriers to successful reading, and how you can benefit from defining a purpose when you read. You will also explore the PQ3R study technique and see how critical reading can help you maximize your understanding of any text.

HOW ARE YOU AFFECTED BY YOUR READING BACKGROUND?

Most likely, you've been a reader for quite some time. Many students take their reading skills for granted and don't think to give them the attention they may give to other, newer college skills. Successful reading in college, however, demands focus and energy. Not all reading backgrounds prepare students equally for the new challenges of college reading.

Why might your past as a reader not fully prepare you for reading in postsecondary settings? Students come to college with a variety of reading strategies, but some of your strategies that may have worked in the past may not be as efficient and effective as you'd like them to be now. Some elementary and even secondary reading programs were driven by textbook or teacher-made questions, resulting in the misconception that "good readers" are the ones that can *answer the questions*. In high school, you generally had more time to read less material, and less necessity for deep-level **understanding** .

Understanding,
Perceiving and comprehending the nature and significance; knowing thoroughly.

Part of your challenge to become a better reader in college is to consider new reading strategies and to define reading as a step-by-step process *aimed at the construction of meaning*, which is a more complex task than answering someone else's questions. Study guides, worksheets, and other aids to guide your reading are helpful, even comforting. However, college reading requires a whole new approach—an approach to reading based on *self-reliance*.

WHAT NEW CHALLENGES DOES COLLEGE READING PRESENT?

Whatever your skill level, you will encounter new challenges that make reading more difficult, such as an excess of reading assignments, difficult texts, distractions, a lack of speed and comprehension, and perhaps an insufficient vocabulary. Challenges in reading fall into two categories: on the page and off the page. All readers must strategically control both sorts of problems. This chapter will give you ideas for alleviating these problems and overcoming reading and studying challenges.

Following are some ideas about how to meet different kinds of challenges. Note that if you have a reading disability, if English is not your primary language, or if you have limited reading skills, you may need additional support and guidance. Most colleges provide services for students through a reading center or tutoring program. Take the initiative to seek help if you need it. Many accomplished learners have benefited from help in specific areas.

Dealing With Reading Overload

Reading overload is part of almost every college experience. On a typical day, you may be faced with reading assignments that look like this:

➤ an entire textbook chapter on the causes of the Civil War (American history)

➤ an original research study on the stages of sleep (psychology)

➤ pages 1–50 in Arthur Miller's play *Death of a Salesman* (American literature)

Reading all this and more leaves little time for anything else unless you read selectively and skillfully. You can't control your reading load. You can, however, improve your reading strategies. Following are techniques that can help you read and study as efficiently and effectively as you possibly can, while still having time left over for other things.

Working Through Difficult Texts

While many textbooks are useful teaching tools, some may be poorly written and organized. They are written by experts on the subject who may not explain the information in the friendliest manner for non-experts. Students using texts that aren't well written may blame themselves for the difficulty they're experiencing. Additionally, because texts are often written with the purpose of challenging the intellect, even well-written, well-organized texts may be difficult and dense to read.

Generally, the further you advance in your education, the more complex your required reading is likely to be. For example, your sociology professor may assign a chapter on the dynamics of social groups, including those of dyads and triads. When is the last time you heard the terms *dyads* and *triads* in normal conversation? You may feel at times as though you are reading a foreign language as you encounter new concepts, words, and terms. However, the good news is that as you get into your major field of study, you will become accustomed to the vocabulary of your discipline.

Assignments can also be difficult when the required reading is from primary sources rather than from texts. *Primary sources* are original documents rather than another writer's interpretation of these documents. They include:

➤ historical documents

➤ works of literature (novels, poems, and plays)

➤ scientific studies, including laboratory reports and accounts of experiments

➤ journal articles

The academic writing found in journal articles and scientific studies is different from other kinds of writing. Some academic and scientific writers assume that readers understand sophisticated concepts. They may not begin with explanations of basic terms, provide background information, or supply a wealth of examples to support their ideas. As a result, concepts may be difficult to understand.

Making your way through poorly written or difficult reading material is hard work that can be accomplished by setting purposes for reading, using prereading and active reading strategies, and taking ownership of the material that you read. The following strategies may help you with your overall motivation and focus.

Approach your reading assignments head-on.   Be careful not to prejudge them as impossible or boring before you even start to read. Pre-reading helps you realize that you can master the text!

Accept the fact that some texts may require extra work and concentration. Set goals; make plans to work your way through the material and learn. Understand that reading for understanding requires more than tracking your eyes over the words.

When a primary source discusses difficult concepts that it does not explain, put in some extra work to enrich your background and to define such concepts on your own.   Ask your instructor or other students for help. Sometimes successful reading begins with finding a simpler source: Consult reference materials in that particular subject area, other class materials, dictionaries, and encyclopedias. For convenience, try creating your own mini-library at home. Collect reference materials that you use often, such as a dictionary, a thesaurus, a writer's style handbook, and maybe an atlas or computer manual. You may also benefit from owning reference materials in your particular areas of study. "If you find yourself going to the library to look up the same reference again and again, consider purchasing that book for your personal or office library," advises library expert Sherwood Harris.[2]

Look for order and meaning in seemingly chaotic reading materials.   The information you will find in this chapter on the PQ3R reading technique and on using writing to enhance critical reading will help you discover patterns and achieve a greater depth of understanding. Finding order within chaos is an important skill, not just to construct meaning in reading, but also in all life endeavors. This skill can give you power through helping you "read" (think through) work dilemmas, personal problems, and educational situations.

Managing Distractions

With so much happening around you, it's often hard to keep your mind on what you are reading. Distractions take many forms. Some are external: the sound of a telephone, a friend who sits next to you at lunch and wants to talk, a young child who asks for help with homework. Other distractions come from within. As you try to study, you may be thinking about your parent's health, an argument you had with a friend or partner, a paper due in art history, or a site on the Internet that you want to visit.

Identify the Distraction and Choose a Suitable Action

Pinpoint what's distracting you before you decide what kind of action to take. If the distraction is *external* and *out of your control*, such as construction outside your building or a noisy group in the library, try to move away from it. If the distraction is *external* but *within your control*, such as the television, telephone, or children, take action. For example, if the TV or phone is a problem, turn off the TV or unplug the phone for an hour. Figure 4-1 explores some ways that parents or other people caring for children may be able to maximize their study efforts.

If the distraction is *internal*, there are a few strategies to try that may help you clear your mind. You may want to take a break from your studying and tend to one of the issues you are worrying about. Physical exercise may relax you and bring back your ability to focus. For some people, studying while listening to music helps to quiet a busy mind. For others, silence may do the trick. If you need silence to read or study and cannot find a truly quiet environment, consider the purchase of sound-muffling headphones or even earplugs.

Find the Best Place and Time to Read: Set the Context for Success

Any reader needs focus and discipline in order to concentrate on the material. Finding a place and time that minimizes outside distractions will help you achieve that focus. Here are some suggestions:

Read alone unless you are working with other readers. Family members, friends, or others who are not in study mode may interrupt your concentration. If you prefer to read alone, establish a relatively interruption-proof place and time, such as an out-of-the-way spot at the library or an after-class hour in an empty classroom. If you study at home and live with other people, you may want to place a "Quiet" sign on the door. Some students benefit from reading together with one or more other students. If this helps you, schedule a group meeting where you read sections of the assigned material and then break to discuss them.

Find a comfortable location. Many students study in the library on a hard-backed chair. Others prefer a library easy chair, a chair in their room, or even the floor. The spot you choose should be comfortable enough for hours of reading, but not so comfortable that you fall asleep. Make sure you have adequate lighting and aren't too hot or too cold.

Choose a regular reading place and time. Choose a spot or two you like and return to them often. Also, choose a time when your mind is alert and focused. If possible, the best time to read for particular classes is just before or after the class for which the reading is assigned. Eventually, you will associate preferred places and times with focused reading.

FIGURE 4–1   MANAGING CHILDREN WHILE STUDYING

Managing Children While Studying

Explain what your education entails. Tell them how it will improve both your life and theirs. This applies, of course, to older children who can understand the situation and compare it to their own schooling.

Keep them up to date on your schedule. Let them know when you have a big test or project due and when you are under less pressure, and what they can expect of you in each case.

Keep them active while you study. Give them games, books, or toys to occupy them. If there are special activities that you like to limit, such as watching videos on TV, save them for your study time.

Find help. Ask a relative or friend to watch your children or arrange for a child to visit a friend's house. Consider trading baby sitting hours with another parent, hiring a sitter to come to your home, or using a day care center that is private or school-sponsored.

Offset study time with family time and rewards. Children may let you get your work done if they have something to look forward to, such as a movie night, a trip for ice cream, or something else they like.

Study on the phone. You might be able to have a study session with a fellow student over the phone while your child is sleeping or playing quietly.

Special Notes for Infants

Study at night if your baby goes to sleep early, or in the morning if your baby sleeps late.

Study during nap times if you aren't too tired yourself.

Lay your notes out and recite information to the baby. The baby will appreciate the attention, and you will get work done.

Put baby in a safe and fun place while you study, such as a playpen, motorized swing, or jumping seat.

Consider a set of class notes as a study guide to your textbooks.   Your professors don't have time or the desire to "retell" your textbooks, but reading a good set of notes along with a chapter gives you a more complete picture of how the lecture and the text fit. Sometimes hearing a teacher discuss a subject is a good pre-reading strategy.

If it helps you concentrate, listen to soothing background music.   The right music can drown out background noises and relax you. However, the wrong music can make it impossible to concentrate, and for some people, silence is best. Experiment to learn what you prefer; if music helps, stick with the type that works best. A personal headset makes listening possible no matter where you are.

Turn off the television.   For most people, reading and TV don't mix.

Building Speed and Comprehension

Most students lead busy lives, carrying heavy academic loads while perhaps working a job or even caring for a family. It's difficult to make time to study at all, let alone handle the enormous reading assignments for your different classes. Increasing your reading speed and comprehension will save you valuable time and effort.

Rapid reading won't do you any good if you can't remember the material and answer questions about it. However, reading too slowly can be equally inefficient because it often eats up valuable study time and gives your mind space to wander. Your goal is to read for maximum speed *and* comprehension. Because greater comprehension is the primary goal and actually promotes faster reading, make comprehension your priority over speed.

Methods for Increasing Reading Speed

The average American adult reads between 150 and 350 words per minute. Slower readers fall below this range, while faster readers are capable of speeds of 500 to 1000 words per minute and sometimes faster.[3] However, the human eye as a lens can only move so fast; reading speeds in excess of 350 words per minute involve "skimming" and "scanning" (see p. 104). The following suggestions will help increase your overall reading speed.

> ➤ Try to read groups of words rather than single words.

> ➤ Avoid pointing your finger to guide your reading, since this will slow your pace.

> ➤ Try swinging your eyes from side to side as you read a passage, instead of stopping at various points to read individual words.

> ➤ When reading narrow columns, focus your eyes in the middle of the column and read down the page. With practice, you'll be able to read the entire column width.

> ➤ Avoid **vocalization** when reading.

> ➤ Avoid thinking each word to yourself as you read it, a practice known as *subvocalization*. Subvocalization is one of the primary causes of low reading speed.

> " No barrier of the senses shuts me out from the sweet, gracious discourse of my book friends. They talk to me without embarrassment or awkwardness."
> Helen Keller

Vocalization, The practice of speaking the words and/or moving your lips while reading.

Methods for Increasing Reading Comprehension

Remember, comprehension is more important then mere speed! Following are some specific strategies for increasing your understanding of what you read:

Continually build your knowledge through reading and studying. More than any other factor, what you already know before you read a passage will determine your ability to understand and remember important ideas. Previous knowledge, including vocabulary, facts, and ideas, gives you a **context** for what you read.

> **Context,**
> Parts of written or spoken material that surround a word or passage and can throw light on its meaning.

Establish your purpose for reading. (A detailed discussion on defining purposes for reading follows on p. 102.) When you establish what you want to get out of your reading, you will be able to determine what level of understanding you need to reach and, therefore, on what you need to focus.

Remove the barriers of negative self-talk. Instead of telling yourself that you cannot understand, think positively. Tell yourself: *I can learn this material. I am a good reader.*

Think critically. Take advantage of titles, headings, and subheadings that indicate important concepts. Ask yourself questions. Do you understand the sentence, paragraph, or chapter you just read? Are ideas and supporting examples clear to you? Could you clearly explain what you just read to someone else?

Expanding Your Vocabulary—A Challenge That Is Part of Comprehension Work

Lifelong learners consider their vocabularies works in progress, because they never finish learning new words. A strong vocabulary increases reading speed and comprehension—when you understand the words in your reading material, you don't have to stop as often to think about what they mean. No matter how strong or weak your vocabulary is, you can improve it by reading and writing words in context, using a dictionary, and using the context of the passage to "get the gist" of the unfamiliar word.

Use a Dictionary Sparingly, But Strategically

When reading a textbook, the first "dictionary" to search is the text glossary. Textbooks often include an end-of-book glossary that explains technical words and concepts. The definitions there are usually limited to the meaning of the term as it is used in the text.

Standard dictionaries provide a broader treatment. They give you all kinds of information about each word, including its origin, pronunciation, part of speech, synonyms (words with similar meanings), antonyms (words with opposite meanings), and multiple meanings. By using a dictionary sparingly and strategically whenever you read, you will increase your general comprehension. Buy a standard dictionary and keep it nearby. Don't hesitate to make notations in it when you need to. Consult your dictionary when you need help understanding a passage that contains unfamiliar key words that are central to the main idea of the work, but don't spend too much time in the dictionary.

You may not always have time for the following suggestions, but if and when you can use them, they will make your dictionary use as productive as possible.

Read every meaning of a word, not just the first. Think critically about which meaning suits how the word in question is used, and choose the one that makes the most sense to you.

Substitute a word or phrase from the definition for the word. Use the definition you have chosen. Imagine, for example, that you encounter the following sentence and do not know what the word "indoctrinated" means:

The cult indoctrinated its members to reject society's values.

When you search the dictionary, you find several alternate definitions including "brainwashed," "instructed," and "trained exhaustively." You decide that the definition closest to the correct meaning is "brainwashed." Substituting this term, the sentence reads:

The cult brainwashed its members to reject society's values.

Reading and Writing Words in Context: Natural Language Development

Most people learn words best when they read and use them in written or spoken language. Although reading a definition tells you what a word means, you may have difficulty remembering that definition because you have no former knowledge, or context, to which to connect or compare it. Using a word in context after defining it will help to anchor the information so you can continue to build upon it.

Here are some strategies for using context to solidify your learning of new vocabulary words.

Use new words in a sentence or two right away. Do this immediately after reading their definitions, while everything is still fresh in your mind.

Reread the sentence where you originally saw the word. Go over it a few times to make sure you understand how the word is used.

Use the word over the next few days whenever it may apply. Try it while talking with friends, writing letters or notes, or in your own thoughts.

Consider where you may have seen or heard the word before. When you learn a word, going back to sentences you previously didn't understand may help you to broaden your understanding of its meaning. For example, when most children learn the Pledge of Allegiance, they memorize the words by rote without understanding exactly what "allegiance" means.

Later, when they learn the definition of "allegiance," the pledge provides a context for the word that is now understandable to them.

Seek knowledgeable advice.   If after looking up a word you still have trouble with its meaning, ask your instructor or a friend if they can help you figure it out.

If you keep a vocabulary journal, include sentences that place the word in context.   Write sentences near the word's definition.

Facing the challenges of reading is only the first step. The next important step is to examine why you are reading any given piece of material.

WHY AND HOW DO YOU DEFINE YOUR PURPOSES FOR READING?

As with all other aspects of your education, asking important questions will enable you to make the most of your efforts. When you define your purpose, you ask yourself *why* you are reading a particular piece of material.

One way to do this is by completing this sentence: "In reading this material, I intend to define/learn/answer/achieve . . ." With a clear purpose in mind, you can decide how much time and effort to expend on various reading assignments. You also need to ask: "Ultimately, how will I be using this information? Will I have to include it in an essay, use it to apply on a multiple-choice test, or will I need it for an in-class discussion? Should I write or draw some sort of a visual representation of the material that makes good sense to me?"

Establishing and achieving your reading purpose requires adapting to different types of reading materials. Being a flexible, versatile reader—adjusting your reading strategies and pace—will help you to adapt successfully.

Purpose Determines Reading Strategy

With purpose comes direction and a goal, and with direction come strategies for reading. Following are four reading purposes, examined briefly. You may have one or more purposes and goals for each reading event you approach.

Purpose 1: Always read for understanding.   Unlike high school reading, in college, all of the studying you do involves reading for the purpose of comprehending the material. The two main components of comprehension are *general ideas* and *specific facts/examples*. These components depend on one another. Facts and examples help to explain or support ideas, and ideas provide a framework that helps the reader to remember facts and examples.

General Ideas. General-idea reading is rapid reading that seeks an overview of the material. You may skip entire sections as you focus on headings, subheadings, and summary statements in search of general ideas.

Specific Facts/Examples. At times, readers may focus on locating specific pieces of information—for example, the stages of intellectual development in young children. Often, a reader may search for examples that support or explain more general ideas—for example, the causes of economic recession. Because you know exactly what you are looking for, you can skim the material at a rapid rate. Reading your texts for specific information may help before taking a test.

> "In books, I could travel anywhere, be anybody, understand worlds long past and imaginary colonies in the future."
>
> Rita Dove

Purpose 2: Read to evaluate critically. Critical evaluation involves understanding first and foremost, and also approaching the material with an open mind, examining causes and effects, evaluating ideas, and asking questions that test the strength of the writer's argument and that try to identify assumptions. Critical reading is essential for you to demonstrate an understanding of material that goes beyond basic understanding of information, because critical reading requires a personal connection and response. You will read more about critical reading later in the chapter.

Purpose 3: Read for practical application of specifics. A third related purpose for reading is to gather usable information that you can apply toward a specific goal. When you read a computer software manual, an instruction sheet for assembling a gas grill, or a cookbook recipe, your goal is to learn how to do something. Reading and action usually go hand in hand. However, a certain degree of comprehension is necessary to remember the specifics.

Purpose 4: Read for pleasure. Some materials you read for entertainment, such as *Sports Illustrated* magazine or the latest John Grisham courtroom thriller. Recreational reading may also go beyond materials that seem obviously designed to entertain. Whereas some people may read a Jane Austen novel for comprehension, as in a class assignment, others may read Austen books for pleasure.

So far, this chapter has focused on reading as a deliberate, purposeful process of meaning construction. Recognizing obstacles to effective reading and defining the various purposes for reading is the groundwork for effective *studying*—the process of *owning* the concepts and skills contained in your texts.

HOW CAN PQ3R HELP YOU OWN WHAT YOU READ?

When you study, you take *ownership* of the material you read. You learn it well enough to apply it to what you do. For example, by the time students studying to be computer-hardware technicians complete their course work, they should be able to assemble various machines and analyze hardware problems that lead to malfunctions.

Studying to truly understand and learn also gives you mastery over *concepts*. For example, a dental hygiene student learns the causes of gum disease, a biology student learns what happens during photosynthesis, and a business student learns about marketing research.

This section will focus on a technique to help you understand, learn, study, and remember more effectively as you read your college textbooks.

Preview-Question-Read-Recite-Review (PQ3R)

PQ3R is a technique that will help you grasp ideas quickly, remember more, and review effectively and efficiently for tests. The symbols P-Q-3-R stand for *preview, question, read, recite, review,* which are steps in the studying process. Developed more than fifty-five years ago by Francis Robinson, and originally named SQ3R, the technique is still being used today because it works.[4] It is particularly helpful for studying all kinds of texts. When reading literature, for example, you may read the work once from beginning to end to appreciate the story and language. Then, reread it using PQ3R to master the material. Remember, however, that PQ3R is applicable to all types of texts and reading experiences.

Moving through the stages of PQ3R entails learning the techniques of skimming and scanning. **Skimming** involves rapid reading of various chapter elements, including introductions, conclusions, and summaries; the first and last lines of paragraphs; boldface or italicized terms; pictures, charts, and diagrams. The goal of skimming is a quick construction of the main ideas. In contrast, **scanning** involves the careful search for specific details. You will probably use scanning during the *review* phase of PQ3R when you need to locate and remind yourself of particular information. In a chemistry text, for example, you may scan for examples of how to apply a particular formula.

Skimming,
Rapid, superficial reading of material that involves glancing through to determine central ideas and main elements.

Scanning,
Reading material in an investigative way, searching for specific information.

Preview

The best way to ruin a "whodunit" novel is to flip through the pages to find out "whodidit." However, when reading textbooks, previewing can help you learn and is encouraged. *Previewing* refers to the process of surveying, or pre-reading, a book before you actually study it. Most textbooks include devices that give students an overview of the text as a whole as well as of the contents of individual chapters. As you look at Figure 4-2, think about how many of these devices you already use.

Question

Your next step is to examine the chapter headings and, on your own paper, write *questions* linked to those headings. If your reading material has no headings, develop questions as you read. These questions will focus your attention and increase your interest, helping you relate new ideas to what you already know, and building your comprehension. You can take

FIGURE 4-2   TEXT AND CHAPTER PREVIEWING DEVICES

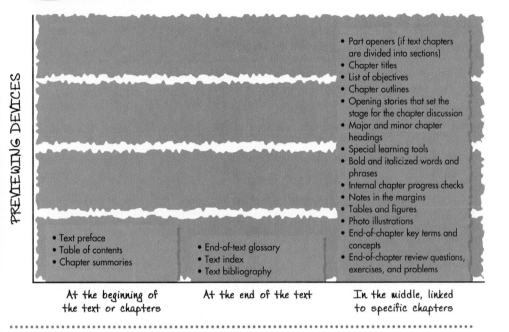

PREVIEWING DEVICES

- Part openers (if text chapters are divided into sections)
- Chapter titles
- List of objectives
- Chapter outlines
- Opening stories that set the stage for the chapter discussion
- Major and minor chapter headings
- Special learning tools
- Bold and italicized words and phrases
- Internal chapter progress checks
- Notes in the margins
- Tables and figures
- Photo illustrations
- End-of-chapter key terms and concepts
- End-of-chapter review questions, exercises, and problems

- Text preface
- Table of contents
- Chapter summaries

- End-of-text glossary
- Text index
- Text bibliography

At the beginning of the text or chapters | At the end of the text | In the middle, linked to specific chapters

questions from the textbook, from your lecture notes, or come up with them on your own when you preview, based on what ideas you think are most important.

Here is how this technique works. The column on the left contains primary- and secondary-level headings from a section of *Business,* an introductory text by Professors Griffin and Ebert. The column on the right rephrases these headings in question form.

I. THE CONSUMER BUYING PROCESS	I. WHAT IS THE CONSUMER BUYING PROCESS?
A. Problem/Need Recognition	A. Why must consumers first recognize a problem or need before they buy a product?
B. Information Seeking	B. What is information seeking and who answers consumers' questions?
C. Evaluation of Alternatives	C. How do consumers evaluate different products to narrow their choices?
D. Purchase Decision	D. Are purchasing decisions simple or complex?
E. Post-purchase Evaluations	E. What happens after the sale?

There is no "correct" set of questions. Given the same headings, you would create your own particular set of questions. The more useful kinds of questions are ones that engage the critical-thinking mind actions and processes found in Chapter 3.

Read

Your questions give you a starting point for *reading,* the first *R* in PQ3R. Read the material with the purpose of answering each question you raised. Pay special attention to the first and last lines of every paragraph, which should tell you what the paragraph is about. As you read, record key words, phrases, and concepts in your notebook. Some students divide the notebook into two columns, writing questions on the left and answers on the right. This method, known as the Cornell note-taking system, is described in more detail in Chapter 6.

If you own the textbook, marking it up—in whatever ways you prefer—is a must, if done sensibly. The notations you make will help you to interact with the material and make sense of it. You may want to write notes in the margins, circle key ideas, or selectively highlight key sections. Some people prefer to underline, although underlining adds more ink to the lines of text and may overwhelm your eye. Bracketing an entire key passage is a good alternative to underlining because it requires you to reread for understanding. Although writing in a textbook makes it difficult to sell the book back to the bookstore, the increased depth of understanding you can gain is worth the investment.

Selective highlighting may help you pinpoint material to review before an exam. Excessive highlighting is not a comprehension strategy! Here are some additional tips on highlighting and bracketing:

Get in the habit of marking the text *after* you read the material. If you do it while you are reading, you may wind up marking less-important passages.

Highlight key terms and concepts. Mark the examples that explain and support important ideas. You might try highlighting ideas in one color and examples in another.

Bracket figures and tables. They are especially important if they summarize text concepts.

Avoid overmarking. A phrase or two is enough in most paragraphs. Set off long passages with brackets rather than marking every line.

Write notes in the margins with a pen or pencil. Comments such as "key point" and "important definition" will help you find key sections later on.

Be careful not to mistake highlighting for learning. You will not learn what you highlight unless you review it carefully. You will benefit more from writing the important information you have highlighted into your lecture notes.

One critical step in the reading phase is to divide your reading into digestible segments. Many students read from one topic heading to the next, then stop. Pace your reading so that you understand as you go. If you find you are losing the thread of the ideas you are reading, you may want to try smaller segments, or you may need to take a break and come back to it later. Try to avoid reading in mere sets of time—such as, "I'll read for 30 minutes and then quit"—or you may destroy the meaning by stopping in the middle of a key explanation.

Recite

Once you finish reading a topic, stop and answer the questions you raised about it in the Q stage of PQ3R. You may decide to *recite* each answer aloud, silently speak the answers to yourself, tell the answers to another person as though you were teaching him or her, or write your ideas and answers in brief notes. Writing is undoubtedly the most effective way to solidify what you have read, because writing from memory checks your understanding. Use whatever techniques best suit your learning-style profile (see Chapter 1).

After you finish one section, move on to the next. Then repeat the question-read-recite cycle until you complete the entire chapter. If during this process you find yourself fumbling for thoughts, it means that you do not yet "own" the ideas. Reread the section that's giving you trouble until you master its contents. Understanding each section as you go is crucial because the material in one section often forms a foundation for the next.

Review

Review soon after you finish a chapter. Here are some techniques for re-viewing.

> ➢ Skim and reread your notes. Then, try summarizing them from memory.

> ➢ Answer the text's end-of-chapter review, discussion, and application questions.

> ➢ Quiz yourself using the questions you raised in the Q stage. If you can't answer one of your own or one of the text's questions, go back and skim or scan the material for answers.

> ➢ Review and summarize in writing the sections and phrases you have highlighted or bracketed.

➤ Create a chapter outline in standard outline form or think-link form.

➤ Reread the preface, headings, tables, and summary.

➤ Recite important concepts to yourself, or record important information on a cassette tape and play it on your car's tape deck or your portable cassette player.

➤ Make flashcards that have interrelated sets of ideas or words on one side and examples, the definitions, and other related information on the other. Test yourself.

➤ Think critically: Break ideas down into examples; consider similar or different concepts; recall important terms; evaluate ideas; and explore causes and effects.

➤ Make think links that show how important concepts relate to one another.

Remember that you can ask your instructor if you need help clarifying your reading material. Your instructor is an important resource. Pinpoint the material you want to discuss, schedule a meeting with him or her during office hours, and come prepared with a list of questions. You may also want to ask what materials to focus on when you study for tests.

If possible, you should review both alone and with study groups. Reviewing in as many different ways as possible increases the likelihood of retention. Figure 4-3 shows some techniques that will help a study group maximize their time and efforts.

Repeating the review process renews and solidifies your knowledge. That is why it is important to set up regular review sessions—for example, once a week. As you review, remember that refreshing your knowledge is easier and faster than learning it the first time.

As you can see in Table 4-3, using PQ3R is part of being an active reader. Active reading involves the specific activities that help you retain what you learn.

HOW CAN YOU RESPOND CRITICALLY TO WHAT YOU READ?

Your textbooks will often contain features that highlight important ideas and help you determine questions to ask while reading. As you advance in your education, however, many college reading assignments will not be so clearly marked, especially if they are primary sources. Your professors won't give you "worksheets" that point you to the important ideas. Therefore, you will need critical-reading skills in order to select the impor-

FIGURE 4-3 | STUDY GROUPS

Increased motivation. Because others will see your work and preparation, you may become more motivated.

Solidifying knowledge. When you discuss concepts or teach them to others, you reinforce what you know and how to think.

Group size. Limiting the group to two to five people is usually best.

Benefits

Be careful about...

Sharing each other's knowledge. Each student has a unique body of knowledge, and students can learn from each other's specialties.

Studying with friends. Resist your temptation to socialize until you are done.

Preparation. Members should study on their own before the meeting, so that everyone can be a team player.

Study Groups

Choose a leader for each meeting. Rotating the leadership helps all members take ownership of the group. Be flexible. If a leader has to miss class for any reason, choose another leader for that meeting.

Set a regular meeting schedule. Try every week, every two weeks, or whatever the group can manage.

Set general goals. Determine what the group wants to accomplish over the course of a semester.

Tips for Success

Set meeting goals. At the start of each meeting, compile a list of questions you want to address.

Share the workload. The most important factor is a willingness to work, not a particular level of knowledge.

Adjust to different personalities. Respect and communicate with members whom you would not necessarily choose as friends. The art of getting along will serve you well in the workplace, where you don't often choose your co-workers.

TABLE 4–3 USE PQ3R TO BECOME AN ACTIVE READER

ACTIVE READERS TEND TO . . .

Divide material into manageable sections	Answer end-of-chapter questions and applications
Write questions	Create a chapter outline
Answer questions through focused note-taking	Create think links that map concepts in a logical way
Recite, verbally and in writing, the answers to questions	Make flashcards and study them
Highlight key concepts	Recite what they learned into a tape recorder and play the tape back
Focus on main ideas found in paragraphs, sections, and chapters	Rewrite and summarize notes and highlighted materials from memory
Recognize summary and support devices	Explain what they read to a family member or friend
Analyze tables, figures, and photos	Form a study group

tant ideas, identify examples that support them, and ask questions about the text without the aid of any special features or tools provided by the teacher.

Critical reading enables you to consider reading material carefully, developing a thorough understanding of it through evaluation and analysis. A critical reader is able to discern the main idea of the piece as well as identify what in that piece of reading material is true or useful, such as when using material as a source for an essay. A critical reader can also compare one piece of material to another to find common attributes or to evaluate which makes more sense, which proves its thesis more successfully, or which is more useful for the reader's purposes.

Critical reading is reading that transcends rote memorization (just taking in and regurgitating material). Critical reading is both making meaning of the original text and adding your own "take" on the material to that meaning. You can read critically by using PQ3R to get a basic idea of the material and asking questions based on the critical-thinking mind actions, which simultaneously engages your critical-thinking processes. Remember that critical reading yields some retelling of the original work, but it also requires an answer that includes a personal response. As you read critically, remember a most important question: "So what?"

Use PQ3R to "Taste" Reading Material

Sylvan Barnet and Hugo Bedau, authors of *Critical Thinking, Reading, and Writing—A Brief Guide to Argument,* suggest that the active reading of

PQ3R will help you form an initial idea of what a piece of reading material is all about. Through previewing, skimming for ideas and examples, highlighting and writing comments and questions in the margins, and reviewing, you can develop a basic understanding of its central ideas and contents.[5]

Summarizing, part of the review process in PQ3R, is one of the best ways to develop an understanding of a piece of reading material. To construct a summary, focus on the central ideas of the piece and the main examples that support those ideas. A summary does *not* contain any of your own ideas or your evaluation of the material. It simply condenses the material, making it easier for you to focus on the structure of the piece and its central ideas when you go back to read more critically. At that point, you can ask "So what?" and begin to evaluate the piece and introduce your own ideas. Using the mind actions will help you.

> **Summary,**
> A concise restatement of the material, in your own words, that covers the main points.

Ask Questions Based on the Mind Actions

The essence of critical reading, as with critical thinking, is asking questions. Instead of simply accepting what you read, seek a more thorough understanding by questioning the material as you go along. Using the mind actions of the Thinktrix to formulate your questions will help you understand the material.

What parts of the material you focus on will depend on your purpose for reading. For example, if you are writing a paper on the causes of World War II, you might spend your time focusing on how certain causes fit your thesis. If you are comparing two pieces of writing that contain opposing arguments, you may focus on picking out their central ideas and evaluating how well the writers use examples to support these ideas.

You can question any of the following components of reading material:

> ➤ The central idea of the entire piece

> ➤ A particular idea or statement

> ➤ The examples that support an idea or statement

> ➤ The proof of a fact

> ➤ The definition of a concept

Following are some ways to critically question your reading material, based on the mind actions that focus on relationships between and among ideas. Apply them to any component you want to question by substituting the component for the words "it" and "this."

Similarity: What does this remind me of, or how is it similar to something else I know?

Difference: What different conclusions are possible?
How is this different from my experience?

<u>Cause and Effect</u>: Why did this happen, or, what caused this?
What are the effects or consequences of this?
What effect does the author intend, or, what is the purpose of the material?
What effects support a stated cause?

<u>Example to Idea</u>: How would I classify this, or, what is the best idea to fit this (these) example(s)?
How would I summarize this, or, what are the key ideas?
What is the thesis or central idea?

<u>Idea to Example</u>: What evidence supports this, or, what examples fit this idea?

<u>Evaluation</u>: How would I evaluate this? Is it valid or pertinent?
Does this example support my thesis or central idea?

Engage Critical-Thinking Processes

Certain thinking processes from Chapter 3 can help to deepen your analysis and evaluation of what you read. These processes are establishing truth, constructing an argument, and shifting perspective. Within these processes you will ask questions that use the mind actions.

Establishing Truth

With what you know about how to seek truth, you can evaluate any statement in your reading material, identifying it as fact, opinion, or assumption and challenging how it is supported. Evaluate statements, central ideas, or entire pieces of reading material using questions such as the following:

➢ Is this true? How does the writer know?

➢ How could I test the validity of this?

➢ What assumptions underlie this?

➢ What else do I know that is similar to or different from this?

➢ What information that I already know supports or disproves this?

➢ What examples disprove this as fact or do not fit this assumption?

For example, imagine that a piece of writing states, "The dissolving of the family unit is the main cause of society's ills." You may question the truth of this statement by looking at what facts and examples support it.

You may question the writer's sources of information. You may investigate its truth by reading other materials. You could discern that some hidden assumptions underlie this statement, such as an assumed definition of what a family is or of what constitutes "society's ills." You could also find examples that do not fit this assumption, such as successful families that don't fit the definition of "family" used by the writer.

Constructing an Argument

An argument is a proven point of view. Another way of defining an argument is as a main idea with compelling proof, often in the form of details. A strong argument includes a nod to the opposing point of view. When your reading material contains one or more arguments, you can use what you know about arguments to evaluate whether the writer has constructed his or her argument effectively. Ask questions like the following:

> ➤ What is the purpose of the writer's argument?
>
> ➤ Do I believe this? How is the writer trying to persuade me?
>
> ➤ If the author uses cause-and-effect reasoning, does it seem logical?
>
> ➤ Do the examples adequately support the central idea of the argument?
>
> ➤ What different and perhaps opposing arguments are included to add credibility?
>
> ➤ If I'm not sure whether I believe this, how could I construct an opposing argument?

"With one day's reading a man may have the key in his hands."

Ezra Pound

Don't rule out the possibility that you may agree wholeheartedly with an argument. However, use critical thinking to make an informed decision, rather than accepting the argument outright.

Shifting Perspective

Your understanding of perspective will help you understand that many reading materials are written from a particular perspective. Perspective often has a strong effect on how the material is presented. For example, if a recording artist and a music censorship advocate were to each write a piece about a controversial song created by that artist, their different perspectives would result in two very different pieces of writing.

To analyze perspective, ask questions such as the following:

What perspective is guiding this? What are the underlying ideas that influence this material?

Who wrote this, and what may be the author's perspective? For example, a piece on a new drug written by an employee of the drug manufacturer may differ from a doctor's evaluation of the drug.

What does the title of the material tell me about its perspective? For example, a piece entitled "New Therapies for Diabetes" may be more informational; "What's Wrong With Insulin Injections" may intend to be persuasive.

How does the material's source affect its perspective? For example, an article on health management organizations (HMOs) published in an HMO newsletter may be more favorable and one-sided than one published in the *New York Times*.

Seek Understanding

The fundamental purpose of all college reading is basic understanding of the material. Reading critically, though, allows you to investigate what you read so you can reach the highest possible level of understanding. Think of your reading process as an archaeological dig. The first step is to excavate a site and uncover the artifacts. In reading, that corresponds to your initial preview and reading of the material. As important as the excavation is, the process would be incomplete if you stopped there and just took home a bunch of items covered in dirt. The second half of the process is to investigate each item, evaluate what all of those items mean, and derive new knowledge and ideas from what you discover. Critical reading allows you to complete that crucial second half of the process.

As you work through all of the different requirements of critical reading, remember that critical reading takes *time* and *focus*. Finding a time, place, and purpose for reading, covered earlier in the chapter, is crucial to successful critical reading. Give yourself a chance to gain as much as possible from what you read. Read to read more effectively by reading more!

читать

This word may look completely unfamiliar to you, but anyone who can read the Russian language and alphabet will know that it means "read." People who read languages that use different kinds of characters, such as Russian, Japanese, or Greek, learn to process those characters as easily as you process the letters of your native alphabet. Your mind learns to process

REAL WORLD PERSPECTIVE

· ·

How can I cope with a learning disability?

Clacy Albert, Washington State University—Pullman, Washington, Communications Major

All my life I've felt different. I just couldn't seem to learn the way other kids did. I felt stupid and afraid that other people would think I couldn't do any-thing right. I wouldn't raise my hand in class because I was afraid of being laughed at. I wouldn't volunteer for games because I was afraid I'd let my team down. Study groups were impossible for me. I didn't want anyone to know that I was different. Because of this, my self-esteem really suffered. I became very quiet.

It wasn't until I was a sophomore in high school that a teacher recognized something was wrong with the way I learned. It was my math teacher who saw that I couldn't recognize certain patterns. I would see things in reverse or not be able to recognize a pattern at all. He sat down with my parents and helped them understand something was wrong. Unfortunately, the school I attended didn't have any testing for learning disabilities, so I let it go until I was in college. When I enrolled at WSU they told us about the learning-disability resource center. My mom suggested I finally get the testing I needed. I'm glad I did, because now I know that I have dyslexia and need special assistance to handle my studies. I wish there was mandatory testing for this disability in grade school. If there had been

I wouldn't have suffered so deeply all these years. What suggestions do you have for helping me cope with this disability?

Edith Hall, Senior Sales Representative—Prentice Hall

I have a different disability but one that causes similar problems. I have Attention Deficit Hyperactivity Disorder, and the fact that it was undiagnosed and untreated for many years has caused lots of problems in my life. It wasn't until I was six years out of college that I was diagnosed with  ADHD. And the great thing about it is I don't feel crazy any more. Now I know why I can't sit still for long periods and why I can't complete large and/or long projects like other non-ADHD people can.

I think acknowledging that I had a disorder and then accepting it were the biggest steps to coping and living with this disorder. The other thing I have done is to get educated. I have read almost anything I can get my hands on. I am also involved in a support group. Having other people I can talk with about how my brain affects my behavior and my life truly is one of the best coping strategies I know.

Having a disability or disorder is not a bad thing. Ennis Cosby, slain son of comedian Bill Cosby, said of his dyslexia, "The day I found out I had dyslexia was the best day of my life." Finding out he had dyslexia relieved him of the belief that he was dumb or stupid or slow. For me, like Ennis Cosby, finding out I had ADHD was a great day in my life because I now had tools and help to be different . . . and I no longer felt alone.

individually each letter or character you see. This ability enables you to move to the next level of understanding—making sense of those letters or characters when they are grouped to form words, phrases, and sentences.

Think of this concept when you read. Remember that your mind is an incredible tool, processing unmeasurable amounts of information so you can understand the concepts on the page. Give it the best opportunity to succeed by reading as often as you can and by focusing on all of the elements that help you read to the best of your ability.

Chapter 4: Applications

Name _____ Date _____

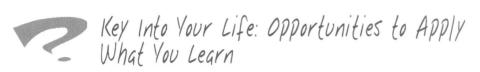 Key Into Your Life: Opportunities to Apply What You Learn

Exercise 1: Previewing Your Textbook[6]

Previewing is an important step in PQ3R *(preview, question, read, recite, review)*. Use the following form to conduct this preview on one of the most important texts you are using this semester or term:

TEXTBOOK PREVIEW FORM

1. Textbook title and authors: _____

2. Describe the mission of the book as defined in the Preface. (*Mission* is defined by the scope of the book's contents, what it is trying to accomplish, and the readers for whom it is intended):

   _____

   _____

3. List three important features that will help you study the material covered in the text. (You will find a list of these features in the Preface):

   a. _____

   b. _____

   c. _____

4. What does the Table of Contents tell you about the contents and focus of the book? Does the book intend a comprehensive overview of the field or does it focus on a narrow part of the field?

   _____

   _____

5. Based on your preview, write a short statement about what you expect studying this text will be like.

   _____

   _____

   _____

Exercise 2: Previewing Individual Chapters[7]

Conduct the same type of analysis on an individual chapter of the text you just previewed.

CHAPTER PREVIEW FORM

1. Chapter title: _____
   What does the title tell you about the chapter's focus?

   _____

   _____

   _____

2. From the list below, check the study aids contained in the chapter:

   ☐ list of objectives

   ☐ chapter outline

   ☐ opening vignette

   ☐ major and minor chapter headings

   ☐ bold and italicized words
   and phrases

   ☐ internal chapter reviews

   ☐ marginal notes

   ☐ tables, charts, and figures

   ☐ photo illustrations, including captions

   ☐ end-of-chapter summaries

   ☐ end-of-chapter key terms and concepts

   ☐ end-of-chapter review questions,
   exercises, and problems

   ☐ other

   _____

3. Based on your analysis of these elements, which seem likely to provide you with the most studying assistance? Why?

   _____

   _____

   _____

4. Identify at least three break points in the chapter that will help you divide it into manageable segments. Note the page number and the location on the page.

   a. _____

   b. _____

   c. _____

SOCIAL GROUPS

Virtually everyone moves through life with a sense of belonging; this is the experience of group life. A **social group** refers to *two or more people who identify and interact with one another.* Human beings continually come together to form couples, families, circles of friends, neighborhoods, churches, businesses, clubs, and numerous large organizations. Whatever the form, groups encompass people with shared experiences, loyalties, and interests. In short, while maintaining their individuality, the members of social groups also think of themselves as a special "we."

Groups, Categories, and Crowds

People often use the term "group" imprecisely. We now distinguish the group from the similar concepts of category and crowd.

Category

A *category* refers to people who have some status in common. Women, single fathers, military recruits, homeowners, and Roman Catholics are all examples of categories.

Why are categories not considered groups? Simply because, while the individuals involved are aware that they are not the only ones to hold that particular status, the vast majority are strangers to one another.

Crowd

A *crowd* refers to a temporary cluster of individuals who may or may not interact at all. Students sitting together in a lecture hall do engage one another and share some common identity as college classmates; thus, such a crowd might be called a loosely formed group. By contrast, riders hurtling along on a subway train or bathers enjoying a summer day at the beach pay little attention to one another and amount to an anonymous aggregate of people. In general, then, crowds are too transitory and too impersonal to qualify as social groups.

The right circumstances, however, could turn a crowd into a group. People riding in a subway train that crashes under the city streets generally become keenly aware of their common plight and begin to help each other. Sometimes such extraordinary experiences become the basis for lasting relationships.

Primary and Secondary Groups

Acquaintances commonly greet one another with a smile and the simple phrase "Hi! How are you?" The response is usually a well-scripted "Just fine, thanks. How about you?" This answer, of course, is often more formal than truthful. In most cases, providing a detailed account of how you are *really* doing would prompt the other person to beat a hasty and awkward exit.

Sociologists classify social groups by measuring them against two ideal types based on members' level of genuine personal concern. This variation is the key to distinguishing *primary* from *secondary* groups.

According to Charles Horton Cooley (1864–1929), who is introduced in the box, a **primary group** is *a small social group whose members share personal and enduring relationships*. Bound together by *primary relationships*, individuals in primary groups typically spend a great deal of time together, engage in a wide range of common activities, and feel that they know one another well. Although not without periodic conflict, members of primary groups display sincere concern for each other's welfare. The family is every society's most important primary group.

Cooley characterized these personal and tightly integrated groups as *primary* because they are among the first groups we experience in life. In addition, the family and early play groups also hold primary importance in the socialization process, shaping attitudes, behavior, and social identity.

Source: Sociology, 6/E by John J. Macionis, ©1997. Reprinted by permission of Prentice-Hall, Inc., Upper Saddle River, NJ.

Exercise 3: Studying a Text Page

The excerpt on these pages is from the "Groups and Organizations" chapter in John J. Macionis's *Sociology*, a Prentice Hall text.[8] Using what you learned in this chapter about study techniques, complete the following items:

1. Identify the headings on the page and the relationship among them. Which headings are primary-level headings; which are secondary; which are tertiary (third-level heads)? Which heading serves as an umbrella for the rest?

_____

_____

2. What do the headings tell you about the content of the page? (Answer this question before you read the page.)

_____

_____

3. After reading the chapter headings, write three study questions. List the questions below:

a. _____

b. _____

c. _____

Exercise 4: Focusing on Your Purpose for Reading

For the previous sociology excerpt, how did you go about establishing a purpose for reading?

_____

_____

How would you set your purpose for reading without prompts such as those provided by this text?

_____

_____

KEY TO COOPERATIVE LEARNING: BUILDING TEAMWORK SKILLS

Troublesome Texts: Talk It Over   Break into small groups or pairs. Each group should choose, or be assigned, two or three of the following common reading problems. In your groups or pairs, "brainstorm" solutions to your problems (don't forget to add, and talk about, any problems you have that aren't listed below). Choose one person in your group who will write the answers on a piece of paper. Then, as a class, discuss the ideas you have gathered.

Problem on the Page

1. Stupid, unfamiliar vocabulary
2. Too long to read in one sitting
3. No headings and/or subheadings
4. No diagrams or pictures
5. Lofty language
6. No summary
7. Main ideas embedded and obscure
8. Loads of footnotes or endnotes
9. Print is too small to read comfortably
10. Any other problem that has affected you

KEY TO SELF-EXPRESSION: DISCOVERY THROUGH JOURNAL WRITING

To record your thoughts, use the lined pages preceding the next chapter or a separate journal.

Reading Challenges   What is your most difficult challenge when reading assigned materials? A challenge might be a particular kind of reading material, a reading situation, or the achievement of a certain goal when reading. Considering the tools that this chapter presents, make a plan that addresses this challenge. What techniques might help you most? How and when will you try them out? What positive effects do you anticipate they may have on you?

KEY TO YOUR PERSONAL PORTFOLIO: YOUR PAPER TRAIL TO SUCCESS

End-of-Chapter Cumulative Essay   According to a recent study of first-year college students, many students are unprepared for the "boredom and hard work" involved in reading and studying, and are likely to give up rather than try to tackle the texts. Unlike high school, where teachers explained what students needed from their books, college students are "on their own."

In light of the need for self-reliance in reading and studying, explain different methods you have developed for reading and learning effectively. Your goal is to demonstrate that you are inventing ways to be successful with reading and studying. Use information from your text, class discussion, and your own experience.

Journal Entry

Prentice Hall

Name _____ Date _____

Journal Entry

focus

LISTENING AND MEMORY:

Taking In and Remembering Information

In this chapter, you will explore answers to the following questions:

Why is listening a strategy to be developed?

How can you improve your listening strategies?

How do the memory systems work together?

How can you improve your memory?

When might you use mnemonic devices to boost memory power?

How can tape recorders help you listen, learn, and remember?

Although reading may take up more time than any other college activity, listening comes in a close second. You listen in class as instructors discuss key concepts, while studying as members of your study group share ideas, and while relaxing as friends share thoughts. With so much time spent listening, learning how to focus your listening will enable you to receive messages successfully, much as a photographer focuses a lens to get the clearest image. Compare your listening ability to your reading ability. Both require making sense of information.

Even the best listeners can have trouble remembering what they hear and read. If you forget the information on an exam as soon as you finish it, your victory is short-term—even if you achieve good grades. Memory has to be grounded, for the most part, in *comprehension—understanding*—rather than just remembering. Imagine that you're a nursing student who memorized your way through anatomy. What good is an A on an anatomy exam if you can't remember the location of a leg bone when you meet your first patient with a fractured tibia? This chapter will explore specific techniques to boost your ability to take in, understand, and remember what you learn.

125

WHY IS LISTENING A STRATEGY TO BE DEVELOPED?

Listening,

A process that involves sensing, interpreting, evaluating, and reacting to spoken messages.

The ability to listen is something most people take for granted, because it is common to confuse the act of *hearing* with the act of *listening*. While hearing refers to sensing spoken messages from their source, **listening** is a more complex process of communication. Successful listening results in the speaker's intended message reaching the listener. In school or at home, poor listening results in communication breakdowns and mistakes, while strategic listening promotes progress and success.

Listening is also one of the most important strategies in the workplace. The way in which employees and managers listen to customers and to each other greatly affects their ability to work effectively. If you don't accurately hear what others in your workplace tell you, the quality of your work can be undermined no matter how much effort you put forth. For example, if an order for "twenty thousand" business cards sounds to you like "two thousand," you could have an unhappy customer on your hands! Accurate listening is an important key to workplace success.

Different kinds of thoughts can interfere with effective listening. Understanding the listening process, and the reasons people may have trouble listening well, can help you overcome these barriers.

The Stages of Listening

Listening is made up of four stages that build on one another: sensing, interpreting, evaluating, and reacting. These stages take the message from the speaker to the listener and back to the speaker (see Figure 5-1).

FIGURE 5–1   STAGES OF LISTENING

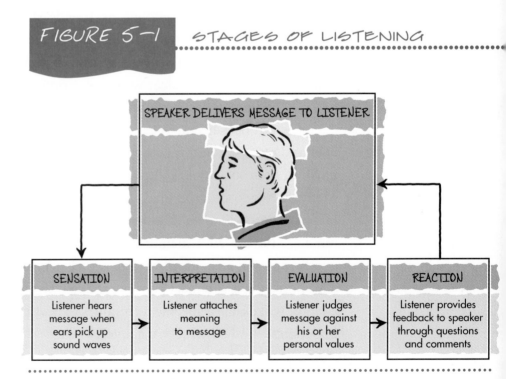

SENSATION	INTERPRETATION	EVALUATION	REACTION
Listener hears message when ears pick up sound waves	Listener attaches meaning to message	Listener judges message against his or her personal values	Listener provides feedback to speaker through questions and comments

During the *sensation stage* (also known as *hearing*), your ears pick up sound waves and transmit them to the brain. For example, you are sitting in class and hear your instructor say, "The only opportunity to make up last week's test is Tuesday at 5 P.M."

In the *interpretation stage*, listeners attach meaning to a message. This involves understanding what is being said and relating the message to what you already know. For example, when you hear this message you relate it to your knowledge of the test, whether you need to make it up, and what you are doing on Tuesday at 5 P.M.

In the *evaluation stage* of listening, you decide how you feel about the message—whether, for example, you like it or agree with it. This involves evaluating the message as it relates to your needs and values. If the message goes against your values or does not fulfill your needs, you may reject it, stop listening, or begin arguing in your mind with the speaker. In this example, if you do need to make up the test but have to work at Tuesday at 5 P.M., you may evaluate that you aren't thrilled with the message. What happens during the evaluation phase can interfere with listening.

The final stage of listening involves a *reaction* to the message in the form of direct feedback. In a classroom, direct feedback often comes in the form of questions and comments. Your reaction, in this example, may be to raise your hand or stick around after class and ask the instructor if there is any alternative to that particular makeup test time.

> "No one cares to speak to an unwilling listener. An arrow never lodges in a stone; often it recoils upon the sender of it."
> St. Jerome

HOW CAN YOU IMPROVE YOUR LISTENING STRATEGIES?

Even though you probably won't find a course in your college catalog entitled "Effective Listening," listening is a teachable—and learnable—skill. According to psychologist Beatrice Harris, "People can be trained to listen to content and tone. But learning takes persistence and motivation."[1] Although becoming a better listener will help in every class, it is especially important in subject areas that are tougher for you. For example, if your natural strengths are in English and communications, your ability to listen effectively to your physics instructor may mean the difference between understanding concepts and never grasping them—between success and failure. Improving your learning skills involves two primary actions: managing listening challenges and becoming an active listener.

Manage Listening Challenges

Communication barriers can interfere at each listening stage. In fact, classic studies have shown that immediately after listening, students are likely to recall only half of what was said. This is partly due to particular listening challenges such as divided attention and distractions, the tendency to shut out the message, the inclination to rush to judgment, and partial hearing loss or learning disabilities.[2]

To help create a positive listening environment, in both your mind and your surroundings, explore how to manage these challenges.

Divided Attention and Distractions

Imagine yourself at a noisy end-of-year party attended by about fifty friends. Relieved that final exams are over, you are talking with a friend about plans for the summer when, suddenly, you hear your name mentioned across the room. Your name was not shouted, and you weren't consciously listening to anything outside your own conversation. However, once you hear your name, you strain to hear more as you now listen with only half an ear to what your friend is saying. Chances are you hear neither person very well.

Situations like this happen often; they demonstrate the consequences of divided attention. While you are capable of listening to more than one message at the same time, you may not completely hear or understand any of these simultaneous messages. Learning to focus your attention—even as it is pulled in different directions—is one of your most important listening challenges.

Internal and external distractions often divide your attention. *Internal distractions* include anything from hunger to headache to personal worries. Something the speaker says may also trigger a recollection that may cause your mind to drift. In contrast, *external distractions* include environmental noises (whispering, honking horns, screaming sirens) and even excessive heat or cold. It is hard to listen effectively in an overheated room that is putting you to sleep.

Your goal is to reduce distractions so you can focus on what you're hearing. Sitting where you can see and hear clearly will help. When you can clearly see and hear your instructors, you have a much better chance of being able to listen well. You may even be more willing to listen, because knowing that instructors can see you may encourage you to take a more active part in receiving their messages. In order to avoid activity that might divide your attention, you may want to sit apart from people who might distract you by chatting or making noise.

Be sure you are as relaxed and alert as possible. Work to concentrate on class when you're in class and save worrying about personal problems for later. Try not to go to class hungry or thirsty. Dress comfortably. Bring a sweater or sweatshirt if you anticipate that the classroom will be too cold. If there's a chance you'll be too warm, wear a removable layer of clothing.

Shutting Out the Message

Instead of paying attention to everything the speaker says, many students fall into the trap of focusing on specific points and shutting out the rest of the message. Worse, if you perceive that a subject is too difficult or uninteresting, you may tune out everything. Shutting out the message makes it tough to listen well from that point on, and the information you miss may be the foundation for what goes on in future classes.

Creating a positive listening environment includes accepting responsibility for listening. While the instructor is responsible for communicating information to you, he or she cannot force you to listen. You are responsible for taking in the information that comes your way during class.

One important motivator is believing that what your instructors say is valuable. For example, some students might assume that anything not covered in the textbook isn't really important. As many people learn the hard way, however, instructors often cover material outside the textbook and test on that material. If you work to take in the whole message in class, you will be able to read over your notes later and think critically about what is most important.

The Rush to Judgment

People tend to stop listening during the evaluation stage when they hear something they don't like. If you rush to judge what you've heard, your focus turns to your personal reaction to what you heard rather than to the content of the speaker's message. Students who disagree during a lecture often spend a lot of their thinking time figuring out exactly how they want to word a question or comment in response.

Judgments also involve reactions to the speakers themselves. If you do not like your instructors or if you have preconceived notions about their ideas or cultural background, you may decide that their words have little value. Anyone whose words have ever been ignored because of race, ethnic background, gender, or disability understands how prejudice can interfere with listening.

Understanding how your emotions and opinions can interfere with listening will help you recognize and control your judgments. Being aware of what you tend to judge will help you avoid putting up a barrier against incoming messages that clash with your opinions or feelings. Keeping an open mind means being aware of the things you believe in as well as your prejudices. It also means defining education as a continuing search for evidence, regardless of whether it supports or negates your point of view.

Partial Hearing Loss and Learning Disabilities

Good listening techniques don't solve every listening problem. Students who have a partial hearing loss have a physical reason for difficulty in listening. If you have some level of hearing loss, seek out special services that can help you listen in class. You may require special equipment or might benefit from tutoring. You may be able to arrange to meet with your instructor outside of class to clarify your notes.

Other disabilities, such as Attention Deficit Disorder (ADD) or a problem with processing heard language, can cause difficulties with both focusing on and understanding that which is heard. People with such disabilities have varied ability to compensate for and overcome them. If you have a disability, don't blame yourself for having trouble listening. Your counseling center, student health center, advisor, and instructors should be able to give you assistance in working through your challenges.

Become an Active Listener

On the surface, listening seems like a passive activity; you sit back and listen as someone else speaks. Effective listening, however, is really an active process that involves setting a purpose for listening, asking questions,

putting "extra" listening time to good use, and paying attention to instructors' nonverbal messages and verbal signposts.

Set Purposes for Listening (Much Like for Reading)

Active listening is difficult to achieve if you don't know or care why you are listening. Think through why you listen in any situation. Establish what you want to achieve by listening, such as greater understanding of the material, a more direct connection with your instructor, a clear understanding of a phone message, staying awake in class, or better note-taking. Just as in active reading, when you set a purpose, you have a goal that you can achieve only through active listening. A purpose for listening motivates you to listen.

Ask Questions

Asking questions is not a sign of stupidity or a reason to doubt your intelligence. Question-asking sets purposes. In fact, a willingness to ask questions shows a desire to learn, and is the mark of an active listener and critical thinker. Some questions are informational—seeking information—such as any question beginning with the phrase, "I don't understand. . . ." Other clarifying questions state your understanding of what you just heard and ask if that understanding is correct. While some clarifying questions focus on a key concept or theme ("So, some learning disorders can be improved with treatment?"), others highlight specific facts ("Is it true that dyslexia can cause people to reverse letters and words?").

While asking questions and making comments indicates that you are an active participant in the listening process, you might spend so much time thinking about what to ask that you stop listening to the continuing message. One way to avoid this is to quickly jot down your questions and come back to them during a discussion period or when you can talk to the instructor one-on-one. When you know that your question is on paper, you may be more able to relax and listen.

Take Cues From Instructors' Nonverbal Messages and Verbal Signposts

Listening between the lines means paying attention to the *way* people speak, through body language and tone of voice, rather than just to what is being said. Even though nonverbal cues can sometimes be difficult to read, you can usually assume that when an instructor emphasizes a point by writing it on the blackboard, by speaking more loudly or softly than usual, or by slowing the rate of speech, the message is important.

You can also identify important facts and ideas and predict test questions by paying attention to the speaker's specific choice of words. For example, an idea described as "new and exciting" or "classic" is more likely to be on a test than one described as "interesting." **Verbal signposts** often involve transition words and phrases that help organize information,

Verbal Signpost, Spoken words or phrases that call your attention to the information that follows.

TABLE 5–1 PAYING ATTENTION TO VERBAL SIGNPOSTS

SIGNALS POINTING TO KEY CONCEPTS	SIGNALS OF SUPPORT
There are two reasons for this . . .	For example, . .
A critical point in the process involves. . .	Specifically, . .
Most importantly, . .	For instance, . .
The result is . . .	Similarly, . .
SIGNALS POINTING TO DIFFERENCES	**SIGNALS THAT SUMMARIZE**
On the contrary, . .	Finally, . .
On the other hand, . .	Recapping this idea, . .
In contrast, . .	In conclusion, . .
However, . .	As a result, . .

Source: Adapted from George M. Usova, *Efficient Study Strategies.* Pacific Grove, CA: Brooks/Cole Publishing Company, p. 69.

connect ideas, and indicate what is important and what is not. Learn to listen for the phrases listed in Table 5-1. Let them direct your attention to the material that follows them.

The habit of effective listening will enable you to acquire knowledge. You also need a good memory, however, so you can remember what you've heard. A good memory is made up of skills that improve with practice.

HOW DO THE MEMORY SYSTEMS WORK TOGETHER?

You need effective memory systems in order to use the knowledge you take in throughout your life. Therefore, listening and memory are powerfully related. Human memory works somewhat like a computer. Both perform essentially the same functions—in stages—to encode, store, and retrieve information.

During the *encoding stage,* information is changed into usable form. On a computer, this occurs when keyboard entries are transformed into electronic symbols, which are then stored on a computer disk. In the brain, sensory information becomes impulses that the central nervous system reads and codes. You are encoding, for example, when you study a list of chemistry formulas.

During the *storage stage,* information is held in memory (the mind's version of a computer hard drive) so it can be used later. In this example, after you complete your studying of the formulas, your mind stores them until you need to use them.

During the *retrieval stage,* stored memories are recovered from storage, just as a saved computer program is called up by name and used again. In this example, your mind would retrieve the chemistry formulas when you had to take a test or solve a problem.

Stored memories are placed in three very different kinds of information storage banks. Each is its own unique system that works together with the other memory systems. The first, called *sensory memory,* is an exact copy of what you see and hear, and lasts for a second or less. Certain information is then selected from sensory memory and becomes part of conscious awareness. This information moves into *short-term memory,* a temporary information storehouse that lasts no more than ten to twenty seconds. You are consciously aware of material in your short-term memory. While unimportant information is quickly dumped, important information may be transferred to *long-term memory*—the mind's more permanent information storehouse. The strategies you choose to employ determine how your memory systems work (or do not work) together.

Suppose your history instructor lists five major causes of the Civil War. As you listen to the causes, the incoming information immediately becomes part of sensory memory and, since you are paying attention, it is quickly transferred to short-term memory. Nearby whispering may never get past the stage of sensory memory, since your mind selectively pays attention to some things while ignoring others. Realizing that you will probably be tested on this information, you consciously decide that it is important enough to remember. Depending on the memory strategy you use, it then may become part of long-term memory.

Having information in long-term memory does not necessarily mean that you will be able to recall it when needed. Particular *active memory* techniques can help you improve your recall.

HOW CAN YOU IMPROVE YOUR MEMORY?

> *"The true art of memory is the art of attention."*
> Samuel Johnson

Your accounting instructor is giving a test tomorrow on the use of bookkeeping programs. You feel confident since you spent hours last week memorizing the material. Unfortunately, by the time you take the test, you may remember very little. That's because most forgetting occurs within minutes after memorization.

In a classic study conducted in 1885, researcher Herman Ebbinghaus memorized a list of meaningless three-letter words such as CEF and LAZ. He then waited and examined how quickly he forgot these words. It happened in a surprisingly short time: Within one hour he had forgotten more than 50 percent of what he learned. After two days, he knew fewer than 30 percent of the memorized words. Although Ebbinghaus's recall of the nonsense syllables remained fairly stable after that, his experiment shows how fragile memory can be—even when you take the time and energy to memorize information.[3]

If forgetting is so common, why do some people have better memories than other people? Some may have an inborn talent for remembering. More often, though, they succeed because they have practiced and mastered techniques for improving recall. Remember that techniques aren't a cure-all for memory difficulties, especially for those who may have disabilities such as ADD. If you have a disability, the following memory techniques may help you but may not be enough. Seek specific assistance if you consistently have trouble remembering.

Use Specific Memory Strategies for Specific Learning Situations

As a student, your job is to understand, learn, and remember a great deal of information—everything from general concepts to specific details. Remembering involves two kinds of memory processes: general remembering (comprehension) and verbatim memorization.

> <u>General remembering, or *comprehension*</u>—the most frequently required type of memory task—involves remembering ideas, but not the exact words in which the ideas are expressed.

> <u>Verbatim memorization</u> involves learning a mathematical formula, an unfamiliar language, the sequence of operating a machine, and so on.

The following suggestions will help improve your recall in both memory processes.

Develop a Will to Remember

Why can you remember the lyrics to dozens of popular songs but not the functions of the pancreas? Perhaps this is because you want to remember them, connect them with a visual image, or have an emotional tie to them. To achieve the same results at school or on the job, tell yourself that what you are learning is important and that you need to remember it. Saying these words out loud can help you begin the active, positive process of memory improvement.

A simple experiment demonstrates what developing the will to remember can do for you. Think for a moment about the common, ordinary U.S. penny. Although it is easy to remember that Abraham Lincoln's picture is engraved on the penny's head, it is hard to recall anything else. Try it yourself by looking at Figure 5-2. Which penny represents the real thing and which are the fakes?[4]

Most people have trouble identifying the correct answer because it was never important for them to focus on the details of the coin's design. Thus, they "forget" because they never created the memory in the first place.

Recite, Rehearse, and Write

When you *recite* material, you repeat it aloud in order to remember it. Reciting helps you retrieve information as you learn it and is a crucial step in studying (see Chapter 4). Frequently stopping to summarize aloud as you

FIGURE 5-2 CAN YOU RECOGNIZE A REAL PENNY?

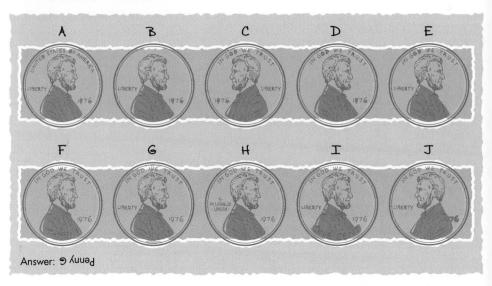

Answer: Penny G

Source: Adapted from R.S. Nickerson and M. J. Adams, "Long-Term Memory for a Common Object," *Cognitive Psychology,* 1979(11) pp. 287–307. Used with permission of Academic Press, Inc.

read can maximize your textbook studying. *Rehearsing* is similar to reciting, but is done silently. It involves the process of mentally repeating, summarizing, and associating information with other information. *Writing* is rehearsing on paper. The act of writing solidifies the information in your memory.

Separate Main Points From Unimportant Details

If you use critical-thinking skills to select and focus on the most important information, you can avoid overloading your memory with extra clutter. To focus on key points, highlight only the most important information in your texts and write notes in the margins about central ideas. When you review your lecture notes, highlight or rewrite the most important information to remember. Figure 5-3 shows how this is done on a section of text that introduces the concept of markets. This excerpt is from the fourth edition of *Marketing: An Introduction,* a Prentice Hall textbook written by professors Philip Kotler and Gary Armstrong.[5]

Study During Short but Frequent Sessions

If you think you have mastered material after studying it once, you might be shortchanging yourself. Research has shown that you can improve your chances of remembering vital material if you learn it more than once. The more you study, the more likely you are to remember at exam time.

To get the most out of your study sessions, spread them over time. A pattern of short sessions followed by brief periods of rest is more effective

FIGURE 5-3 EFFECTIVE HIGHLIGHTING AND MARGINAL NOTES AID MEMORY

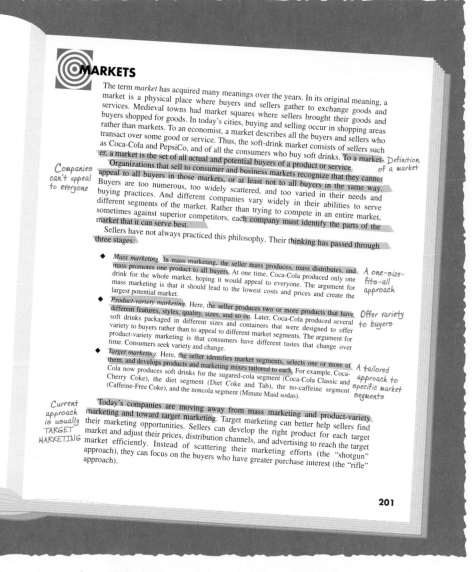

Source: Excerpt from Philip Kotler and Gary Armstrong, *Marketing: An Introduction, 4th ed.,* ©1997, p. 201. Reprinted with permission of Prentice-Hall, Inc., Upper Saddle River, NJ.

than continual studying with little or no rest. Even though you may feel as though you accomplish a lot by studying for an hour without a break, you'll probably remember more from three 20-minute sessions.

With this in mind, try studying during breaks in your schedule. Although studying between classes isn't for everyone, you may find that it can help you remember more of what you study. When studying for several

tests at a time, avoid studying two similar subjects back to back. You'll avoid the interference of one set of related topics with another when you study history right after biology rather than, for example, if you study chemistry after biology.

Separate Material Into Manageable, Interrelated Sections

Generally, when material is short and easy to understand, studying it start to finish improves recall. With longer material, however, you may benefit from dividing it into logical sections, mastering each section, putting all the sections together, and then testing your memory of all the material. Actors take this approach when learning the lines of a play, and it can work just as well for students.

Use Visual Aids

Any kind of visual representation of study material can help you remember. You may want to convert material into a think link or outline. Write material in any visual shape that helps you recall it and link it to other information.

Flashcards are a great memory tool. They give you short, repeated review sessions that provide immediate feedback. Such sessions are usually more effective than long cram sessions.

Make your cards from three-by-five-inch index cards. Use the front of the card to write a word, idea, or phrase you want to remember. Use the back side for a definition, explanation, and other key facts. Figure 5-4 shows two flashcards used to study for a psychology exam.

Here are some suggestions for making the most of your flashcards:

> ➢ *Use the cards as a self-test.* Divide the cards into two piles: the material you know and the material you are learning. You may want to use rubber bands to separate the piles.

> ➢ *Carry the cards with you and review them frequently.* You'll learn the most if you start using cards early in the course, well ahead of exam time.

> ➢ *Shuffle the cards and learn information in various orders.* This will help avoid the problem of weak learning in the middle of your review.

> ➢ *Test yourself in both directions.* First, look at the terms and provide the definitions or explanations. Then turn the cards over and reverse the process.

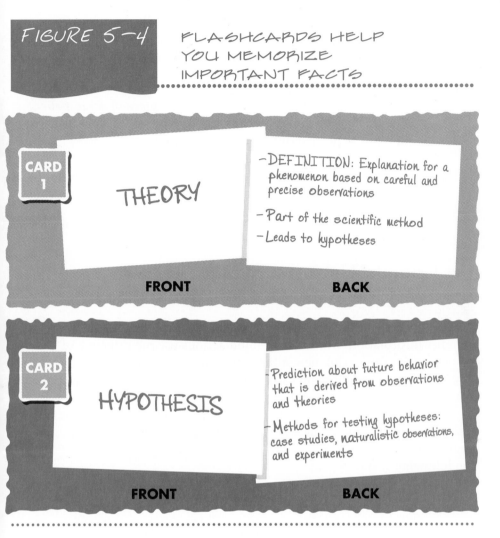

FIGURE 5-4 FLASHCARDS HELP YOU MEMORIZE IMPORTANT FACTS

CARD 1

THEORY

—DEFINITION: Explanation for a phenomenon based on careful and precise observations

—Part of the scientific method

—Leads to hypotheses

FRONT   **BACK**

CARD 2

HYPOTHESIS

—Prediction about future behavior that is derived from observations and theories

—Methods for testing hypotheses: case studies, naturalistic observations, and experiments

FRONT   **BACK**

Make the Most of Last-Minute Review

Last-minute studying, or *cramming*, often results in forgetting much of the material learned. Study conditions, however, aren't always ideal. Sometimes a busy week may leave you only a few hours to prepare for a big exam. Nearly every student crams sometime during college. If you end up with a tight schedule, use these hints to make the most of your study time:

➤ *Go through your flashcards,* if you have them, one last time.

➤ *Resist going through your notes or textbook page by page.* Bracket crucial concepts and don't sweat the rest.

➤ *Create a last-minute study sheet with hard-to-remember material.* On a single sheet of paper, write down key facts, definitions, formulas, and so on. Try to keep the material short and simple. If you prefer visual notes, use think links to map out ideas and their supporting examples (see Chapter 6 for more information about think links).

> *Arrive at the exam room a few minutes early.* Don't study the sheet or your flashcards until you are asked to clear your desk; instead, relax and resist taking on others' anxieties.

> *While it is still fresh in your mind, after the test is distributed, record the study-sheet information on a piece of scrap paper.* Do this before looking at any test questions. Review this information as needed during the test.

After your exam, evaluate the effects cramming had on learning the material and what you will do to improve the situation next time. Set a goal to plan ahead.

> *"memory is the stepping-stone to thinking, because without remembering facts, you cannot think, conceptualize, reason, make decisions, create, or contribute."*
> Harry Lorayne

Use Critical Thinking to Facilitate Memory and Comprehension

Your knowledge of the critical-thinking mind actions can help you remember information. Many of the mind actions use the principle of *association*—considering new information in relation to information you already know. The more you can associate a piece of new information with your current knowledge, the more likely you are to remember it.

Imagine that you have to remember information about a specific historical event—for example, the signing of the Treaty of Versailles, the agreement that ended World War II. You might put the mind actions to work in the following ways:

Recall everything you know about the topic.

Think about how this event is *similar* to other events in history, recent or long ago.

Consider what is *different* and unique about this treaty in comparison to other treaties.

Explore the *causes* that led up to this event, and look at the event's *effects.*

From the general *idea* of treaties that ended wars, explore other *examples* of such treaties.

Think about *examples* of what happened during the treaty signing, and from those examples come up with *ideas* about the tone of the event.

Looking at the facts of the event, *evaluate* how successful you think the treaty was.

Working through every mind action might take time—you don't always have to use every one in every memory situation. Choose the ones that will help you most. The more information and ideas you can associate with the new item you're trying to remember, the more successful you will be.

WHEN MIGHT YOU USE MNEMONIC DEVICES TO BOOST MEMORY POWER?

Certain show business performers entertain their audiences by remembering the names of 100 strangers or flawlessly repeating 30 ten-digit phone numbers. These performers probably have superior memories, but genetics alone can't produce these results. They also rely on memory techniques, known as **mnemonic devices** (pronounced nehMAHNick), for assistance.

Mnemonic devices work by using associations—associating a meaning with the information. Instead of learning new facts by rote (repetitive practice), associations give you a hook on which to hang these facts and retrieve them. Rote memorization is useful primarily when the information to be stored *has no meaning*. That's why we have the "alphabet jingle" to remember those 26 characters. (What does the alphabet *mean*, anyway?) Mnemonic devices work when they create unusual, unforgettable mental associations; involve visual pictures; and make information familiar and meaningful.

> **Mnemonic devices,** Memory techniques that involve associating new information with simpler information or information you already know.

Here's an example of the power of mnemonics. Suppose you want to remember the names of the first six presidents of the United States. You notice that the first letters of their last names—Washington, Adams, Jefferson, Madison, Monroe, and Adams—together read W A J M M A. To remember them, first you might add an "e" after the "J" and create a short nonsense word, "wajemma." Then, to make sure you don't forget the nonsense word, you might picture the six presidents sitting in a row wearing pajamas. To remember their first names—George, John, Thomas, James, James, and John—you might set the names to the tune of "Happy Birthday" or any musical tune that you know.

Different kinds of mnemonic devices exist, including visual images and associations and acronyms. Study how these devices work, then apply them to your own memory challenges.

Create Visual Images and Associations

Visual images are easier to remember than images that rely on words alone. In fact, communication through visual images goes back to the prehistoric era, when people made drawings that still exist on cave walls. It is no accident that the phrase "a picture is worth a thousand words" is so familiar. The best mental images often involve bright colors, three-dimensional images, action scenes, inanimate objects with human traits, and images that are out of proportion, ridiculous, or funny.

Especially for visual learners, turning information into mental pictures helps improve memory. To remember that the Spanish artist Picasso painted "The Three Women," you might imagine the women in a circle dancing to a Spanish song with a pig and a donkey (pig-asso). Don't reject outlandish images—as long as they help you.

Using an Idea Chain to Remember Items in a List

An *idea chain* is a memory strategy that involves forming exaggerated mental images of twenty or more items. The first image is connected to the second image, which is connected to the third image, and so on. Imagine, for example, that you want to remember the seven Thinktrix mind actions that appear in the critical-thinking discussion in Chapter 3: recall, similarity, difference, cause and effect, example to idea, idea to example, and evaluation. You can use the visual icons to form an idea chain that goes like this:

The other end of a string tied around your finger leads to two pyramids

and ends at a black square office building next to one of the pyramids. Inside the building there's a courtyard with a fountain dripping into a pool. On the wall, a painted "ex" and an arrow direct you to a light bulb, which points to another "ex". Lit by the light bulb above, a set of scales weighs mail.

Create Acronyms for Series

Another helpful association method involves the use of the acronym. Physics instructors often supply the acronym "Roy G. Biv" to help students remember the colors of the spectrum. Roy G. Biv stands for Red, Orange, Yellow, Green, Blue, Indigo, Violet. In history, you can remember the big-three Allies during World War II—Britain, America, and Russia—with the acronym BAR.

When you can't create a name like Roy G. Biv, create an acronym from an entire sentence. Here, the first letter of each word in the sentence stands for the first letter of the memorized terms. When science students want to remember the list of planets in order of their distance from the sun, they learn the sentence: My very elegant mother just served us nine pickles. (Mercury, Venus, Earth, Mars, Jupiter, Saturn, Uranus, Neptune, and Pluto.)

Improving your memory requires energy, time, and work. In school, it also helps to master PQ3R, the textbook study technique that was introduced in Chapter 4. By going through the steps in PQ3R and using the specific memory techniques described in this chapter, you will be able to learn more in less time—and remember what you learn long after exams are over.

How can I retain new information for a longer period of time?

Litzka Stark, Sarah Lawrence College, Bronxville, NY

At Sarah Lawrence most of our exams are essay, so I haven't had to expend much effort memorizing facts. When I do, though, I use the standard mnemonic devices and write the information on index cards. Most of the time I try to avoid anything to do with memorization. Maybe I'm in denial, but I personally believe that memorization is not a good way to really learn something. I'd rather learn concepts or integrate the material into my life. I actually learn best when I study themes.

The greatest difficulty I have with memorization is being able to retain what I've learned. In a very short time the information is gone unless it's somehow reinforced. My question is, how do I retain the material or formulas I'm asked to remember, and not forget all of it down the road?

Carlos Vela Shimano, ITESM Campus Queretaro, Mexico

When I was in junior high, I took an alternative class that taught memorization skills. I learned to link random ideas together in a chain. That way I could visualize numerous concepts that were not necessarily related.

Today, in my classes, I create mindmaps during lectures. I draw a circle in the middle of the page representing the main theme. Then I link smaller circles off to one side or the other with related themes. Each one of those has circles of material or ideas relating to it. This really helps me keep the information visually organized. I think for me that is probably the best way I remember things.

I also have another method that helps me to remember dates, phone numbers, combination numbers, and PIN numbers. I link the number with something else in my life. For instance, I play on a soccer team. My PIN number for one of my accounts is the number of my jersey, plus the numbers of my two friends' jerseys who also play on the team. Since I love sports, I link numbers I need to remember with the shirts of famous athletes. My locker combination number has the same numbers as the ones Michael Jordan and Magic Johnson wear.

Finally, if you learn to build ideas from the simplest to the most complex—really understanding the reasons behind the concept and where and why the concepts were developed in the first place—it will really help you retain more of what you study.

HOW CAN TAPE RECORDERS HELP YOU LISTEN AND REMEMBER?

The selective use of a tape recorder can provide helpful backup to your listening and memory skills. It's important, though, not to let tape recording substitute for active participation. Not all students like to use tape recorders, but if you choose to, here are some guidelines and a discussion of potential effects.

Guidelines for Using Tape Recorders

Ask the instructor whether he or she permits tape recorders in class.   Some instructors don't mind, while others don't allow students to use them.

Use a small, portable tape recorder.   Sit near the front for the best possible recording.

Participate actively in class.   Take notes just as you would if the tape recorder were not there.

Use tape recorders to make study tapes.   Questions on tape can be like audio flashcards. One way to do it is to record study questions, leaving ten to fifteen seconds between questions for you to answer out loud. Recording the correct answer after the pause will give you immediate feedback. For example, part of a recording for a writing class might say, "The three elements of effective writing are. . . . (10–15 seconds). . . . topic, audience, and purpose."

Potential Positive Effects of Using Tape Recorders

> ➢ You can listen to an important portion of the lecture over and over again.

> ➢ You can supplement or clarify sections of the lecture that confused you or that you missed.

> ➢ Tape recordings can provide additional study materials to listen to when you exercise or drive in your car.

> ➢ Tape recordings can help study groups reconcile conflicting notes.

> ➢ If you miss class, you might be able to have a friend record the lecture for you.

Potential Negative Effects of Using Tape Recorders

> ➢ You may tend to listen less and take fewer notes in class.

> ➢ You may take terrible notes, figuring that you will rely on your tape.

➤ It may be time-consuming. When you attend a lecture in order to record it and then listen to the entire recording, you have taken twice as much time out of your schedule. Actually, it takes over three hours to transcribe a fifty-minute lecture word for word.

➤ If your tape recorder malfunctions or the recording is hard to hear, you may end up with very little study material, especially if your notes are sparse.

Think critically about whether using a tape recorder is a good idea for you. If you choose to try it, let the tape recorder be an additional resource for you instead of a replacement for your active participation and skills. Tape-recorded lectures and study tapes are just one study resource among many that will be helpful to you.

ཤེས་ས་ཡེངས་ཤིག

In Sanskrit, the written language of India and other Hindu countries, the characters above read *sem ma yeng chik,* meaning "Do not be distracted." This advice can refer to focus for a task or job at hand, the concentration required to critically think and talk through a problem, or the mental discipline of meditation.

Think of this concept as you strive to improve your listening and memory techniques. Focus on the task, the person, or the idea at hand. Try not to be distracted by other thoughts, other people's notions of what you should be doing, or any negative messages. Be present in the moment to truly hear and remember what is happening around you. Do not be distracted.

Chapter 5: Applications

Name _____   Date _____

 Key Into Your Life: Opportunities to Apply What You Learn

Exercise 1: Optimum Listening Conditions

Describe two recent classroom situations in which you had an easy time listening to the instructor:

Situation 1

Where are you? _____

What is the instructor discussing? _____
Is it a straight lecture or is there give and take between instructor and students?

_____

What is your state of mind? (List factors that might affect your ability to listen.)

_____

_____

Are there any external barriers to communication? If yes, what are they, and how do they affect your concentration?

_____

_____

Situation 2

Where are you? _____

What is the instructor discussing? _____
Is it a straight lecture or is there give and take between instructor and students?

_____

What is your state of mind? (List factors that might affect your ability to listen.)

_____

_____

Are there any external barriers to communication? If yes, what are they, and how do they affect your concentration?

_____

_____

Now describe a third situation, one where you have found it more difficult to listen.

Where are you? _____

What is the instructor discussing? _____

Is it a straight lecture or is there give and take between instructor and students?

_____

_____

What is your state of mind? (List factors that might affect your ability to listen.)

_____

_____

Are there any external barriers to communication? If yes, what are they, and how do they affect your concentration?

_____

_____

Examine the situations. Based on your descriptions, name three conditions that seem crucial to effective listening for you.

1. _____

2. _____

3. _____

How might you be able to recreate these conditions in more difficult situations such as the third one you described?

_____

_____

Exercise 2: Create a Mnemonic Device

Using what you learned about mnemonic devices, create a mnemonic that allows you to remember the seven mind actions of the Thinktrix, described in Chapter 3. If your mnemonic device is a mental picture, describe it here. If it is an acronym, write it here and then indicate the word for which each letter stands.

_____

_____

_____

Think of other situations in which you used a mnemonic device to remember something. What was the device? How effective was it in helping you remember the information?

_____

_____

_____

Exercise 3: Create an Idea Chain

Read the following list just once. Then try to recall the items in the order in which they appear: *radio, stapler, computer, Rosa Parks, pen, telephone, Tom Cruise, trombone, index card, orange juice, Maya Lin, Albert Einstein,* and *barbecued chicken.* How many items did you remember? _____ Most people have trouble remembering more than a few items at the beginning or end of the list.

To improve your recall, create an idea chain that links the first item to the second, the second to the third, and so on. The idea chain should paint an unforgettable picture. Describe your idea chain here:

_____

_____

_____

Wait a day, then use the idea chain to remember the list. How many items do you remember now?_____

KEY TO COOPERATIVE LEARNING: BUILDING TEAMWORK SKILLS

Hone Your Listening and Memory Skills   Improve listening and memory through teamwork. Divide into groups of five to nine to play a game called *Celebrity.* Each group will have two or three teams, each with two to three people (for example, a group of seven will have two teams of two and one of three). Using equal-sized scraps of paper, each person must write down the names of five well-known people, one on each scrap. The people may be living or dead and can have achieved celebrity status in any field—sports, entertainment, politics, arts and literature, science and medicine, and so on. Each scrap of paper should be folded to conceal the name written on it. Put all of the scraps together in one container (there will be thirty in all). The only other equipment you need is a watch with a second hand.

Within each team of two, there is a giver and a receiver (team members switch roles every time they have a new turn). Teams take turns guessing. While a member of a non-guessing team times the pair for one minute, the giver of the guessing team picks a scrap of paper and describes the named celebrity to the receiver without saying any part of the person's name. The giver can use words, sounds, motion, singing, anything that will help the receiver. (For Jackie Robinson: "Famous baseball player, first black man on a pro team, first name is the same as President Kennedy's wife," etc.) If and when the receiver guesses correctly, the giver keeps that scrap and chooses another, continuing to go through as many names as possible before the one minute is up. When time is called, the container of names (minus the names guessed) moves to the next team. (If a name remains unguessed when time is called, that scrap has to go back into the container without the giver revealing the name.)

When all the names have been guessed, teams count their scraps to find out their scores. Then come together as a class and take some time to exchange views about your experience. How did the time limit, teamwork atmosphere, or noise affect your ability to listen? Which names were you more able to remember? Which gave you trouble, and why? Evaluate your skills.

KEY TO SELF-EXPRESSION: DISCOVERY THROUGH JOURNAL WRITING

To record your thoughts, use the lined pages preceding the next chapter or a separate journal.

Pushing Past Your Emotions and Opinions   Write about what it is like to listen to an instructor you disagree with. Imagine that your disagreement is so strong that you feel angry about what the instructor is saying. Describe your typical reaction to a situation like this. Do you stop listening? Do you get caught up in an internal argument? Do you try to figure out the words you will use in a question or comment?

Based on what you learned in this chapter, describe how you plan to respond the next time an instructor touches on a sensitive topic. How might a new approach affect your ability to listen?

KEY TO YOUR PERSONAL PORTFOLIO: YOUR PAPER TRAIL TO SUCCESS

End-of-Chapter Cumulative Essay   New students think that if they "work" hard enough, their memories will be limitless and they will be able to "memorize" their way through college and their professional work. Using information from the text, class discussion, and your own experiences, explain how the memory works: When is rote memorization a good idea? When are memory devices such as mnemonics wise? Under what circumstances would you use different learning strategies for memory? Use examples from your different courses to illustrate your answer.

Journal Entry

Prentice Hall

Journal Entry

6

NOTE-TAKING AND RESEARCH:

Learning From Others by Combining Information Sources

In this chapter, you will explore answers to the following questions:

How does taking notes help you?

How can you make the most of class and book notes?

Which note-taking system should you use?

How can you write faster when taking notes?

How do you conduct research?

Both in school and out, you spend much of your time like a detective in search of knowledge. When you listen to your instructors during class lectures, do independent research, or learn on the job, you are uncovering and gathering information that you may put to use, now or in the future. Note-taking and research can empower you to create new ideas from what you learn. The more knowledge you gather in your "detective work," the more resources you have at your disposal when you move into new realms of thinking.

The search for knowledge requires varied skills. First, you need to use different effective note-taking systems to record what you hear or read. Second, you need to know how to harness the vast print and electronic resources of your college library. This chapter will show you note-taking, note-learning, and research skills that can help you successfully search for and use information.

HOW DOES TAKING NOTES HELP YOU?

Note-taking isn't always easy to do. You might feel that it prevents you from watching your instructor, or that you can't write fast enough, or that you seem to remember enough material even when you don't take notes. The act of note-taking, however, involves you in the learning process in many beneficial ways. Whatever you feel are the negative effects of note-taking, try weighing them against the potential positive effects. You may see why good note-taking makes sense (see Table 6-1).

Notes help you learn when you are in class, doing research, or studying. Since it is virtually impossible to take notes on everything you hear or read, the act of note-taking encourages you to think critically and evaluate what is worth remembering. Asking yourself questions like the following will help you judge what is important enough to write down.

> ➢ Do I need this information?

> ➢ Is the information important to the lecture or reading or is it just an interesting comment?

> ➢ Is the information fact or opinion? If it is opinion, is it worth remembering? (To explore this question, use the techniques described in the section entitled "How Do You Establish Truth?" in Chapter 3, pp. 75–79.)

Your responses will guide your note-taking in class and help you decide what to study before an exam. Similarly, the notes you take while doing research will influence your research efforts.

You have a number of different note-taking styles to choose from, including outlines, think links (mind maps), and the Cornell note-taking system. There are also ways to put your lecture notes together with your

TABLE 6-1 THE VALUE OF NOTES

✓ Your notes provide written material that helps you study information and prepare for tests.

✓ When you take notes, you become an active, involved listener and learner.

✓ Notes help you think critically and organize ideas.

✓ The information you learn in class may not appear in any text; you will have no way to study it without writing it down.

✓ If it is difficult for you to process information while in class, having notes to read and make sense of later can help you learn.

✓ Note-taking allows you to compile information from different research sources and use the information in your writing.

✓ Note-taking is a skill you will use on the job and in your personal life.

book notes. After you read about each one, base your choice on what feels right to you and what works best for the situation. For example, a student who generally prefers to take notes in think-link style might feel more comfortable using outline form for research.

Before you decide on a system, explore what class notes and book notes are and how to use each to your advantage.

HOW CAN YOU MAKE THE MOST OF CLASS AND BOOK NOTES?

Your class notes have two purposes: First, they should reflect what you heard in class; second, they should be a resource for studying, writing, or comparing and combining with your text material. Taking good class notes depends on good preparation, including the following:

➤ Preview the text to become familiar with the topic and possible unfamiliar concepts. Visual familiarity helps note-taking during lectures.

➤ Use separate pieces of 8½-by-11-inch paper for each class. If you use a three-ring binder, punch holes in papers your instructor hands out and insert them immediately following your notes for that day.

➤ Take a comfortable seat where you can easily see and hear, and be ready to write as soon as the instructor begins speaking.

➤ Choose a note-taking system that helps you handle the instructor's speaking style (you'll be more able to determine this style after a few classes). While one instructor may deliver organized lectures at a normal speaking rate, another may jump from topic to topic or talk very quickly.

➤ If the lecturer provides any visual organizers (outlines, charts), anticipate using them as a guide to structure your notes.

➤ Don't forget to pay attention to the "real-world" examples; they often become the source of test questions.

➤ Set up a support system with a student in each of your classes. That way, when you are absent, you can get the notes you missed.

What to Do During Class

Because no one has the time to write down everything he or she hears, the following strategies will help you choose and record what you feel is important, in a format that you can read and understand later.

➤ Date each page. When you take several pages of notes during a lecture, add an identifying letter or number to the date on each page: 11/27A, 11/27B, 11/27C, . . . or 11/27—1 of 3, 11/27—2 of 3, 11/27—3 of 3. This will help you keep track of the order of your pages. Add the specific topic of the lecture at the top of the page. For example:

11/27A—<u>U.S. Immigration Policy After World War II</u>

Since an instructor may revisit a topic days or even weeks after introducing it, this suggestion will help you gather all your notes on the same topic when it is time to study.

➤ If your instructor jumps from topic to topic during a single class, it may help to start a new page for each new topic.

➤ Some students prefer to use only one side of the note paper, because this can make notes easier to read and avoid the problem of flipping back and forth when studying. Others prefer to use both sides, which can be a more economical paper-saving option. Choose what works best for you.

➤ Record whatever your instructor emphasizes. See Figure 6-1 for more details about how an instructor might call attention to particular information.

➤ Write down all key terms and definitions. If, for example, your instructor is discussing the stages of mental development in children, as defined by psychologist Jean Piaget, your notes should

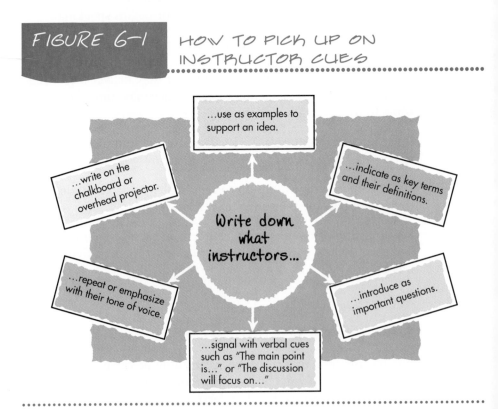

FIGURE 6-1   HOW TO PICK UP ON INSTRUCTOR CUES

...use as examples to support an idea.

...write on the chalkboard or overhead projector.

...indicate as key terms and their definitions.

Write down what instructors...

...repeat or emphasize with their tone of voice.

...introduce as important questions.

...signal with verbal cues such as "The main point is..." or "The discussion will focus on..."

certainly mention the following terms: *sensorimotor, preoperational, concrete operations, formal operations.*

➤ Remember that tests don't just ask for definitions. Record terms in related sets, so you understand comparisons and contrasts among them.

➤ Continue to take notes during class discussions and question-and-answer periods. When your fellow students ask questions, the explanations may help you as well.

➤ Write down all questions raised by the instructor, since the same questions may appear on a test.

➤ Leave one or more blank spaces between major sections. This white space will help you review your notes, since information will be in self-contained segments. (This suggestion does not apply if you are using a think link.)

➤ You may use those white spaces to insert additional material from your text that makes the notes more complete and easier to understand.

➤ Draw pictures and diagrams that help illustrate ideas.

➤ Write quickly but legibly. This may involve using a form of shorthand (see the section on shorthand beginning on p. 163 of this chapter).

➤ If you cannot understand what the instructor is saying, leave a space where the explanation belongs and place a question mark in the margin. Then ask the instructor to explain it again after class, discuss it with a classmate, or consult your textbook. Take advantage of all of your resources (instructor, students, textbook, other materials) when clarifying a question, and fill in the blank when the idea is clear.

➤ Take notes until the instructor stops speaking. Students who stop writing a few minutes before the class is over may miss critical information.

➤ Make your notes as legible, organized, and complete as possible. Your notes are only useful if you can read and understand them. Remember, you always have the option to revise and improve your notes!

➤ Think of the notes you get in a class as a very important part, but not all, of what you need to learn. Adding to the notes from the text after class makes a superior, "deeper and wider" set of information to be learned.

"Consistency is important. If you use the same system of indicating importance, such as indenting, spacing, or underlining on each page of your notes, your mind will perceive the key information with a minimum of effort."
William H. Armstrong and M. Willard Lampe II
(Source: From *A Pocket Guide to Study Tips* by W. H. Armstrong, M.W. Lampe, and G. Ehrenhaft. Copyright © 1997 by Barrons Educational Series, Inc.)

Make Notes a Valuable After-Class Reference: Add Text Material

Class notes, along with additions and further explanations added from your print sources, are a valuable study tool when you review them regularly. As mentioned above, you can include book information in your notes by using a format that allows you to add or clarify points easily. Empty lines between main points leaves a good place to insert book information. The act of reviewing (after the class and on a regular basis) helps you remember important concepts and links new information to information you already know. Invent a system that works for you and allows easy consolidation of lecture and text.

If you can, try to begin your review the same day of the lecture, as soon as possible after the class. Read over your notes to learn the information and to clarify difficult concepts and shorthand abbreviations. Fill in missing information by referring to your text; underline or highlight key points. You may also want to add headings and subheadings and insert clarifying phrases or sentences. Besides day-to-day keeping up, try to review each week's notes at the end of that week. Think critically about the material, in writing, study-group discussions, or quiet reflective thought. You might use critical-thinking actions to add on to your notes in the following ways:

 Consider how easily you can recall the facts and figures in your notes.

 Brainstorm and write down examples that illustrate central ideas.

 Evaluate how important the ideas are in your notes, and highlight or rewrite the most important ones.

 Think of similar facts or ideas that will help you understand your notes.

 Consider what in your class notes might differ from your book notes, and why.

 Write down any new ideas that come up when rereading your notes.

 Look at cause-and-effect relationships in the material. Note how ideas, facts, and examples relate to one another.

Writing a **summary** of your notes is another important review technique. Summarizing involves critically evaluating what ideas and examples are most important and then rewriting the material in a shortened form, focusing on those important ideas and examples. You may prefer to summarize as you review your notes, although you might also try summarizing your notes from memory after you review them.

Study groups can be a useful way to review notes, because group members can benefit from each other's different perspectives and abilities. For example, if you happened to focus well on one particular part of the lecture and lost concentration during another, a fellow student may have been taking good notes on the part you missed. If you are a part of a study group, compare your notes with the notes of other group members to make sure they are complete and accurate. If there are gaps, fill them in. If another explanation seems to make more sense than the one you have, copy it down.

Your class and book notes will help you study for tests. Use them along with your textbook, text study notes, and other sources. Your combined "deeper and wider" notes may help you predict what will be covered on a test and may even point to specific test questions. Remember, tests are derived from a combination of lecture and book material—therefore, the sources should be studied together.

Summary,
The substance of a body of material, presented in a condensed form by reducing it to its main points.

WHICH NOTE-TAKING SYSTEM SHOULD YOU USE?

There are many ways to take notes; the choice is yours. You will benefit most from the system that feels most comfortable to you and makes the best sense for the type of content covered in any given course. For example, you might take notes in a different style for a history class than for a foreign language class. As you consider each system, remember the learning-styles profile you compiled in Chapter 1. Everyone has a different learning and working style, so don't wedge yourself into a system that doesn't work for you. The most common note-taking systems include outlines, the Cornell system, and think links.

Taking Notes in Outline Form

When a reading assignment or lecture seems well organized, you may choose to take notes in outline form. *Outlining* shows the relationships among ideas and their supporting examples through the use of line-by-line phrases set off by varying indentations. When you use an outline, you construct a line-by-line representation of how ideas relate to one another and are supported by facts and examples. Obviously, if a lecturer offers the class an outline to follow, you should use it to your advantage. When outlining textbook chapters, use headings and subheadings as your guide.

Formal Versus Informal Outlines

Formal outlines indicate ideas and examples using Roman numerals, capital and lowercase letters, and numbers. The rules of formal outlines require at least two headings on the same level. That is, if you have a II A, you must also have a II B. Similarly, if you have a III A 1 you must also have a III A 2. In contrast, *informal outlines* show the same relationships but replace the formality with a system of consistent indenting and dashes. Informal outlining goes a lot faster in a lecture setting.

Figure 6-2 shows the difference between the two outline forms. Because making a formal outline can take time and focus, many students find that the time pressures of in-class note-taking make using formal outlines unwise and inefficient. You might be more able to keep up if you use an informal outline instead. Note how informal outlining uses space on the page, rather than numbers or letters, to show how concepts relate to one another.

Figure 6-3 shows how a student has used the structure of a formal outline to write notes on the topic of civil-rights legislation.

FIGURE 6-2 THE STRUCTURE OF AN OUTLINE

FORMAL OUTLINE	INFORMAL OUTLINE
TOPIC	**TOPIC**
I. First Main Idea	First Main Idea
A. Major supporting fact	—Major supporting fact
B. Major supporting fact	—Major supporting fact
1. First reason or example	—First reason or example
2. Second reason or example	—Second reason or example
a. First supporting fact	—First supporting fact
b. Second supporting fact	—Second supporting fact
II. Second Main Idea	Second Main Idea
A. Major supporting fact	—Major supporting fact
1. First reason or example	—First reason or example
2. Second reason or example	—Second reason or example
B. Major supporting fact	—Major supporting fact

FIGURE 6-3   SAMPLE FORMAL OUTLINE

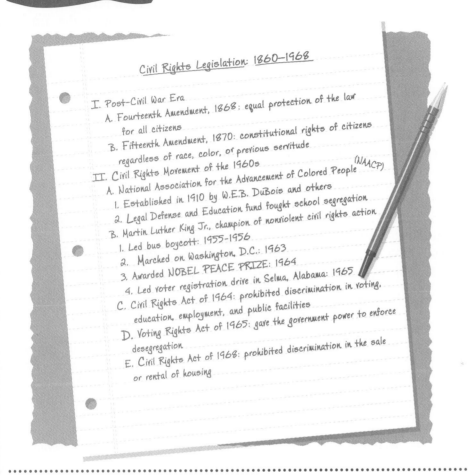

Pay attention to how successful you are when you attempt to use an outline to write class notes. If the material does not lend itself to an outline, try to focus on capturing the information in "chunks" of key topics, use arrows to show relationships, and know that after class you can reorganize the information by rewriting it.

Guided Notes

From time to time, an instructor may give you a guide to help you take notes in the class, usually in the form of an outline. This outline may be on a page that you receive at the beginning of the class, on the board, or on an overhead projector. Visuals from professors can be extremely helpful!

Although *guided notes* help you follow the lecture and organize your thoughts during class, they do not replace your own notes. Because they are more of a basic outline of topics than a comprehensive coverage of information, they require that you fill in the information presented in class. If you think that the guided notes are all you need, you will miss out on important information.

When you receive guided notes on paper, write directly on the paper if there is room. If not, use a separate sheet and write on it the outline categories that the guided notes suggest. If the guided notes are on the board or overhead, copy them down, leaving plenty of space in between for your own notes. If the professor leaves the outline in sight for the entire lecture, use it as you go rather than copying it at the beginning of the lecture. Copying the whole outline right away might result in your missing the first part of the lecture, which is often key to understanding the content of the entire class period.

"What sculpture is to a block of marble, education is to a human soul."
Joseph Addison

Using the Cornell Note-Taking System

The *Cornell note-taking system,* also known as the T-note system, was developed more than forty-five years ago by Walter Pauk at Cornell University.[1] Since then, the system has become widely accepted, and is now used and modified by students throughout the world.

The system is successful because it is simple—and because it works. It consists of three sections on ordinary note paper:

> ➤ *Section 1,* the largest section, is on the right. Here you record your notes in informal outline form.

> ➤ *Section 2,* to the left of your notes, is known as the *cue column.* Leave it blank while you read or listen, then fill it in later as you review. You might fill it with comments that highlight main ideas, clarify meaning, suggest examples, or link ideas and examples. You can even draw diagrams.

> ➤ *Section 3,* at the bottom of the page, is known as the *summary area.* Here you use a sentence or two to summarize the notes on the page. Use this section during the review process to reinforce concepts and provide an overview of what the notes are saying.

When you use the Cornell system, create the note-taking structure before class begins. Picture an upside-down letter *T* as you follow these directions, and use Figure 6-4 as your guide.

> ➤ Start with a sheet of standard loose-leaf paper. Label it with the date and title of the lecture.

> ➤ To create the *cue column:* Draw a vertical line about 2-½ inches from the left side of the paper. End the line about 2 inches from the bottom of the sheet.

> ➤ To create the *summary area:* Starting at the point where the vertical line ends (about two inches from the bottom of the page), draw a horizontal line that spans the entire paper.

Figure 6-4 shows how a student used the Cornell system to take notes in an introduction-to-business course.

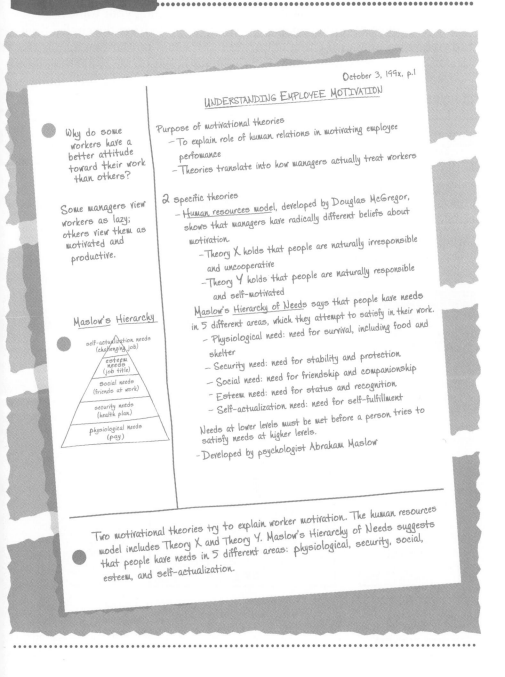

FIGURE 6-4   NOTES TAKEN USING THE CORNELL SYSTEM

October 3, 199x, p.1

<u>UNDERSTANDING EMPLOYEE MOTIVATION</u>

Why do some workers have a better attitude toward their work than others?

Some managers view workers as lazy; others view them as motivated and productive.

Maslow's Hierarchy

- self-actualization needs (challenging job)
- esteem needs (job title)
- social needs (friends at work)
- security needs (health plan)
- physiological needs (pay)

Purpose of motivational theories
- To explain role of human relations in motivating employee performance
- Theories translate into how managers actually treat workers

2 specific theories
- <u>Human resources model</u>, developed by Douglas McGregor, shows that managers have radically different beliefs about motivation
    - Theory X holds that people are naturally irresponsible and uncooperative
    - Theory Y holds that people are naturally responsible and self-motivated
<u>Maslow's Hierarchy of Needs</u> says that people have needs in 5 different areas, which they attempt to satisfy in their work.
    - Physiological need: need for survival, including food and shelter
    - Security need: need for stability and protection
    - Social need: need for friendship and companionship
    - Esteem need: need for status and recognition
    - Self-actualization need: need for self-fulfillment
Needs at lower levels must be met before a person tries to satisfy needs at higher levels.
- Developed by psychologist Abraham Maslow

Two motivational theories try to explain worker motivation. The human resources model includes Theory X and Theory Y. Maslow's Hierarchy of Needs suggests that people have needs in 5 different areas: physiological, security, social, esteem, and self-actualization.

Creating a Think Link

A *think link,* also known as a mind map, is a visual form of note-taking. When you draw a think link, you diagram ideas using shapes and lines that link ideas and supporting details and examples. Think links show relationships between and among concepts and ideas. The visual design makes the connections easy to see, and the use of shapes and pictures extends the material beyond just words. Many learners respond well to the power of **visualization**. You can use think links to brainstorm ideas for paper topics as well.

> **Visualization,**
> The interpretation of verbal ideas through the use of mental visual images.

One way to create a think link is to start by circling your topic in the middle of a sheet of unlined paper. Next, draw a line from the circled topic and write the name of the first major idea at the end of that line. Circle the idea also. Then draw lines from that circle, noting at the ends of those lines specific facts related to the circled idea. Continue the process, connecting thoughts to one another using circles, lines, and words. Figure 6-5 shows a think link on social stratification—a concept presented during a sociology class—that follows this particular structure.

You can design any kind of think link that feels comfortable to you. Different examples include stair steps showing connected ideas that build toward a conclusion, a tree shape with roots as causes and branches as effects, or a sun shape with a central idea and facts radiating out from the center. Figure 6-6 shows a type of think link sometimes referred to as a "jellyfish."

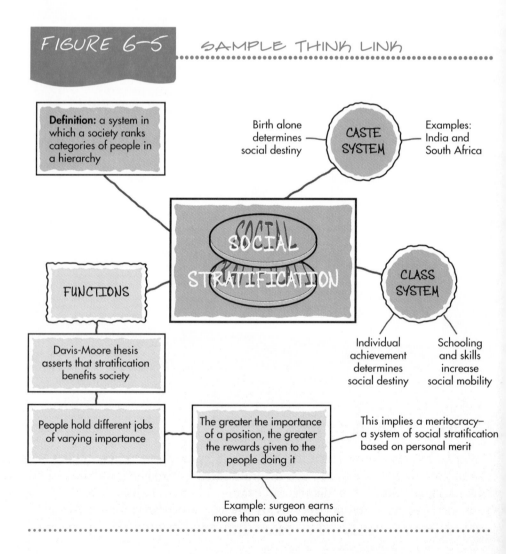

FIGURE 6-5   SAMPLE THINK LINK

Definition: a system in which a society ranks categories of people in a hierarchy

Birth alone determines social destiny — CASTE SYSTEM — Examples: India and South Africa

SOCIAL STRATIFICATION

CLASS SYSTEM

Individual achievement determines social destiny

Schooling and skills increase social mobility

FUNCTIONS

Davis-Moore thesis asserts that stratification benefits society

People hold different jobs of varying importance

The greater the importance of a position, the greater the rewards given to the people doing it

This implies a meritocracy–a system of social stratification based on personal merit

Example: surgeon earns more than an auto mechanic

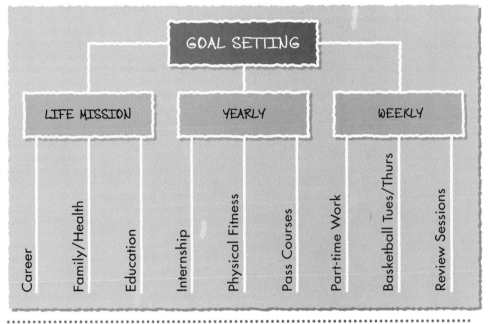

FIGURE 6-6   THE "JELLYFISH" THINK LINK

A think link may be difficult to construct in class, especially if your instructor talks quickly. In this case, use another note-taking system during class. Then make a think link as part of the process of reviewing your notes.

Once you choose a note-taking system, your success will depend on how well you use it to record vital information. Learning some form of personal shorthand will help you make the most of whatever system you choose.

HOW CAN YOU WRITE FASTER WHEN TAKING NOTES?

When taking notes in class, many students have trouble keeping up with the instructor. You may have had this feeling, hurrying along in a game of catch-up, sensing that you are always a few sentences behind. Using some personal **shorthand** (not standard secretarial shorthand) can help to push the pen faster.

Personal shorthand uses abbreviations and shortened words, in addition to replacing words or parts of words with symbols. Because you are the only intended reader, you can misspell and abbreviate words in ways that only you understand. The only danger to shorthand is that you might forget what your writing means. To avoid this problem, review your short-

Shorthand,
A system of rapid handwriting employing symbols to represent words, phrases, and letters.

hand notes while your abbreviations and symbols are fresh in your mind. If there is any confusion, spell out words as you review.

Here are some suggestions that will help you master personal shorthand:

1. Use the following standard abbreviations in place of complete words:

w/	with	c͞b	compare; in comparison to
w/o	without	ﬀ	following
→	means; resulting in	Q	question
←	as a result of	p.	page
↑	increasing	∗	most importantly
↓	decreasing	<	less than
∴	therefore	>	more than
∵	because	=	equals
≈	approximately	%	percent
+ OR &	and	△	change
—	minus; negative	2	to; two; too
NO. OR #	number	VS	versus; against
i.e.	that is,	eg	for example
etc.	and so forth	c/o	care of
ng	no good	lb	pound

2. Shorten words by removing vowels from the middle of words:

prps	=	purpose
knlge	=	knowledge
lwyr	=	lawyer
hstry	=	history

3. Substitute word beginnings for entire words:

assoc	=	associate; association
info	=	information
subj	=	subject
chem	=	chemical; chemistry
rep	=	representative
max	=	maximum

4. Form plurals by adding *s* to shortened words:

prblms	=	problems
mchns	=	machines
drctrys	=	directories
prntrs	=	printers

5. Make up your own symbols and use them consistently:

   b/4   =   before
   4tn   =   fortune
   2thake =   toothache

6. Learn to rely on key phrases instead of complete sentences.
   For example, write "German—nouns capitalized" instead of "In the German language, all nouns are capitalized."

7. Use standard or informal abbreviations for proper nouns such as places, people, companies, scientific substances, events, and so on.
   LA—Louisiana
   D.C.—Washington, D.C.
   It.—Italy
   FMC—Ford Motor Company
   H_2O—water
   Moz.—Wolfgang Amadeus Mozart
   WWII—World War II

8. If you know you are going to repeat a particular word or phrase often throughout the course of a class period, write it out once at the beginning of the class and then establish an abbreviation that you will use through the rest of your notes, writing that abbreviation in parentheses following the full name. For example, if you are taking notes on the rise and fall of Argentina's former first lady Eva Peron, you might start out writing "Eva Peron (EP)" and then use "EP" throughout the rest of the class period.

One important reason for taking notes is to record information you gather during research. Research involves a systematic search for information.

HOW DO YOU CONDUCT RESEARCH?

When you use sources available at your library and through your computer to systematically search for information, you are engaged in the *research process*. Through this process, you attempt to find information that will answer your research question. The most useful research sources are usually those that are well known, well supported, balanced, and current. Asking the following questions will help you get a general idea of the research sources available to you and how you might begin to find them.

1. Where is the general reference collection?

2. Where is the specialized reference collection?

3. Is the book catalog computerized or on cards? Is there an open-stack system for books (you are allowed to find materials on your own), or are some areas closed, in which holdings are off

limits to everyone but library staff, who retrieve for you what you need?

4. Does the library have any special collections, including files of corporate annual reports and local, state, and federal government documents?

When you have a general idea of where everything is, you can begin your search for information. This involves following a specific *search strategy*—a step-by-step method for finding information that takes you from general to specific sources as you investigate your research question. Starting with general sources usually works best, because they give you an overview of your research topic and lead you to more specific information. For example, an encyclopedia article on your topic may include the name of an important book or expert in that area which you can then track down.

A library search strategy involves checking general and specific reference works, the catalog of books, periodical indexes, and electronic sources, including the Internet (see Figure 6-7). When you have gathered your resources, then you need to take research notes.

Use General Reference Works

Begin your research with *general reference works.* These works cover hundreds, sometimes thousands, of different topics in a broad, nondetailed way. General reference guides are found in the front of most libraries and

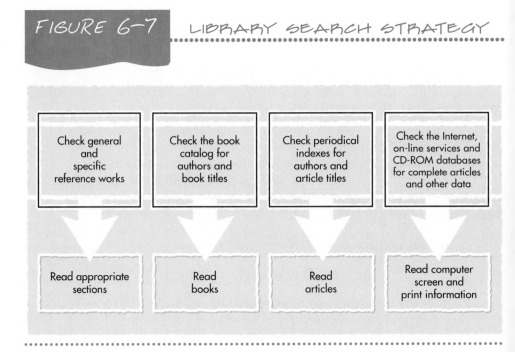

FIGURE 6-7 LIBRARY SEARCH STRATEGY

Check general and specific reference works	Check the book catalog for authors and book titles	Check periodical indexes for authors and article titles	Check the Internet, on-line services and CD-ROM databases for complete articles and other data
Read appropriate sections	Read books	Read articles	Read computer screen and print information

are often available on **CD-ROM**. You access this information by inserting the disk into a specially designed computer. Among the works that fall into this category are:

> ➤ encyclopedias—for example, the multivolume *Encyclopaedia Britannica* and the single-volume *New Columbia Encyclopedia*
>
> ➤ almanacs—*The World Almanac and Book of Facts*
>
> ➤ yearbooks—*The Statistical Abstract of the United States*
>
> ➤ dictionaries—*Webster's New World College Dictionary*
>
> ➤ biographical reference works—*Who's Who in America* and *Webster's Biographical Dictionary*
>
> ➤ bibliographies—*Books in Print*

CD-ROM,

A compact disk, containing millions of words and images, that can be read by a computer (CD-ROM stands for "compact disk read-only memory").

Search Specialized Reference Works

After you have a general overview of your topic, look at *specialized reference works* to find more specific facts. Specialized reference works include encyclopedias and dictionaries that focus on a narrow field. Although the entries you find in these volumes are short summaries, they focus on critical ideas and on the key words you will need to conduct additional research.

Bibliographies that accompany the articles point you to the names and works of recognized experts. Here are some titles of specialized reference works:

> ➤ *Oxford Companion to Art*
>
> ➤ *Encyclopedia of American History*
>
> ➤ *Encyclopedia of Computer Science and Technology*
>
> ➤ *Dictionary of Education*
>
> ➤ *Encyclopedia of Psychology*

Use the Library Book Catalog

Usually found near the front of the library, the *book catalog* lists every book the library owns. The listings usually appear in three separate categories: authors' names, book titles, and subjects. Not too long ago, most libraries stored their book catalog on index-sized cards in hundreds of small drawers. Today, many libraries have replaced these cards with computer systems. Using a terminal that has access to the library's computer records, you can conduct an electronic search by specific author, title, and subject.

The computerized catalog in your college library is probably connected to the holdings of other college and university libraries. This gives you an on-line search capacity, which means that if you don't find the book you want in your local library, you can track it down in another library and request it through an interlibrary loan. *Interlibrary loan* is a system used by many colleges to allow students to borrow materials from a library other than the one at their school. Students request materials through their own library, where the materials are eventually delivered by the outside library. When you are in a rush, keep in mind that it may take a substantial amount of time for you to receive the materials you request via interlibrary loan.

Use Periodical Indexes to Search for Periodicals

Microfilm,

A reel of film on which printed materials are photographed at greatly reduced size for ease of storage.

Periodicals are magazines, journals, and newspapers, which are published on a regular basis throughout the year. Examples include *Time, Newsweek, Business Week, Journal of the American Medical Association,* and *Science.* Many libraries display periodicals up to one or two years old and convert older copies to **microfilm** or **microfiche**. Reading microfilm or microfiche requires special viewing machines, available in most libraries.

Finding articles in publications involves a search of periodical indexes. The most widely used general index is the *Reader's Guide to Periodical Literature,* which is available on CD-ROM and in book form. The *Reader's Guide* indexes articles in more than 100 general-interest magazines and journals. Two general indexes that appear only in computerized form are *Info-trac* and *Academic Abstracts.*

Microfiche,

A card or sheet of microfilm that contains a considerable number of pages of printed text and/or photographs in reduced form.

Specialized periodical indexes focus on magazines and journals in narrow subject areas, such as history, art, and nursing. Many of the following indexes can be found in electronic or book form:

Business and Economics	*ABI-Inform*	*Art Index*
Education Index	*Humanities Index*	*Music Index*
Medicine and Nursing	*Medline*	*Psychological Abstracts*
Religion and History	*Science and Technology*	*Social Science Index*

Almost no library owns all the publications listed in these and other specialized indexes. However, journals that are not part of your library's collection may be available through interlibrary loan.

Conduct Electronic Research

You will also find complete source material through a variety of electronic sources, including the Internet, on-line services, and CD-ROM. Here is a sampling of the kind of information you will find:

> ➤ complete articles from thousands of journals and magazines

> ➤ complete articles from newspapers around the world

> ➤ government data on varied topics such as agriculture, transportation, and labor

> ➤ business documents, including corporate annual reports

How can I conduct a successful research project?

Kathleen Cole, **Gonzaga University**

I returned to school when I was 41 years old. My marriage had broken up so I wanted to develop new skills that would help me better provide for myself and my daughter. I had already gone to school for three years when I was just out of high school, but it was a con-
servatory of music and I didn't have to use any research or study skills, other than to memorize songs. Now that I'm at a university, I'm realiz-ing just how limited I am at some of these skills. I'd eventually like to go on to get a

master's degree, so it is crucial I learn how to function in the library and research in-formation.

Whenever I'm given a research project, I go right to the help desk, and whoever is there finds everything I need for me. I'd like to be able to do it myself. After that, I check out the books, take them home, and read the chapters I think are relevant to my paper. But here's the dilemma: I don't know how to reference the materials I use. If I summarize, do I still need to refer to the author? Also, how much of my research paper should be about what others believe? Am I supposed to just quote the current and past beliefs or do I add my own opinions and conclusions? Finally, when I reference, do I put the small numbers at the bottom of the page or do I write a full bibliography in the back?

Giuseppe Morella, **Public Relations Major, Gonzaga University**

Most libraries provide orientation sessions to show students how to use the library. A library worker can help you learn to find what you need. Even if you know a lot about libraries in general, getting to know your school's library is essential, since each library has special resources that you might never find out about if you don't ask.

Before you take books home from the library, you can skim them to see which will be most useful. Then, at home, you can take notes on index cards so that it will be easier to organize and reference your paper. Label a top corner of each card with the general topic of the fact or quotation. In another corner, write the name of the book you're citing from; in a third corner, mark the page number. As for referencing, you need to cite everything that is not either your own idea or general knowledge. If you summarize another's material, you do not need to use quotation marks, but you still need to cite the author. You can use either footnotes, parentheticals, or endnotes, de-pending on what your professor wants. You also need a bibliography or "works cited" page at the end. There are many good style-books that give detailed instructions for citing all kinds of material.

Deciding how much of your own opinion to use can be tricky. If you are unsure about a particular assignment, you can check with the professor. In general, a "research paper" indicates that you are sup-posed to find out what others believe. But you should also think critically. After as-sessing the information, what conclusions do you reach, and why? A research paper is an exercise in learning from others and then deciding for yourself.

Your library is probably connected to the Internet, a worldwide computer network that links government, university, research, and business computers along an electronic network often referred to as the "Information Superhighway." Tapping into the World Wide Web—a tool for searching the huge libraries of information stored on the Internet—gives you access to billions of written words and graphic images.

As a researcher, your main challenge is to navigate the Internet without wasting hours trying to find what you need. Because the Internet is so vast, this book contains an Internet Research Appendix to help you explore it. After reading this Appendix, you will have many tools to aid you on your journeys along the Information Superhighway. A good place to begin is with your own school. If your library or computer room has Internet access, ask someone to help you learn how to explore and research on-line. If your college has its own Internet home page, spend some time browsing through it.

Although most libraries do not charge a fee to access the Internet, they do charge when you connect to commercial on-line services, including Nexis, CompuServe, and Prodigy. When you use these services, you may have to pay for time used and/or for the number of requests you make. To minimize your expense, see your librarian before you begin and ask about all fees and restrictions. If there is a fee, using an efficient key-word search will slash your on-line time (the final section of this chapter will look at key-word searches).

Libraries also have electronic databases on CD-ROM. A database is a collection of data—in most library cases, a list of related resources that all focus on one specific subject area—arranged so that you can search through it and retrieve specific items easily. For example, the DIALOG Information System includes hundreds of small databases in specialized areas, including databases on business, psychology, and science. CD-ROM databases are generally smaller than on-line databases and are updated less frequently. However, there is never a user's fee.

> "Seeing research as a quest for an answer makes clear that you cannot know whether you have found something unless you know what it is you are looking for."
> Lynn Quitman Troyka
> (Source: Simon & Schuster Concise Handbook by Troyka, © 1990. Reprinted by permission of Prentice-Hall, Inc., Upper Saddle River, NJ.)

Conduct a Key-Word Search

Knowing how to conduct a *key-word search* will help you find what you are looking for on the Internet and in the book catalog and other print and electronic library indexes. Key words are codes that give you access to information. Without these codes, it may be difficult to tap into the library's vast resources to find the exact spot that contains the information you need.

How do you find key words? The best way is to search a multivolume catalog, known as the *Library of Congress Subject Headings (LCSH),* which is available in book and electronic form. Although you won't find any authors or titles in this volume, you will find a list of subject headings that are used consistently in all library indexes. Keeping a list of these words and using them in your research can avoid hours of frustration. For example, although the library card catalog doesn't list any volumes that deal with the topic of "ghost towns," it covers the topic under the Library of Congress Subject Heading: "Cities and Towns: Ruined and Extinct." Figure 6-8 shows how the LCSH system works.

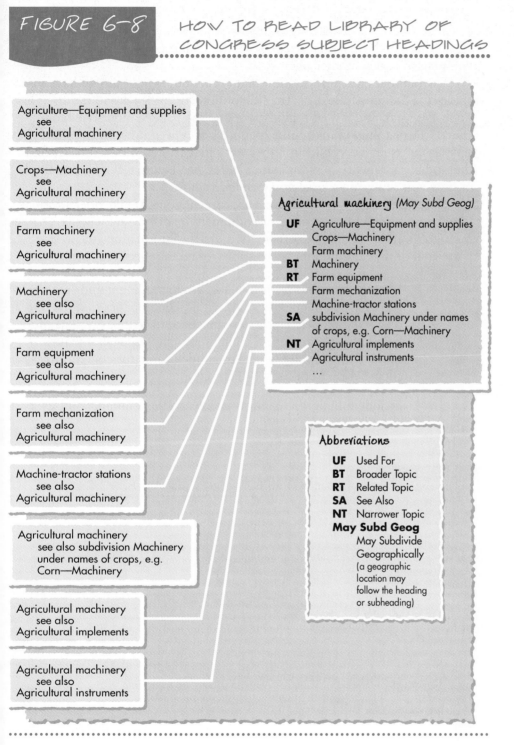

FIGURE 6–8 HOW TO READ LIBRARY OF CONGRESS SUBJECT HEADINGS

Agriculture—Equipment and supplies
  see
Agricultural machinery

Crops—Machinery
  see
Agricultural machinery

Farm machinery
  see
Agricultural machinery

Machinery
  see also
Agricultural machinery

Farm equipment
  see also
Agricultural machinery

Farm mechanization
  see also
Agricultural machinery

Machine-tractor stations
  see also
Agricultural machinery

Agricultural machinery
  see also subdivision Machinery
  under names of crops, e.g.
  Corn—Machinery

Agricultural machinery
  see also
Agricultural implements

Agricultural machinery
  see also
Agricultural instruments

Agricultural machinery *(May Subd Geog)*
- **UF** Agriculture—Equipment and supplies
  - Crops—Machinery
  - Farm machinery
- **BT** Machinery
- **RT** Farm equipment
  - Farm mechanization
  - Machine-tractor stations
- **SA** subdivision Machinery under names of crops, e.g. Corn—Machinery
- **NT** Agricultural implements
  - Agricultural instruments
  - …

Abbreviations
- **UF** Used For
- **BT** Broader Topic
- **RT** Related Topic
- **SA** See Also
- **NT** Narrower Topic
- **May Subd Geog** May Subdivide Geographically (a geographic location may follow the heading or subheading)

Take Research Notes

Research notes are the notes you take while gathering information to answer a research question. Research notes take two forms: source notes and content notes.

   Source notes are the preliminary notes you take as you review available research. They include vital bibliographic information as well as a short summary and critical evaluation of the work. Write these notes when you consider a book or article interesting enough to look at again. They do not signal that you have actually read something all the way through, only that you plan to review it later on.

The bibliographic information that every source note should have includes the author's full name; the title of the work; the edition (if any); the publisher, year, and city of publication; and the page numbers you consulted. (Depending on the source, you may also need other information, such as an issue and volume number for a magazine.) Many students find that index cards work best for source notes. See Figure 6-9 for an example of how you can write source notes on index cards.

The second type of research notes are content notes. Unlike brief informational source notes, *content notes* provide an in-depth look at the source, taken during a thorough reading. Use them to record the information you need to write your draft. Here are some suggestions for taking effective content notes:

> When a source looks promising, begin reading it and summarizing what you read. Use standard notebook paper that fits into a three-ring binder. This gives you space to write as well as the flexibility to rearrange the pages into any order that makes sense. (If you prefer using large index cards for content notes, choose 4-by-6- or 5-by-8-inch sizes.)

> Include bibliographic information and page numbers for every source.

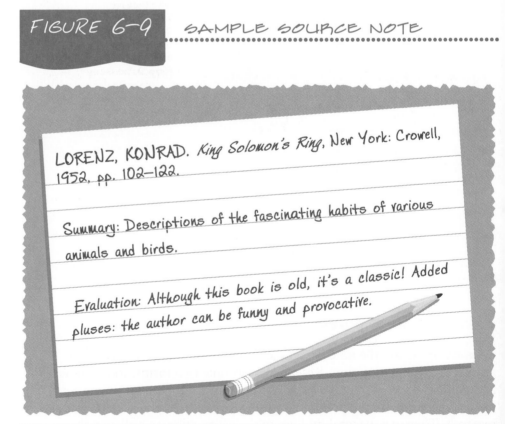

FIGURE 6-9   SAMPLE SOURCE NOTE

LORENZ, KONRAD. *King Solomon's Ring*, New York: Crowell, 1952, pp. 102–122.

Summary: Descriptions of the fascinating habits of various animals and birds.

Evaluation: Although this book is old, it's a classic! Added pluses: the author can be funny and provocative.

> Limit each page to a single source.

> If you take notes on more than one subject from a single source, create a separate page for each subject.

> If the notes on a source require more than one page, label the pages and number them sequentially. Reference the title of the source in how you label the pages. For example, if the particular source is a magazine entitled *Business Week*, your pages might be labeled BW1, BW2, BW3, and so on.

> Identify the type of note that appears on each page. Evaluate whether it is a summary in your own words, a quotation, or a paraphrase .

> Write your summary notes in any of the note-taking systems described later in the chapter.

Paraphrase,
A restatement of a written text or passage in another form or other words, often to clarify meaning.

Different kinds of notations that you make directly on photocopies of sources—marginal notes, highlighting, and underlining—can supplement your content notes. Say, for example, that you are writing a paper on the psychological development of adolescent girls. During your research you photocopy an article written by Dr. Carol Gilligan, an expert in the field. On the photocopy, you highlight important information and make marginal notes that detail your immediate reactions to some of the author's key points. Then, you take content notes on the article. When it is time to write your paper, you have two different and helpful resources to consult.

Try to divide your time as equally as possible between photocopy notes and content notes. If you use photocopies as your primary reference without making any of your own content notes, you may have more work to do when you begin writing, because you will need to spend time putting the source material into your own words. Writing paraphrases and summaries in content notes ahead of time will save you some work later.

Gestalt

The German word *gestalt* refers to a whole that is greater than the sum of its parts. When you can think in terms of *gestalt*, you are able to see both the whole picture and how each individual part contributes to that whole. To refer to a common phrase, *gestalt* is seeing the whole forest as well as individual trees.

Think of this concept as you consider how note-taking and research can help you build your knowledge and store of information. When you're reading your notes, ask yourself: Do I truly understand the material, or am I just trying to cram facts into my head? When you're writing a paper from your research, ask yourself: Am I stepping back to see the central idea clearly, so that I can express my thoughts in the best way possible? As important as the individual facts and examples may be, the *gestalt* is what helps the individual parts of your notes and your research gain a new and important meaning as a whole.

Chapter 6: Applications

Name   Date

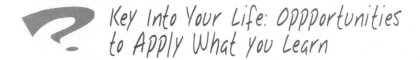

Key Into Your Life: Oppportunities to Apply What You Learn

Exercise 1: How Good Are Your Notes?

Look back at two sets of notes that you recently took in two different courses. For each set, evaluate your level of success, using the questions given.

First set of notes

Do these notes make sense to you? Why or why not? If they aren't as clear as you'd like them to be, evaluate why that happened (fatigue, distraction, dislike of class material, etc.)

_____

_____

_____

Are these notes complete and accurate? Why or why not?

_____

Did you feel that you kept up with the lecture? If not, how does that show in the notes?

_____

How do you evaluate your handwriting?

_____

What note-taking system did you use? Did it work for this class or not, and why?

_____

_____

Did you give supporting facts and examples to back up important ideas?

_____

Do you feel comfortable studying from these notes? Why or why not? If not, what do you need to do to make them complete?

_____

_____

_____

<u>Second set of notes</u>

Do these notes make sense to you? Why or why not? If they aren't as clear as you'd like them to be, evaluate why that happened (fatigue, distraction, dislike of class material, etc.)

_____

_____

_____

Are these notes complete and accurate? Why or why not?

_____

Did you feel that you kept up with the lecture? If not, how does that show in the notes?

_____

How do you evaluate your handwriting?

_____

What note-taking system did you use? Did it work for this class or not, and why?

_____

_____

Did you give supporting facts and examples to back up important ideas?

_____

Do you feel comfortable studying from these notes? Why or why not? If not, what do you need to do to make them more complete?

_____

_____

_____

Based on the information you have just provided, answer the following questions.

What are your strengths and weaknesses as a note-taker?

_____

_____

_____

Identify two goals for improving your note-taking ability.

<u>First goal:</u> _____

_____

<u>Second goal:</u> _____

_____

Exercise 2: Follow a Search Strategy

Choose a research topic that interests you—anything from how the Super Bowl has changed sports in America to the communication differences between men and women. Take a trip to the library and use the search strategy described in this chapter to identify the different sources you could use to research your topic. At the library, list three sources in each of the following categories:

TOPIC: _____

_____

General reference works: _____

_____

_____

Specialized reference works: _____

_____

_____

Books found by searching the book catalog: _____

_____

_____

Periodicals found by searching periodical indexes: _____

_____

_____

Sources found on the Internet and/or through on-line services: _____

_____

_____

KEY TO COOPERATIVE LEARNING: BUILDING TEAMWORK SKILLS

This teamwork exercise will show you how your note-taking techniques compare with those of other students. It will also help you analyze what makes one set of notes more useful than another set:

> Start by choosing a two- to three-page excerpt from your text. The excerpt should contain a lot of "meaty" information, but should have no tables or figures. Don't read the excerpt before you start the exercise.

> Form groups of three to four students. Within each group, one student will play the role of "instructor" and the other two or

three will be "students." Assign different note-taking strategies to each student—one will use outlining, one the Cornell system, and one think links. The "instructor" will read the excerpt as if he or she were delivering a classroom lecture. The "students" will take notes on the material. You will then have three different sets of notes on the same material.

➤ Now come together with all group participants to review and compare all three versions. Read each version carefully and answer the following questions:

1. Did all three note-takers record all the important information? If there are differences in the versions, why do you think these differences occurred? (You can ask the note-takers to explain why they chose to include some information and omit others.)

_____

_____

_____

2. How did each student feel about his or her note-taking strategy? Who felt comfortable and who didn't, and why?

_____

_____

3. Evaluate the different sets of notes. For this material and situation, which set of notes is likely to be the most helpful study tool for you?

_____

_____

KEY TO SELF-EXPRESSION: DISCOVERY THROUGH JOURNAL WRITING

To record your thoughts, use the lined page preceding the next chapter or a separate journal.

Read the following statements:

➤ "When I use a library search strategy, I feel like an investigative reporter in search of the facts I need to write a successful story. The more useful sources I find, the better."

➤ "When I use a library search strategy, I feel like I'm overdoing it. I can usually find everything I need in one source, and looking for more information seems like a waste of time."

Which of these statements reflects your attitude toward library research? Describe in more detail how you feel about research. How do you think you might use research skills both in school and on the job? How did reading this chapter affect your attitude toward the usefulness of library research skills?

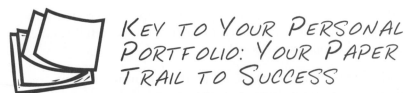

KEY TO YOUR PERSONAL PORTFOLIO: YOUR PAPER TRAIL TO SUCCESS

End-of-Chapter Cumulative Essay   According to a source on college-level learning, most college classes are focused on lectures and texts combined, unlike high-school classes that focus on what the teachers say (often out of the book). To test your ability to learn from others by combining sources, explain and illustrate a complete and efficient learning system. Utilize your own experiences as well as incorporating ideas from your text and class discussions. Demonstrate that you have a system that allows for day-to-day new learning and effective review. Be sure to explain how you may wish to modify the Cornell system for your own purposes.

Name _____ Date _____

Journal Entry

Express

7

EFFECTIVE WRITING:

Communicating Your Message and Making Sound Arguments

In this chapter, you will explore answers to the following questions:

Why does good writing matter?

What are the elements of effective writing?

What is the writing process?

Words, joined to form ideas, have enormous power. As a writer, you can use and shape that power. Far more than a skill just for school-work, writing is as important today as it has ever been. Instead of disappearing in an age that celebrates computer technology, writing has become the communication tool of choice for people using the Internet, as well as for workers in a wide variety of fields.

Words allow you to take your ideas out of the realm of thought and give them a form that other people can read and consider. A written piece is like a building on your campus. It requires a solid foundation (thesis), trustworthy materials (ideas and examples), and reliable construction (putting the words together so they communicate understandable concepts to others).

Whether you are zapping electronic mail across the globe or using a pencil and pad to write a research paper for your history professor, your level of successful communication depends on your ability to express your written ideas completely and well. In this chapter, you will explore the many aspects of learning to be a good writer.

WHY DOES GOOD WRITING MATTER?

In school, almost any course you take will require you to write essays or papers in order to communicate your knowledge and thought process. In order to express yourself successfully in those essays and papers, you need good writing skills. Knowing how to write and express yourself is essential outside of school as well. Good writing is a primary key to success in all life endeavors—educational, professional, and personal.

Good writing depends upon and reflects clear thinking. Therefore, a clear thought process is the best preparation for a well-written document, and a well-written document shows the reader a clear thought process. Good writing also depends on reading. Exposing yourself to the work of other writers helps you learn more words, experience new ideas, and discover all the different ways that a writer can put words together to *express* ideas. In addition, critical reading generates new ideas inside your mind, ideas that you can use in your writing. Actually, *the processes of reading and writing are interrelated* and very similar. The skills in one process tend to enhance the skills in the other.

WHAT ARE THE ELEMENTS OF EFFECTIVE WRITING?

Every writing situation is different, dependent upon three elements. Your goal is to understand each element before you begin to write:

> *Your purpose:* What do you want to accomplish with this particular piece of writing?

> *Your audience:* Who will read your writing?

> *Your topic:* What is the subject about which you will write?

Figure 7-1 shows how these elements are dependent upon one another. As a triangle needs three points to be complete, a piece of writing needs these three elements. Consider purpose and audience even before you begin to plan. Topic will come into play during the planning stage, which is the first stage of the writing process.

Writing Purpose

Writing without having set your purpose first is like driving without deciding where you want to arrive. You'll get somewhere, but chances are it won't be where you needed to go. Therefore, just as you do in the process of reading, always define what you want to accomplish before you start to write. The task of both readers and writers is *making meaning*—making sense of the world.

There are many different purposes for writing. However, the two purposes that you will use most commonly in class work and on the job are to inform and to persuade.

FIGURE 7-1   THE THREE ELEMENTS
OF WRITING

The purpose of *informative writing* is to present and explain ideas. A research paper on how hospitals use donated blood to save lives tries to inform readers without molding opinion. The writer presents facts in an unbiased way, without introducing a particular point of view. Most newspaper articles, except those on the opinion and editorial pages, are examples of informative writing.

Persuasive writing has the purpose of convincing readers that your point of view is correct. Often, persuasive writing seeks to change the mind of the reader. For example, as a member of the college committee on student health, you write a newspaper column asking for blood donations. Through facts, statistics, expert opinion, and examples, you attempt to persuade readers to take action and give blood. Other examples include a history paper on the causes of the Vietnam War, newspaper editorials, business proposals, and books and magazine articles with a point of view.

Additional possible writing purposes include *entertaining* the reader and *narrating* (describing an image or event to the reader). Although most of your writing in school will inform or persuade, you may occasionally need to or wish to entertain or narrate as well. Sometimes purposes will even overlap—you certainly might write an informative essay that entertains at the same time.

Knowing Your Audience

In almost every case, a writer creates written material so that it can be read by others. Therefore, two partners exist in the writing process: the writer and the audience. Successful writing communicates messages that are meaningful to readers. Knowing who your audience is will help you construct the most appropriate message. Initially, of course, you are also your own audience.

Audience, The reader or readers of any piece of written material.

Key Questions About Your Audience

In school, your primary audience is your instructors. For many assignments, instructors will want you to assume that they are typical readers rather than informed instructors. Writing for typical readers usually means that you should be as complete as possible in your explanations.

At other times, you may write papers that intend to address informed instructors or a specific reading audience other than your instructors. In such cases, you may ask yourself some or all of the following questions, depending on which are relevant to your topic:

> ➤ How old are my readers? Are they male or female? What are their cultural backgrounds, interests, experiences, and political views?

> ➤ What are their roles? Are they instructors, students, employers, customers?

> ➤ How much do they know about my topic? Are they experts in the field or beginners? Do they have general or specialized knowledge? Do they expect me to use jargon or to explain every term?

> ➤ Are they already interested in what I am writing or do I have to convince them that my paper is worth reading?

> ➤ Who will grade the paper? What are his or her standards for "good writing"?

> ➤ Can I expect my audience and my grader to have an open or closed mind?

After you answer the questions about your audience, take what you have discovered into consideration as you write. For example, if you are writing a letter to the editor of a computer magazine about Windows 98, the computer operating system developed by Microsoft Corporation, you can safely assume that magazine readers know what Windows 98 is and that they understand specialized computer language. Show the same letter to people who have never used a computer and they won't understand much of what they are reading.

Your Commitment to Your Audience

Your goal is to be as complete as possible in your writing and to organize your ideas so that readers can follow them. Suppose, for example, you are writing an informative research paper for a nonexpert audience on using on-line services to get a job. One way to accomplish your goal is to first explain what these services are and the kinds of help they offer, then describe each service in greater detail, and finally conclude with how these services will change job hunting in the twenty-first century. Although this is not the only way to approach this topic, it is one option that moves readers from idea to idea in a logical way.

Making your writing the best that it can be involves following the steps of the *writing process*.

WHAT IS THE WRITING PROCESS?

The writing process provides an opportunity for you to state and refine your thoughts until you have expressed yourself as clearly as possible. Critical thinking plays an important role every step of the way. You might think of the writing process as beginning when you pick up a pen or start keyboarding words into a computer and finishing when you write the last word of your first draft. However, drafting is only one stage of the journey. The four main parts of the process are planning, drafting, revising, and editing.

As you read about these four parts, keep in mind that the writing process is really more cyclical than linear. Writers move in and out of different parts of the process as they work toward their goals.

Planning

Planning gives you a chance to think about what to write and how to write it so that the final product will communicate your message successfully. Planning involves brainstorming for ideas, establishing guidelines, defining and narrowing your topic by using prewriting strategies, conducting research if necessary, writing a thesis statement, writing a working outline, and completing your research. A lot of excellent planning goes on in the head of the writer. Some planning involves doodling, drawing, or other messy written forms.

Although the steps in preparing to write are listed in sequence, in real life the steps overlap one another as you plan your document. For example, although brainstorming is listed below as the first planning step, you may first want to use other prewriting strategies—listed as the second planning step—to learn where your interests lie.

Open Your Mind Through Brainstorming

In many writing situations, your instructor will assign a topic. For example, your accounting instructor may ask you to write about the role of ethics in corporate accounting practices. Or your health instructor may ask for a written explanation of the causes of diabetes. In other cases, your instructor may assign a broader category and give you the freedom to decide on a topic. *The key to any successful paper or any other writing endeavor is a choice of topic that has meaning, holds a potential for interest, and (in the best of circumstances) provides some fun for the writer.*

Whether your instructor assigns a specific topic (Toni Morrison's message in the novel *Beloved*), a partially defined topic (novelist Toni Morrison), or a general category within which you make your own choice (any of the authors you've studied over the semester), you should brainstorm to develop more specific ideas about what you want to write. Brainstorming is a creative technique that involves generating ideas about a subject without making judgments. Brainstorming is often best achieved by talking your ideas through with a friend. See Chapter 3 for more details about brainstorming.

First, let your mind wander! Step one may be to write down any ideas on the assigned subject that come to mind, in no particular order. Step two is to organize that list into an outline or think link that helps you see the possibilities and relationships more clearly. To make the outline or think link, separate list items into general ideas or categories and sub-ideas or examples. Then associate the sub-ideas or examples with the ideas they support or fit.

FIGURE 7-2   BRAINSTORMING

Write your ideas in the order they occur to you

* What traditional career planning does: career counseling, help in writing a résumé and cover letter, help in locating actual job openings
* What electronic career counseling adds: help in sending a résumé and cover letter via the Internet within seconds of learning about a job
* Companies post help-wanted notices electronically to broadcast their job openings all over the world
* Wave of the future
* Easy to use
* Traditional career services offer face-to-face meetings
* Counselors and job hunters have electronic "conversations" online
* Job seekers go online to learn about thousands of job listings from all over the world
* History of America Online's Career Center: started with a list of 1,000 jobs a week; two years later there were 10,000 weekly listings

Organize your ideas into categories, associating ideas with sub-ideas and examples

1. What traditional and online career planning offer
   - Career counseling
   - Help in writing a résumé and cover letter
   - Help in locating actual job openings
   - Help in sending a résumé and cover letter via the Internet within seconds of learning about a job

2. Differences between traditional and online career services
   - Face-to-face meetings in traditional services
   - "Conversations" take place electronically in electronic services

3. Posting help-wanted notices electronically
   - Companies instantaneously broadcast news of a job opening all over the world
   - Job seekers learn about tens of thousands of job listings from all over the world
   - It is easy for both parties

4. Future trends
   - Electronic job hunting is the wave of the future
   - America Online's Career Center started with a list of 1,000 jobs a week; two years later there were 10,000 weekly listings

Figure 7-2 shows an uncensored brainstorming list on the subject of on-line job hunting, reworked into a list consisting of four logical groupings.[1]

Establish Guidelines

Before narrowing your topic, establish your guidelines by defining the writing context and any special requirements of the assignment. The *writing context* includes:

➤ The course for which the paper is written

➤ The person for whom the paper is written

➤ The deadline—how much time you have to complete the material

➤ Whether the paper will stand alone or be part of a series of related assignments

➤ How long the paper is supposed to be

Special requirements refer to any specific audience or purpose requirements assigned by the instructor. For example, is your assignment a research paper that requires library research? An essay based on readings? A business memo? A letter of complaint?

The writing context and special requirements influence your choice of a final topic. For example, if you had a month and twenty pages in which to write an informative paper on learning disabilities, you might choose to do more research and then discuss the symptoms, diagnosis, effects, and treatment of Attention Deficit Disorder. If you were given a week and five pages to write a persuasive essay, you might write about how elementary students with ADD need special training.

Regardless of the due date, one key requirement of any writing situation is to give yourself plenty of time to think, investigate, and share your writing with others.

"Clear a space for the writing voice. . . . You cannot will this to happen. It is a matter of persistence and faith and hard work. So you might as well just go ahead and get started."

Anne Lamott
(Source: *Bird by Bird* by Anne Lamott, © 1994, Pantheon Books, a division of Random House, Inc.)

Narrow Your Topic Through Prewriting Strategies

When you have established the writing context and requirements, and your brainstorming has generated some possibilities, you can begin to narrow your topic. Focus on the sub-ideas and examples from your initial brainstorming session. Because they are relatively specific, they will be more likely to point you toward possible topics.

Choose one or more sub-ideas or examples that you like and explore them using **prewriting strategies** such as brainstorming, freewriting, and asking journalists' questions. Prewriting strategies will help decide which topic you would most like to pursue. They are especially helpful with papers that don't involve research.

Prewriting strategies, Techniques for generating ideas about a topic and finding out how much you already know before you start your research and writing.

Brainstorming. The same process you used to generate ideas will also help you narrow your topic further. You need to have a reasonable level of interest in your topic. Generate thoughts about the possibility (or possibilities) you have chosen and write them down. Then, organize them into

FIGURE 7-3   PART OF A BRAINSTORMING OUTLINE

Boot camp
- physical conditioning
  ∘ swim tests
  ∘ intensive training
  ∘ ENDLESS push-ups!
- Chief who was our commander
- mental discipline
  ∘ military lifestyle
  ∘ perfecting our appearance
- self-confidence
  ∘ walk like you're in control
  ∘ don't blindly accept anything

categories, noticing any patterns that appear. See if any of the sub-ideas or examples seem as if they might make good topics.

Figure 7-3 shows a portion of the prewriting brainstorming outline that the student editor for this book, Michael B. Jackson, constructed from his brainstorming list. The assignment is a five-paragraph essay on a life-changing event. Michael chose to brainstorm the topic of "boot camp" and organized the ideas he came up with into categories.

Freewriting.   Another stream-of consciousness technique that encourages you to put ideas down on paper as they occur to you is called *freewriting*. When you freewrite, you write whatever comes to mind without censoring your ideas or worrying about grammar, spelling, punctuation, or organization. Freewriting helps you think creatively and gives you an opportunity to begin weaving in information and evidence that you know or have gathered. Freewrite on the sub-ideas or examples you have created to see if you want to pursue any of them. Here is a sample of freewriting from Michael's work:

> Boot camp for the Coast Guard really changed my life. First of all, I really got in shape. We had to get up every morning at 5 a.m., eat breakfast, and go right into training. We had to do endless military-style push-ups—but we later found out that these have a purpose, to prepare us to hit the deck in the event of enemy fire. We had a lot of aquatic tests, once we were awakened at 3 a.m. to do one in full uniform! Boot camp also helped me with feel confident about myself and be disciplined. Chief Marzloff was the main person who made that happen. He was tough but there was always a reason. He got angry when I used to nod my head whenever he would speak to me, he said that made it seem like I was blindly accepting whatever he said, which was a weakness. From him I have learned to keep an eye on my body's movements when I communicate. I learned a lot more from him too.

Asking journalists' questions. When journalists start working on a story, they ask themselves *Who? What? Where? When? Why?* and *How?* You can use these *journalists' questions* to focus your thinking. Ask these questions about any sub-idea or example to discover what you may want to discuss. Don't forget to ask "So what?" For example:

Who?	Who was at boot camp? Who influenced me the most?
What?	What about boot camp changed my life? What did we do?
When?	When in my life did I go to boot camp, and for how long? When did we fulfill our duties?
Where?	Where was camp located? Where did we spend our day-to-day time?
Why?	Why did I decide to go there? Why was it such an important experience? So I went to boot camp—so what?
How?	How did we train in the camp? How were we treated? How did we achieve success?

Through all of your prewriting work, you will be able to develop a topic broad enough to give you something with which to work but narrow enough to be manageable. See Table 7-1 for an overview of how two different topics can be narrowed from broad ideas to possible paper topics.

Prewriting also helps you see what you know about a topic and—just as important—what you don't know. What you don't know may lead to research.

TABLE 7-1	HOW TO DEFINE AND NARROW YOUR WRITING TOPIC	
FOCUS ON...	EXAMPLE 1	EXAMPLE 2
BROAD TOPIC	computers	families
WRITING CONTEXT	business communication course	sociology course
PURPOSE	informative	informative
AUDIENCE	instructor and classmates	instructor
LENGTH	1500 words	1000 words
DEADLINE	2 weeks	1 week
POSSIBLE TOPICS	■ using on-line services to find work	■ major changes in the American family since 1970
	■ using on-line services to conduct business research	■ how shifts in government welfare policies during the early 1990s affected families in poverty

Conduct Research to Gather Possibilities

Much of the writing you do in college will rely on what you already know about a subject, such as when you must write a short essay for freshman composition or for an exam. In these cases, prewriting strategies may generate all the ideas and information you need.

For other writing assignments, however, outside sources are necessary. In such cases, your prewriting exercises help guide your research by identifying where you need more information. Research may take the form of a trip to the library, an interview with an expert, or a connection to an on-line research source. (See Chapter 6 for a detailed description of how to conduct library research.)

Try doing your research in several stages. In the first stage, look for a basic overview that can help you write a thesis statement. Then write an outline or think link that identifies information gaps you still need to fill. Finally, go into more depth in your research, tracking down information that will help you complete your thoughts and take care of the gaps you identified.

Always remember that research can help you find *direction* for your writing, not just support. When you begin research for a writing assignment, one source may lead your inquiry and your thinking in new directions. As you proceed in your inquiry you may adopt a different point of view about your topic, and you may even head toward a new thesis statement.

Write a Thesis Statement

All your work to this point prepares you to write a *thesis statement,* the central message you want to communicate. The thesis statement states your subject and point of view, reflects your writing purpose and audience, and acts as the organizing principle of your paper. A well-written thesis statement summarizes what you want your readers to know and serves as your guide as you write. Here is an example from Michael's paper:

<u>Topic</u>	Coast Guard boot camp
<u>Purpose</u>	To inform and narrate
<u>Audience</u>	Instructor with unknown knowledge about the topic
<u>Thesis statement</u>	Chief Marzloff, our Basic Training Company Commander at the U.S. Coast Guard Basic Training Facility, shaped my life through physical conditioning, developing our self-confidence, and instilling strong mental discipline.

A thesis statement is just as important in a short document—a letter, for example—as it is in a long paper. For example, when you write a job application letter, a clear thesis statement will help you tell the recruiter why you deserve the job. Always make very clear to your reader what your intentions are.

Write a Working Outline and Complete Your Research

The final step in the preparation process involves writing a working outline (in outline or think-link form, whichever you prefer) and completing your research. Think of the working outline as a loose guide, rather than a finalized structure, to how your ideas will be expressed on paper. As you draft your paper, your ideas and structure may change many times. Only by allowing changes and refinements to happen can you get closer and closer to what you really want to say.

An outline is important for short documents as well as long ones. It can help to point out holes in your research that you can fill by making a trip to the library. (See Chapter 6 for a complete discussion on outline writing.)

Create a Checklist

It's a good idea to envision the due date earlier than it actually is. That way, if the computer labs are full of other students who also have papers due, you won't get shut out and end up with a late paper. Also, if you finish your paper early, there's always that one last chance for a trusted friend or a writing tutor to read it. Use the checklist in Table 7-2 to make sure that your preparation is complete. Under "Date Due," create your own writing schedule, giving each task its own intended completion date. Work backwards from the date the assignment is due and figure out how long it will take to complete each step. Refer to Chapter 2 for time-management skills that will help you schedule your writing processes.

TABLE 7-2 PREPARATION CHECKLIST

DATE DUE	TASK	IS IT COMPLETE?
	Brainstorm.	
	Define and narrow.	
	Use prewriting strategies.	
	Conduct research, if necessary.	
	Write thesis statement.	
	Write working outline.	
	Complete research.	

For example, if on May 1 you learn that a research paper is due on May 21, you may decide to schedule your work this way:

May 2: Define and narrow

May 3: Use prewriting strategies

May 4–5: Conduct research

May 6: Write thesis statement and working outline

May 7: Complete research

May 8–11: Write first draft

May 12–14: Revise and write second draft

May 15–17: Revise, edit, and write third (final) draft

May 18–20: Final edits and proofreading of final draft

As you develop your schedule, keep in mind that you'll probably move back and forth between tasks. You might even find yourself doing two and even three things on the same day. Stick to the schedule as best you can, while balancing the other demands of your busy life, and check off your accomplishments on the list as you complete them.

Drafting

Some people aim for perfection when they write a first draft. They want to get everything right, from word choice to tone to sentence structure to paragraph organization to spelling, punctuation, and grammar. Perfection in a first draft is nearly impossible. Try to resist seeking perfection in your first drafts, because it may cause you to shut the door on ideas before you even know they are there.

As its name implies, a *first draft* involves putting your ideas on paper for the first time—but not the last! You may write many different versions of the assignment until you like what you see. Each version moves you closer to communicating exactly what you want to say in the way you want to say it. The process is like starting with a muddy pond and gradually clearing the mud away until your last version is a clear body of water, showing the rocks and the fish beneath the surface. Think of your first draft as a way of establishing the pond before you start clearing it up.

How you structure the ideas in the body of your paper is important, especially for long documents such as research papers and business reports. When you think of drafting, imagine that you are creating a kind of "writing sandwich." The bottom slice of bread is the introduction; the top slice is the conclusion; and the sandwich stuffing is made of central ideas and supporting examples (see Figure 7-4).

The elements of writing a first draft are freewriting, crafting an introduction if you are ready to write one, organizing the ideas in the body of the paper, formulating a conclusion, and citing sources in the required correct format.

Freewriting Your Draft

If the introduction, body, and conclusion are the three parts of the sandwich, freewriting is the process of searching the refrigerator for the ingredients and laying them all out on the table. Take everything that you have developed in the planning stages and freewrite a very rough draft. Don't censor yourself. For now, don't consciously think about your introduction, conclusion, or structure within the paper body. Focus on getting your ideas

FIGURE 7-4   CREATE A "WRITING SANDWICH" IN YOUR FIRST DRAFT

out of the realm of thought and onto the paper, in whatever form is easiest at the moment.

When you have the beginnings of a paper in your hands, you can start to shape it into something with a more definite form. First, work on how you want to begin your paper.

Crafting an Introduction

Think of the introduction as your message to readers in which you tell them, in broad terms, what the rest of the paper will contain. Including the thesis statement is essential. Here, for example, is a draft of an introduction for Michael's paper about the Coast Guard. The thesis statement is underlined at the end of the paragraph:

> Chief Marzloff took on the task of shaping the lives and careers of the youngest, newest members of the U.S. Coast Guard. During my eight weeks in training, he was my father, my instructor, my leader, and my worst enemy. He took his job very seriously and demanded that we do the same. <u>The Chief was instrumental in conditioning our bodies, developing our self-confidence, and instilling mental discipline within us.</u>

Hooks,

Elements— including facts, quotes, statistics, questions, stories, or statements— that catch the reader's attention and encourage him or her to want to continue to read.

When you write an introduction, you might try to draw the reader in with an anecdote—a story that is directly related to the thesis. You can try other **hooks** including a relevant quotation, dramatic statistics, and questions that encourage critical thinking. Whatever strategy you choose, be sure it is linked to your thesis statement. In addition, try to state your purpose without referring to its identity as a purpose. For example, in an introductory paragraph, a student might write, "Computer technology is infiltrating every aspect of business," instead of, "In this paper, my purpose is to prove that computer technology is infiltrating every aspect of business."

After you have an introduction that seems to establish the purpose of your paper, work on making sure the body fulfills that purpose. Some writers get blocked on their introductions; sometimes you can write the introduction later in the process.

Creating the Body of a Paper

Evidence,

Proof that informs or persuades, consisting of facts, statistics, examples, and expert opinion.

The body of the paper contains your main points and supporting **evidence**. For evidence to work as a communication tool, it has to be organized into clear, logical patterns that are easy to follow. Look at the array of ideas and evidence within your draft in its current state. Think about how you might group certain items of evidence with the particular ideas they support. Then, when you see the groups that form, try to find a structure that helps you to organize them into a clear pattern. The pattern you choose will determine how you arrange your ideas from beginning to end. The body of the paper should have a particular order for a particular effect. Here are some strategies to consider:

Arrange ideas by chronological time. Describe a series of events in the order in which they occurred or in reverse order. This arrangement is commonly used when writing history papers.

Arrange ideas by steps in a process. This organization would be appropriate for an American government paper that describes the process by which a bill is passed into a law.

Arrange ideas by location. Here your organizational pattern is determined by geography. You may choose, for example, to write a paper in your sociology course on differences in the out-of-wedlock birth rate in five selected cities: Los Angeles, Denver, Chicago, Cleveland, and New York. Your discussion moves from west to east along with the cities.

Arrange ideas according to importance. You can choose to start with the idea that carries the most weight and move to ideas with less value or influence. For instance, in a paper for your marketing course on the most common advertising media, you decide to start with the medium that consumes the most advertising dollars each year and then move to those where less money is spent.

On the other hand, you can also choose to save the best for last by moving from the least important to the most important idea. This approach may encourage readers to continue reading since you have informed them that the best is yet to come. Your readers are often impressed by the last points you make in your paper.

Arrange ideas by problem and solution. Start with a specific problem, then discuss one or more suggested solutions. For example, in a paper for your health course, you introduce the problem of alienation and loneliness on campus. Among the solutions you suggest are joining clubs, participating in student government, and seeking professional counseling.

Formulating the Conclusion

The conclusion is a statement or paragraph that communicates that your paper is complete. In your conclusion, aim to summarize the information in the body of your paper, as well as to critically evaluate what is important about that information. Try one of the following devices:

- ➤ a summary of main points (if material is longer than three pages)

- ➤ a story, statistic, quote, or question that makes the reader think

- ➤ a call to action

- ➤ a look to the future

- ➤ an answer to "So what?" (why is what you've said *important?*)

As you work on your conclusion, try not to introduce new facts or restate what you feel you have proved ("I have successfully proven that violent cartoons are related to increased violence in children.") Let your ideas as they are presented in the body of the paper speak for themselves. Readers should feel that they have reached a natural point of completion.

Crediting Authors and Citing Sources

When you write a paper using any materials other than your own thoughts and recollections, you make the ideas you gathered in your research part of your own writing. This does not mean that you can claim these ideas as your own or fail to attribute them to someone. You need to credit authors for their ideas and words in order to avoid **plagiarism** .

Plagiarism,
The act of using someone else's exact words, figures, unique approach, or specific reasoning without giving appropriate credit.

Writers own their writings just as a computer programmer owns a program that he or she designed or a photographer owns an image that he or she created. A piece of writing and its enclosed ideas are the writer's products, or intellectual property. Using an idea, phrase, or word-for-word paragraph without crediting its author is the same as using a computer program without buying it or printing a photograph without paying the photographer. It is just as serious as any other theft, and will have unfavorable consequences. Most colleges have stiff penalties for plagiarism as well as for any other cheating offense.

To avoid plagiarism, know the difference between a quotation and a paraphrase. A *quotation* refers to a source's exact words, which are set off from the rest of the text by quotation marks. A *paraphrase* is a restatement of the quotation in your own words, using your own sentence structure. Restatement means to completely rewrite the idea, not just to remove or replace a few words. A paraphrase may not be acceptable if it is too close to the original. Figure 7-5 demonstrates these differences.

Plagiarism often begins by accident when you take research notes. You may forget to include quotation marks around a word-for-word pickup from the source, or you may intend to cite or paraphrase but never find the time to do it. To avoid forgetting, you may want to write something like "Quotation from original—rewrite later" next to quoted material and note at that time the specifics of the original document (title, author, source, page number, etc.) so you don't spend hours trying to locate it later.

Even an acceptable paraphrase requires a citation of the source of the ideas within it. Take care to credit any source that you quote, paraphrase, or use as evidence. To credit sources, write a footnote or endnote that describes the source. Use the format preferred by your instructor. Some citation styles require internal parenthetical citations ("author, p.____," for example). Writing handbooks such as the *MLA Handbook* contain acceptable formats.

Continue Your Checklist

Create a checklist for your first draft (see Table 7-3). The elements of a first draft do not have to be written in order. Remember, many writers prefer to write the introduction after they complete the body of the paper, so that the introduction accurately reflects the paper's content and tone. Whatever order you choose, make sure your schedule allows enough time to get everything done—with enough time left over for revisions and/or sharing your writing with other readers.

FIGURE 7-5   AVOID PLAGIARISM BY LEARNING HOW TO PARAPHRASE

QUOTATION

> "The most common assumption that is made by persons who are communicating with one another is . . . that the other perceives, judges, thinks, and reasons the way he does. Identical twins communicate with ease. Persons from the same culture but with a different education, age, background, and experience often find communication difficult. American managers communicating with managers from other cultures experience greater difficulties in communication than with managers from their own culture."[3]

UNACCEPTABLE PARAPHRASE
(the underlined words are taken directly from the quoted source)

> When we communicate, we assume that the person to whom we are speaking perceives, judges, thinks, and reasons the way we do. This is not always the case. Although identical twins communicate with ease, persons from the same culture but with a different education, age, background, and experience often encounter communication problems. Communication problems are common among American managers as they attempt to communicate with managers from other cultures. They experience greater communication problems than when they communicate with managers from their own culture.

ACCEPTABLE PARAPHRASE

> Many people fall into the trap of believing that everyone sees the world exactly as they do and that all people communicate based on the same assumptions. This belief is difficult to support even within our own culture as African-Americans, Hispanic-Americans, Asian-Americans, and others often attempt unsuccessfully to find common ground. When intercultural differences are thrown into the mix as they are when American managers, working abroad, attempt to communicate with managers from other cultures, clear communication becomes even harder.

Revising

When you *revise,* you critically evaluate the word choice, paragraph structure, and style of your first draft to see how it works. Any draft, no matter how good, can always be improved. Be thorough as you add, delete, replace, and reorganize words, sentences, and paragraphs. You may want to print out your draft and then spend time making notes and corrections on that hard copy before you make changes on a typewritten or computer-printed version. Figure 7-6 on page 200 shows a paragraph from Michael's first draft, with revision comments written in.

TABLE 7–3   FIRST DRAFT CHECKLIST

DATE DUE	TASK	IS IT COMPLETE?
	Freewrite a draft.	
	Plan and write the introduction.	
	Organize the body of the paper.	
	Include research evidence in the body.	
	Plan and write the conclusion.	
	Check for plagiarism and rewrite passages to avoid it.	
	Credit your sources.	

Although you should always revise on your own, some of your classes may include peer review (having students read each other's work and offer suggestions). A peer reviewer can offer valuable perspective about what comes across well and what may be confusing. Even if you don't have an organized peer review system, you may want to give a friend with a good "editor's eye" a hard copy to review as a favor to you.

The elements of revision include being a critical writer, evaluating paragraph structure, and checking for clarity and conciseness.

Being a Critical Writer

Critical thinking is as important in writing as it is in reading. Thinking critically when writing will help your papers move beyond simply restating what you have researched and learned. Of course, your knowledge is an important part of your writing. What will make your writing even more important and unique, however, is how you use critical thinking to construct your own new ideas and knowledge from what you have learned. In a sense, the task of writing requires you to play two roles: writer and reader, or creator and audience.

The key to critical writing is asking and answering the question, "So what?" For example, if you were writing a paper on nutrition, you might discuss a variety of good eating habits. Asking "So what?" could lead you into a discussion of *why* these habits are helpful, or what positive effects they have. If you were writing a paper on egg imagery in the novel *All the President's Men* by Robert Penn Warren, you might list all the examples of where you noticed that imagery. Then, asking "So what?" could lead you to evaluate why that imagery is so strong and what idea you think those examples convey about the message of the book. Asking "So what?" is the key to creating new knowledge and making meaning.

"See revision as 'envisioning again.' If there are areas in your work where there is a blur or vagueness, you can simply see the picture again and add the details that will bring your work closer to your mind's picture."

Natalie Goldberg

(Source: From *Writing Down the Bones* by Natalie Goldberg © 1986. Reprinted by arrangement with Shambhala Publications, Inc., 300 Massachusetts Avenue, Boston, MA 02115.)

How can I improve my writing?

Erica Epstein, Ithaca College—Ithaca, New York, Education Major

I don't know if it was the school's fault or mine, but by the time I was in high school, I didn't do homework or reading. I just stopped paying attention. The classes were too boring. Fifteen weeks of the same topic was redundant. I think education should be interesting. The material should be tied in with something else so it has meaning. Instead, the teacher feeds you the information so you don't really have to put much effort in. But now, even though I do all right, I have to work really hard to write a good paper. I think if I'd had a better start I wouldn't have to spend so much time rewriting my papers.

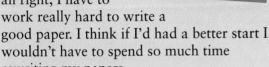

My teachers say the main problem is with my grammar. I tend to go from the past tense to the present tense in the wrong places. I just don't make proper sentences. I also have trouble organizing my material. I jump in and start writing. But I end up starting somewhere in the middle when I should be somewhere else. This is really frustrating. I had to take the writing class twice because I didn't get a high enough score the first time. I passed it this semester. I go to the writing center. They help me outline what I'm going to write. But I still end up rewriting my work before it's what I want. It's been really helpful but I know I still need to do more. What suggestions do you have?

Tom Smith, University of Wyoming, Administration of Justice

First of all, just like you, I get help from the writing center at my school. They know a lot about what the different teachers expect of you; particularly the technical stuff like footnote and bibliography requirements. They also give great advice about phrasing and punctuation. I also ask several of my friends to edit my papers. Usually, they'll focus on the weaker points and then I can make the changes and strengthen my work. If your papers are sounding too chatty, this would probably be the best thing for you to do. They'll be able to show you where you've gotten off the point. I'm never bothered by their comments. In fact, I'm grateful because it helps my papers be more professional.

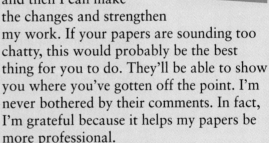

By the time three or four people have read my work, I'm usually pretty sure I've handled the problems. I also personally edit my papers about three or four times before I turn them in. I make sure I got my point across. I also try and look at my paper from an opposing perspective or different viewpoint. That way I can be sure my arguments are clear. Finally, if you don't have a reference book for writers, I suggest you go to your college bookstore and get one. And don't forget to use your spell-check and thesaurus. That way you'll be sure your spelling is correct and you can increase your vocabulary with every paper you write.

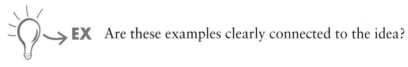

FIGURE 7-6   REVISING A FIRST DRAFT

military recruits
undergo

Of the changes that ~~happened to us,~~ the physical transformation is

most evident

the ~~biggest.~~ ~~When we arrived at the training facility, it was January, cold~~

Too   much.↗   *Maybe— upon my January arrival at the*

~~and cloudy. At the time,~~ I was a little thin, but I had been working out

training facility,

and thought that I could physically do anything. Oh boy, was I wrong!

← his trademark
phrase

The Chief said to us right away: "Get down, maggots!" Upon this

were   *endless*

command, we all to drop to the ground and do military-style push-ups.

∧   ∧

Water survival tactics were also part of the training ~~that we had to complete.~~

unnecessary

Occasionally, my dreams of home were interrupted at 3 a.m. when we

resented

had a surprise aquatic test. Although we ~~didn't feel too happy about~~ this

sub-human treatment at the time, we learned to appreciate how the

conditioning was turning our bodies into fine-tuned machines.

∧

mention how chief was involved   *say more about this*
(swimming in
uniform incident?)

....

As you revise, ask yourself questions that can help you think
through ideas and examples, come up with your own original insights
about the material, and be as complete and clear as possible. Use the
mind actions to guide you. Here are some examples of questions you
may ask:

 **EX** Are these examples clearly connected to the idea?

△ △ Are there any similar concepts or facts I know of that
can add to how I support this?

What else can I recall that can help to support this idea?

 In evaluating any event or situation, have I clearly indicated the causes and effects?

 What new idea comes to mind when I think about these examples or facts?

How do I evaluate any effect/fact/situation? Is it good or bad, useful or not?

What different arguments might a reader think of that I should address here?

Finally, critical thinking can help you evaluate the content and form of your paper. As you start your revision, ask yourself the following questions:

> Will my audience understand my thesis and how I've supported it?

> Does the introduction prepare the reader and capture attention?

> Is the body of the paper organized effectively?

> Is each idea fully developed, explained, and supported by examples?

> Are my paragraphs and ideas connected to one another through logical transitions?

> Do I have a clear, concise, simple writing style?

> Does the paper fulfill the requirements of the assignment?

> Does the conclusion provide a natural and satisfying ending to the paper?

Evaluating Paragraph Structure

Think of your individual paragraphs as mini-versions of your paper as a whole, each with an introduction, a body, and a conclusion. Make sure each paragraph has a *topic sentence* that states the paragraph's main idea (a topic sentence does for a paragraph what a thesis statement does for an entire paper). The rest of the paragraph should support that idea by presenting examples and other evidence. Although some topic sentences may occur just after the first sentence of a paragraph, or even at the end, most of them occur at the beginning. For example:

> <u>Chief Marzloff played an integral role in the development of our self-confidence.</u> He taught us that anything less than direct eye contact was disrespectful to both him and ourselves. He encouraged us to be confident about our own beliefs and to think about what was said to us before we decided whether to accept it. Furthermore, the Chief reinforced self-confidence through his own example. He walked with his chin up and chest out, like the proud parent of a newborn baby. He always gave the appearance that he had something to do and that he was in complete control.

Examine how your paragraphs flow one into the other by evaluating your use of transitions . Transitions help readers to move through the text in a natural, logical way. For example, words like *also, in addition,* and *next* indicate that another idea is coming. Similarly, *finally, as a result,* and *in conclusion* tell readers a summary is on its way. *However* and *on the other hand* signal contrasts rather than similarities.

Transitions, Words and phrases that build bridges between ideas, leading the reader from one idea or paragraph to the next.

Check for Clarity and Conciseness

Aim to say what you want to express in the clearest, most efficient way. A few well-chosen words will do your ideas more justice than a flurry of language. Try to state your thoughts in as few words as possible by eliminating extra words and flowery phrases. Other readers may be better at finding wordiness than you, the writer. Table 7-4 shows how some phrases can be rewritten in a more concise, conversational way.

Some wordy expressions can be eliminated altogether. For example, instead of writing:

> In the case of political reform, the new law applies to both the Republican and Democratic parties.

TABLE 7-4 SHORTEN WORDY EXPRESSIONS

INSTEAD OF ...	WRITE ...
in the event that	if
10:20 A.M. in the morning	10:20 A.M.
past experience	experience
this point in time	now
due to the fact that	because
are in the process of	are
call your attention to the fact that	remind you

Write:

> The new political reform law applies to Republicans and Democrats.

Editing

In contrast to the critical thinking of revising, *editing* involves correcting technical mistakes in spelling, grammar, punctuation, and style consistency for elements such as abbreviations and capitalizations. Editing may very well come last, after you are satisfied with your ideas, organization, and style of writing, unless you have strong first-draft editing skills. If you use a computer, you might want to use the grammar-check and spell-check functions to find mistakes. Remember, though, that you still need to check your work on your own. While a spell-checker won't pick up the mistake in the following sentence, someone who is reading for sense will:

> They are not hear on Tuesdays.

Look also for *sexist language,* which characterizes people based on their gender. Sexist language often involves the male pronoun *he* or *his*. For example, the sentence "An executive often spends hours each day going through his electronic mail" implies that executives are always men. A simple change, such as those shown in either of the following sentences, will eliminate the sexist language:

> Executives often spend hours each day going through their electronic mail.

or

> An executive often spends hours each day going through his or her electronic mail.

Try to be sensitive to words that slight women. *Mail carrier* is preferable to *mailman; student* to *coed*.

Proofreading is usually the final stage of editing, occurring when you have a final version of your paper. Proofreading means reading every word and sentence in the final version to make sure it is accurate. Look for technical mistakes, run-on sentences, and sentence fragments. Look for incorrect word usage and references that aren't clear. Reading your paper out loud can help you "hear" things your eyes don't catch. Reading the paper backwards from the last word to the first is a good way to find spelling errors.

Teamwork can be a big help as you edit and proofread, because another pair of eyes may see errors that you didn't notice on your own. If possible, have someone look over your work, throughout the writing process. Ask for feedback on what is clear and what is confusing. Then, ask the reader to edit and proofread for errors.

A Final Checklist

You're now ready to complete your revising and editing checklist. All the tasks listed in Table 7-5 should be complete when you submit your final paper.

Your final paper reflects all the hard work you put in during the writing cycle. Figure 7-7 shows the final version of Michael's paper.

> "Omit needless words. . . . This requires not that the writer make all his sentences short, or that he avoid all detail and treat his subjects only in outline, but that every word tell."
>
> William Strunk, Jr.
> (Source: William Strunk, Jr., and E.B. White, *The Elements of Style,* 3rd ed. Copyright © 1979. All rights reserved. Reprinted by permission from Allyn & Bacon.)

TABLE 7-5 EDITING CHECKLIST

DATE DUE	TASK	IS IT COMPLETE?
	Check the body of the paper for clear thinking and adequate support of ideas.	
	Finalize introduction and conclusion.	
	Check word spelling and usage.	
	Check grammar.	
	Check paragraph structure.	
	Make sure language is familiar and concise.	
	Check punctuation.	
	Check capitalization.	
	Check transitions.	
	Eliminate sexist language.	

FIGURE 7-7   A SAMPLE ESSAY

March 19, 1997

Michael B. Jackson

BOYS TO MEN

His stature was one of confidence, often misinterpreted by others as cockiness. His small frame was lean and agile, yet stiff and upright, as though every move were a calculated formula. For the longest eight weeks of my life, he was my father, my instructor, my leader, and my worst enemy. His name is Chief Marzloff, and he had the task of shaping the lives and careers of the youngest, newest members of the U.S. Coast Guard. As our Basic Training Company Commander, he took his job very seriously and demanded that we do the same. Within a limited time span, he conditioned our bodies, developed our self-confidence, and instilled within us a strong mental discipline.

Of the changes that recruits in military basic training undergo, the physical transformation is the most immediately evident. Upon my January arrival at the training facility, I was a little thin, but I had been working out and thought that I could physically do anything. Oh boy, was I wrong! The Chief wasted no time in introducing me to one of his trademark phrases: "Get down, maggots!" Upon this command, we were all to drop to the ground and produce endless counts of military-style push-ups. Later, we found out that exercise prepared us for hitting the deck in the event of enemy fire. Water survival tactics were also part of the training. Occasionally, my dreams of home were interrupted at about 3 a.m. when our company was selected for a surprise aquatic test. I recall one such test that required us to swim laps around the perimeter of a pool while in full uniform. I felt like a salmon swimming upstream, fueled only by natural instinct. Although we resented this sub-human treatment at the time, we learned to appreciate how the strict guidance of the Chief was turning our bodies into fine-tuned machines.

Beyond physical ability, Chief Marzloff also played an integral role in the development of our self-confidence. He would often declare in his raspy voice, "Look me in the eyes when you speak to me! Show me that you believe what you're saying!" He taught us that anything less was an expression of disrespect. Furthermore, he appeared to attack a personal habit of my own. It seemed that whenever he would speak to me individually, I would nervously nod my head in response. I was trying to demonstrate that I understood, but to him, I was blindly accepting anything that he said. He would roar, "That is a sign of weak-ness!" Needless to say, I am now conscious of all bodily motions when commu-nicating with others. The Chief also reinforced self-confidence through his own example. He walked with his square chin up and chest out, like the proud parent of a newborn baby. He always gave the appearance that he had some-thing to do, and that he was in complete control. Collectively, all of the methods that the Chief used were successful in developing our self-confidence.

Perhaps the Chief's greatest contribution was the mental discipline that he instilled in his recruits. He taught us that physical ability and self-confidence were nothing without the mental discipline required to obtain any worthwhile goal. For us, this discipline began with adapting to the military lifestyle. Our day began promptly at 0500 hours, early enough to awaken the oversleeping roosters. By 0515 hours, we had to have showered, shaved, and perfectly donned our uniforms. At that point, we were marched to the galley for chow, where we learned to take only what is necessary, rather than indulging. Before each meal, the Chief would warn, "Get what you want, but you will eat all that you get!" After making good on his threat a few times, we all got the point. Throughout our stay, the Chief repeatedly stressed the significance of self-discipline. He would calmly utter, "Give a little now, get a lot later." I guess that meant different things to all of us. For me, it was a simple phrase that would later become my personal philosophy on life. The Chief went to great lengths to ensure that everyone under his direction possessed the mental discipline required to be successful in boot camp or in any of life's challenges.

Chief Marzloff was a remarkable role model and a positive influence on many lives. I never saw him smile, but it was evident that he genuinely cared a great deal about his job and all the lives that he touched. This man single-handedly conditioned our bodies, developed our self-confidence, and instilled a strong mental discipline that remains in me to this day. I have not seen the Chief since March 28, 1992, graduation day. Over the years, however, I have incorporated many of his ideals into my life. Above all, he taught us the true meaning of the U.S. Coast Guard slogan, "Semper Peratus" (Always Ready).

Suà

Suà is a Shoshone Indian word, derived from the Uto-Aztecan language, meaning "think." While much of the Native American tradition in the Americas focuses on oral communication, written languages have allowed Native American perspectives and ideas to be understood by readers outside the Native American culture. The writings of Leslie Marmon Silko, J. Scott Momaday, and Sherman Alexis have expressed important insights that all readers can consider.

Think of *suà*, and of how thinking can be communicated to others through writing, every time you begin to write. The power of writing allows you to express your own insights so that others can read them and perhaps benefit from knowing them. Explore your thoughts, sharpen your ideas, and remember the incredible power of the written word. Remember that you learn to write by *writing*—for different purposes, various audiences, and diverse academic requirements.

Chapter 7: Applications

Name _____   Date _____

 Key Into Your Life: Opportunities to Apply What You Learn

Exercise 1: Audience Analysis

As a reporter for your college newspaper, you have been assigned the job of writing a story about some aspect of campus life. You submit the following suggestions to your editor-in-chief:

- The campus parking lot squeeze: too many cars and too few spaces

- Diversity: how students accept differences and live and work together

- Drinking on campus: Is the problem getting better or worse?

Use the following questions to analyze how various readership groups would respond to each article idea. Readership groups include students, faculty and administrators, community members, and students' family members. (Your editor-in-chief is likely to ask you these and other questions before assigning the story.)

1. Would readers care enough about each subject to read the entire article?

_____

_____

_____

2. How would you adjust your writing according to whether readers know or don't know about the subject?

_____

_____

_____

3. Which article idea is likely to have the greatest appeal to all the audiences? Why?

_____

_____

_____

4. For each topic, name the audience (or audiences) that you think would be most interested. If you think one audience would be equally inter-

ested in more than one topic, you can name that audience more than once.

Campus parking lot: _____

Student diversity: _____

Drinking on campus: _____

5. If an idea has narrow appeal, should you write about it anyway? Why or why not?

_____

_____

_____

6. How can you make a narrow-interest article interesting to a general audience?

_____

Exercise 2: Prewriting

Choose a topic you are interested in and know something about—for example, college sports, handling stress in a stressful world, our culture's emphasis on beauty and youth, or child rearing. Narrow your topic, then use the following prewriting strategies to discover what you already know and what you would need to learn if you had to write an essay about the subject for one of your classes. (If necessary, continue this prewriting exercise on a separate sheet of paper):

Brainstorm your ideas: _____

_____

_____

_____

_____

Freewrite: _____

_____

_____

_____

_____

_____

Ask journalists' questions: _____

_____

_____

_____

Exercise 3: Writing a Thesis Statement

Write two thesis statements for each of the following topics. The first statement should try to inform the reader, while the second should try to persuade. In each case, writing a thesis statement will require that you narrow the topic:

> ➤ *The rising cost of a college education*
> Thesis with an informative purpose _____
> _____
>
> Thesis with a persuasive purpose _____
> _____

> ➤ *Taking care of your body and mind*
> Thesis with an informative purpose _____
> _____
>
> _____
>
> Thesis with a persuasive purpose _____
> _____

> ➤ *Career choice*
> Thesis with an informative purpose _____
> _____
>
> Thesis with a persuasive purpose _____
> _____

Exercise 4: Drafting an Introduction and Conclusion

Imagine that one of the topics you explored in Exercise 2 or 3 is the basis for a short paper in one of your courses. Use what you learned in the chapter to write an introduction and conclusion to that paper. (If necessary, continue the exercise on a separate sheet of paper.)

Introduction

_____
_____
_____
_____
_____
_____
_____
_____

<u>Conclusion</u>

_____

_____

_____

_____

_____

_____

_____

KEY TO COOPERATIVE LEARNING: BUILDING TEAMWORK SKILLS

Collaborative Writing   In many jobs, you may be asked to work with other employees to produce written documents, including reports, proposals, procedure manuals, and even important letters and memos. Writing in groups, also known as *collaborative writing,* involves planning, drafting, revising, and editing.

To see what collaborative writing is like, join with three classmates and choose a general topic you are all interested in—for example, "What Colleges Can Do to Help Students Juggle School, Work, and Family" or "Teaching Safe Sex in an Age When Sex Isn't Safe." Now imagine that you and other group members have to write a persuasive paper on some aspect of this topic. Writing the paper involves the following steps:

> ➢ Each group member should spend an hour in the library to get an overview of the topic so that everyone is able to write about it in general terms.

> ➢ The group should come together to brainstorm the topic, narrow its focus, and come up with a thesis. Use your research and thesis to write a working outline that specifies what the paper will say and the approach it will take. Divide the writing assignment into parts and assign a part to each group member.

> ➢ Each group member should *draft* his or her portion of the paper. Each section should be about two to three paragraphs long.

> ➢ Photocopy each draft and hand a copy to each group member. Working independently, each person should use the suggestions in this chapter to *evaluate* and *revise* each section. After the independent revision work is done, come together as a group to hammer out differences and prepare a final, unedited version.

> ➢ Photocopy this version and distribute it to group members. Have everyone *edit* the material, looking for mistakes in

spelling, grammar, punctuation, and usage. Incorporate the group's changes into a final version you all agree on, and ask every group member to read it. The group's goal is to produce a finished paper that satisfies the thesis and that also looks good.

➤ Working alone, each group member should answer the following questions. Finally, compare your responses with those of other group members:

1. What do you see as the advantages and disadvantages of collaborative writing? Is it difficult or easy to write as a team member?

_____

_____

_____

2. What part of the collaborative writing project worked best? Where did you encounter problems?

_____

_____

_____

3. What did you learn from this experience that will make you a more effective collaborative writer on the next project?

_____

_____

_____

KEY TO SELF-EXPRESSION: DISCOVERY THROUGH JOURNAL WRITING

To record your thoughts, use the lined page preceding the next chapter or a separate journal.

Your Relationship With Words   Some people love to work with words—writing them, reading them, speaking them—while others would rather do anything else. Do you enjoy writing in school, or does writing intimidate you? Do you write anything outside of school, either at work or at home? Discuss how you feel about writing. What sorts of experiences did you have in your K-to-12 schooling with reading and writing? Did they move you ahead or make you a reluctant writer or reader?

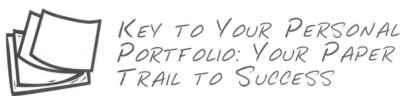

KEY TO YOUR PERSONAL
PORTFOLIO: YOUR PAPER
TRAIL TO SUCCESS

End-of-Chapter Cumulative Essay   Many people think that the process of reading is the opposite of the process of writing. They perceive reading as *taking in* information, while writing is *transmitting out* information. The truth is that reading and writing are *both meaning making, active processes whose aim is communication.* Review Chapter 4 on the reading process, and then compose an essay that shows you understand the similarities between reading for meaning and writing to communicate your message. Note that there are many similar stages in both processes. You may wish to discuss this question with peers in the class before you begin to write.

Journal Entry

APPLY

TEST PREPARATION AND TEST TAKING:

Knowing and Showing What You Know

In this chapter, you will explore answers to the following questions:

How and why does strategic test preparation—prediction and practice—help improve test scores?

How can you deal with test anxiety?

What general test-taking strategies can help you succeed on tests?

How can you master specific types of test questions?

How can you learn from test mistakes and modify your preparation and test-taking strategies for future success?

Testing is a fact of student life, even though many students don't look forward to taking tests. Part of the remedy for dreading tests lies in how you perceive them. If you think of doing well on a test as your ultimate educational goal, having an off day that results in a low grade might stop you in your tracks. Rather than seeing exams as the end of the trip, think of them as a bridge that leads you toward your goals. Taking tests is preparation for life. When you get a job, act as a volunteer, or even work through your family budget, you'll have to apply what you know and put your skills into action—exactly what you do when you take a test.

In this chapter, you will explore strategies that focus on preparation, test taking, and learning from test results. You will learn that your test-taking abilities will benefit strongly from predicting test format and questions as well as practicing course material, often in a testlike setting.

HOW AND WHY DOES STRATEGIC TEST PREPARATION—PREDICTION AND PRACTICE—HELP IMPROVE TEST SCORES?

Your success on tests is directly and powerfully related to the methods you use, on an ongoing day-to-day basis, to construct strategies that prepare you adequately for "training for the task." Training for the task means that you keep the specifics of the task in mind when you study—that is, each time you work on learning material, you carefully consider test formats, time constraints, and other factors that determine test success.

Consider this analogy: You didn't get ready to pass your driver's test just by reading the driver's manual. You knew that much of your success on that test would be determined by how well you could drive a car in specific situations. By comparison, if you have a history essay test in which you must write a proven point of view within a time limit, why would you study only by reading and rereading details? That's not training to the reality of the task.

Think of the following equation as it applies to success on tests:

$$P1 + P2 = T3$$

PREDICTION AND PRACTICE = TERRIFIC TEST TAKING

Although you will often be predicting and practicing at the same time, the following sections will first cover predicting strategies and then practicing strategies.

Predict Test Type and Material

Coming at a test from different angles will help you get the clearest possible picture of what it will involve. Prediction means identifying test type, taking time early in the term to talk to your instructors during office hours, using your studying techniques to anticipate test questions, talking to other students, and looking at old tests.

Identify Test Type

Before you begin studying, try to determine what will be covered on the test and the type of test it will be:

> Will it be a short-answer test with true/false and multiple-choice questions, an essay test, or a combination?

> Will the test cover everything you studied since the semester began or will it be limited to a more narrow topic?

> Will the test cover only what you learned in class and in the text or will it also cover outside readings?

Your instructors can answer many of these questions for you. Even though they may not tell you the specific questions that will be on the test, they will let you know what blocks of information will be covered, the question formats, and numbers of items on exams. Some instructors may even give you a study guide or drop hints throughout the semester about possible test questions. While some comments are direct ("I might ask a question on the subject of _____ on your next exam"), other clues are subtle. For example, when instructors repeat an idea or when they express personal interest in a topic ("One of my favorite theories is . . ."), they are often letting you know that the material may be on the test.

Use Your Instructors' Office Hours Early in the Term

Interacting with your instructors outside of the normal classroom constraints is an important way for you to understand an instructor's intentions for the course, and an important first step in their getting to know you. Often, an instructor's personality is not revealed in the classroom, and if students care enough to seek out their instructors early, instructors often respond with gracious assistance. The following are specific ideas for interacting with your instructors in powerful and effective ways:

> ➢ Go to office hours *before the first test* to get an idea of the instructor's preferred sources for questions.

> ➢ Make sure your instructors know your name.

> ➢ When you meet with your instructor, take your class notes and books as a focus for the conversation; that way, the instructor can assess your note-taking style.

> ➢ After a first test, review your test with your instructor.

> ➢ Take notes in office-hour visits.

> ➢ Find out if instructors or teaching assistants are willing to hold test reviews.

Use PQ3R to Identify Important Ideas and Facts

Often, the questions you write and ask yourself when you read assigned materials may be part of the test. Textbook study questions may seem like good candidates for test material, but college tests are usually different from practice questions in your textbooks.

Consult Fellow Students

If you know people who have taken the instructor's course before, ask them about the tests. Try to find out how difficult the tests are, whether they focus more on assigned readings or class notes, what materials are usually covered, and what types of questions occur on the tests. This information can help you decide which materials to focus on during your study time. Ask also about instructor preferences. For example, if you learn that the instructor pays close attention to factual and grammatical accuracy, you will be wise to focus on details and grammar as you study. Find out if certain instructors tend to ask exam questions about the "real-world" examples that they use to illustrate their lectures.

Examine Old Tests

Instructors often make these tests available in class or on reserve in the library. Studying these exams can help you learn what type and level of questions to expect. Old tests help to answer the following questions:

> ➤ Does the instructor focus on examples and details, general ideas and themes, a combination of both, or relationships between and among concepts?

> ➤ Can you do well on the test through straight memorization (this is seldom true in college) or does the material require critical thinking?

> ➤ Are the questions straightforward or are they confusing and sometimes tricky because of the wording?

> ➤ Do the tests require the integration of facts from different areas to draw conclusions?

If you can't get copies of old tests and your instructor doesn't give too many details about what the test will cover, use clues from the class and from your course syllabus to predict test questions. After taking the first exam in the course, you will have more information about what to expect in the future. Professors tend to have test-writing styles, and it's your responsibility to figure them out.

Practice the Course Material

> *"A little knowledge that acts is worth infinitely more than much knowledge that is idle."*
> Kahlil Gibran

During and after your prediction of what your test will be like, the other key to your success is practice, practice, practice. Like a runner who prepares for a marathon by exercising, eating right, taking practice runs, and getting enough sleep, you can take steps to master your course material.

The primary step, occupying much of your preparation time, is to study until you know the material that will be on the test (Chapter 4 examines the art of effective reading and studying). Other important steps are the strategies that follow. The most effective practices include carefully choosing study materials, setting a study schedule that works for you, practicing critical thinking, using a pretest to practice under simulated test conditions, using "best studying" techniques, creating a study plan checklist, and preparing physically.

Choose Study Materials

Once you have identified as much as you can about the subject matter of the test, choose the materials that contain the information you need to study. You can save yourself time by making sure you aren't studying anything you don't need to. Go through your notes, your texts, any primary source materials that were assigned, and any handouts from your instructor. Find connections between and among lecture and print sources.

Set a Study Schedule

Use your time-management skills to set a schedule that will help you feel as prepared as you can be. Consider all of the relevant factors—the materials you need to study, how many days or weeks until the test date, and how much time you can study each day. If you establish your schedule ahead of time and write it in your date book, you will be much more likely to follow it. If you can study before and/or right after your classes, learning will come easier.

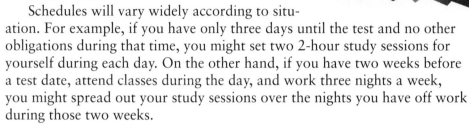

Schedules will vary widely according to situation. For example, if you have only three days until the test and no other obligations during that time, you might set two 2-hour study sessions for yourself during each day. On the other hand, if you have two weeks before a test date, attend classes during the day, and work three nights a week, you might spread out your study sessions over the nights you have off work during those two weeks.

Parents who have to juggle child care with study time can find the challenge especially difficult right before a test. Here are some suggestions that might help:

Tell your children why this test is important. You might explain that doing well on this exam is a step toward a successful education and a better job, which will improve their lives as well as yours. Discuss the situation in concrete terms that they can understand. For example, a better job for you might mean for them a better home, nicer places to play, more money to plan fun outings and vacations, more time to spend as a family, and a happier parent (you)!

Explain the time frame. Tell them when and for how long you will study, and when the test will take place. Although children age nine and older will probably cooperate, younger children may have a harder time accepting that you can't be with them. Plan a reward outing so they can celebrate with you after you finish your test—going for ice cream, seeing a movie, having a picnic.

Keep children active while you study. Stock up on games, books, and videos. If a child is old enough, have him or her invite a friend over.

Find help. Ask a relative or friend to watch the children during the day for a couple of days before your exam, or arrange for your child to visit a friend's house. Consider trading baby-sitting hours with another parent, hiring a baby sitter who will come to your home, or enrolling your child in a day care center.

Prepare Through Practicing Critical Thinking

Using the techniques from Chapter 3, approach your test preparation as an active, critical thinker, working to understand the material rather than to just pass the test by repeating facts. As you study, try to connect ideas to examples, analyze causes and effects, establish truth, and look at issues from different perspectives.

In many courses, instructors want to see evidence that you can link seemingly unrelated ideas into patterns that make sense. As you study, try to explore concepts from different perspectives and connect ideas and examples that, on the surface, appear unrelated. Although you'll probably find answers to these questions in your text or class notes, you may have to work at putting different ideas together. Critical thinking takes work, but may promote a greater understanding of the subject and probably a higher grade on the exam.

Using critical thinking is especially important in your preparation for essay tests that ask you to develop and support a thesis. The best way to prepare for these questions is to identify three or four essay questions your instructor is likely to ask. For each one, decide on your point of view, find the important proof and examples you need to prove your thesis, plan an outline, and write out your responses as part of your test preparation. Be mindful of how long you will have to write the essay as you plan it, and try writing an answer without using cues within that time limit.

Make a Pretest and Practice in Test Conditions

Use questions from your textbook to create your own pretest. Most textbooks, although not all, will include such questions at the ends of chapters. If your course doesn't have an assigned text, develop questions from your notes and from assigned outside readings. Choose questions that are likely to be covered on the test, then answer them under testlike conditions—in quiet, with no books or notes to help you (unless your exam is open-book), and with a clock telling you when to quit. Try to come as close as you can to duplicating the actual test situation.

Keep in Mind What "Best Studying" Entails

Not all studying is equally effective. Mere repetition is not necessarily better, and longer sessions are not necessarily more effective than focused, shorter sessions. The following are some attributes of effective, efficient studying:

> ➤ The best study is short but focused on a particular goal (30–90 minutes is best).

> ➤ The best study is intense, and ends with a testlike use of the material.

> ➤ The best study is done before and/or after a class meets, and the best review is accomplished within twenty-four hours of the lecture.

> ➤ The goal of the best study should be unaided recall of the material.

Prepare Physically

When taking a test, you need to work efficiently under time pressure. If your body is tired or under stress, you will probably not think as clearly or perform as well. If you can, avoid pulling an all-nighter before any test. Get some sleep so that you can wake up rested and alert. If you are one of the many who press the snooze button in their sleep, you may want to set two alarm clocks and place them across the room from your bed. That way you'll be more likely to get to your test on time.

Eating right is also important. Sugar-laden snacks will bring your energy up, only to send you crashing back down much too soon. Similarly, too much caffeine can add to your tension and make it difficult to focus. Eating nothing will leave you drained, but too much food can make you want to take a nap. The best advice is to eat a light, well-balanced meal before a test. When time is short, grab a quick-energy snack such as a banana, some orange juice, or a granola bar.

Despite all your good intentions, you still may feel stressed about your tests. If that stress becomes too intense, it may interfere with your test performance. Some particular strategies will help you combat any anxiety you may feel.

HOW CAN YOU DEAL WITH TEST ANXIETY?

For many students, the time before and during an exam is very stressful. The near-panic these students feel is known as *test anxiety.* Described as a bad case of nerves that makes it hard to think or remember, test anxiety can make your life as a student miserable and affect how well you do on tests. A certain amount of stress is a good thing; your body is on alert, and your energy motivates you to do your best. However, when anxiety blocks performance, you need to take steps to control it. Here are some suggestions:

Predict and prepare so you'll feel in control.   The more you know about what to expect on the exam, the better you'll feel. Find out what material will be covered, the format of the questions, the length of the exam, and the points assigned to each question.

Study in the room where you'll be taking the exam.   Find a class period (or more) when the room is empty and you can spend some time there. This practice will desensitize you to the panic associated with the room itself.

"He has not learned the lesson of life who does not every day surmount a fear."
Ralph Waldo Emerson

Put the test in perspective.   No matter how important it may seem, a test is only a small part of your educational experience and an even smaller part of your life. Your test grade, whether high or low, does not reflect on the kind of person you are or on your ability to succeed in many different areas.

Make a detailed study plan.   Divide the plan into a series of small tasks. As you finish each one, you'll be able to boost your sense of accomplishment and control. Time management is key to managing test anxiety.

Don't assume that anything less than perfection equals failure. Trying for a perfect score might overwhelm you, and the resulting anxiety could lower your score rather than raise it. Successful people aren't perfect people, they are people who constantly aim to do their best.

Practice relaxation. When you feel test anxiety coming on, take some deep breaths, close your eyes, and visualize a positive mental image related to the test. Images like the following can help propel you to success:

> *Your instructor hands your test back with a grade of A.*

> *Your grades in all your courses are so good that you make the dean's list.*

> *When you apply for a job, the employer reviews your college transcript and hires you on the spot.*

Test Anxiety and the Returning Adult Student

If you're returning to school after several years away, you may wonder if you can compete with younger students or if your mind is still able to learn new material. These feelings of inadequacy can block success if you let them. Telling yourself that you can't pass an exam because your test-taking skills are rusty is a formula for failure.

To counteract any negative feelings you may have, focus on how your life experiences have given you skills you can use. For example, managing work and a family requires strong time management, planning, and communication skills that can help you plan your study time, juggle school responsibilities, and interact with students and instructors. These positive feelings can translate into increased ability to achieve your goals. Younger students often assume that nontraditional students are smarter, anyway!

When you have predicted, practiced, and worked through your anxieties using the strategies described above, you are ready to take your exam. Now you can focus on methods to help you succeed when the test begins.

WHAT GENERAL TEST-TAKING STRATEGIES CAN HELP YOU SUCCEED ON TESTS?

Even though every test is different, there are general strategies that will help you handle almost all tests, including multiple choice, true/false, matching, short-answer and essay exams.

Write Down Key Facts: Get What You Know Out Where You Can Use It

Before you even look at the test, write down any key information—including formulas, rules, visual representations, outlines, and/or definitions—that you studied recently, even right before you entered the test room. Use the back of the question sheet or a piece of scrap paper for your notes (make sure it is clear to your instructor that this scrap paper didn't come into the test room already filled in!). Recording this information right at the start will make forgetting less likely.

Begin With an Overview of the Exam

Even though exam time is precious, spend a few minutes at the start of the test to get a sense of the kinds of questions you'll be answering, what type of thinking processes or mind actions they require, the number of questions in each section, and the point value of each section. Use this information to schedule the time you spend on each section. For example, if a two-hour test is divided into two sections of equal point value—an essay section with four questions and a short-answer section with sixty questions—you can divide your time in the following way:

> ➤ An hour on the essay section; no more than fifteen minutes for each question

> ➤ An hour on the short-answer section; one minute for each question

As you make your calculations, think about the level of difficulty of each section. If you think you can handle the short-answer questions in less than an hour and that you'll need more time with the essays, budget your time in a way that works for you.

Read All Test Directions

Although it seems obvious, reading test directions carefully can save you a lot of trouble. For example, while a history test made up of 100 true/false questions and one essay may look straightforward, the directions may tell you that you have to answer 80 of the 100 questions, that you won't be penalized for incorrect answers, and that the essay is a nonrequired bonus question. If the directions indicate that you *are* penalized for incorrect answers—meaning that you will lose points instead of simply not gaining points—you may want to avoid guessing unless you're fairly certain of the answer. For example, incorrect responses may do some damage if you earn two points for every correct answer and lose one point for every incorrect answer.

When you read the directions, you may learn that some questions or sections are weighted more heavily than others. For example, the short-answer questions on a two-part test may be worth only 30 points, while the essays are worth 70 points. In this case, it's smart to spend a lot more time on the essays than the short answers. To keep yourself aware of the specifics of the directions, you may want to circle or underline key words and numbers.

Work From Easy to Hard: Begin With Success

Begin with the parts or questions that seem easiest to you. One advantage of this strategy is that you will tend to take less time to answer the questions you know well, leaving more time to spend on the more difficult questions that may require increased effort and thinking. If you like to work through questions in order, mark difficult questions as you reach them and return to them after you answer the questions you know.

Another advantage of answering the easier questions first is that comfortably knowing answers to questions can boost your confidence early in the test. This confidence can help you to continue to believe in yourself when you launch into the more difficult sections.

Watch the Clock

Part of your test preparation should be practicing the material within appropriate time constraints. You need to enter a test knowing what test-taking time feels like. As you work through the test, keep track of how much time is left and whether your progress is keeping up with your schedule. You may want to plan out your time on a scrap piece of paper, especially if you have one or more essays to write. Wear a watch or bring a small clock with you to the test room. A wall clock may be broken, or there may be no clock at all!

Some students are so concerned about time that they rush through the test and actually have time left over. In situations like this, it's easy to leave early, happy that the test is over. The best move, however, is to take your time. Rushing is almost always a mistake, even if you feel you've done well. Stay till the end so you can refine and check your work—it couldn't hurt, and it might help.

Master the Art of Intelligent Guessing

Nothing can replace your being knowledgeable and well prepared for tests. When you are unsure of an answer on a short-answer test, however, you can leave it blank or you can guess. In most cases, provided that you are not penalized for incorrect answers, guessing will benefit you. "Intelligent guessing," writes Steven Frank, an authority on student studying and test taking, "means taking advantage of what you do know in order to try to figure out what you don't. If you guess intelligently, you have a decent shot at getting the answer right."[1]

Intelligent guessing begins by eliminating all the answers you know—or believe—are wrong. Try to narrow your choices to two possible answers, then choose the one you think is more likely to be correct. Strategies for guessing the correct answer in a multiple-choice test will be discussed later in the chapter.

When you check your work at the end of the test, ask yourself whether you would make the same guesses again. Chances are that you will leave your answers alone, but you may notice something that will make you change your mind. For example, you may have misread or failed to notice a **qualifier** that affects meaning (these are little words such as *always, except, never, best* and so on), recalled a fact that will enable you to answer the question without guessing, miscalculated a step in a math problem, or determined that your guess didn't make sense.

> Qualifier,
> A descriptive word, such as *always, never,* or *often,* that changes the meaning of another word or word group.

Follow Directions on Machine-Scored Tests

Machine-scored tests require that you use a special pencil to fill in a small box on a computerized answer sheet. When the computer scans the sheet, it can tell whether you answered the questions correctly.

Taking these tests requires special care. Use the right pencil (a number-two pencil is usually required) and mark your answer in the correct space. Periodically, check the answer number against the question number to make sure they match. If you mark the answer to question 4 in the space for question 5, not only will you get question 4 wrong, but your responses for every question that follows will be off by a line. One helpful way to avoid getting off track is to put a small dot next to any number that you skip and plan to return to later on.

Neatness counts on these tests, because the computer can misread stray pencil marks or partially erased answers. If you mark two answers to a question and only partially erase one, the computer will read both responses and charge you with a wrong answer. Completely fill each answer space and avoid any other pencil marks that could be misinterpreted by the computer.

Use Critical Thinking to Avoid Errors

When the pressure of a test makes you nervous, critical thinking can help you work through each question thoroughly and avoid errors. Following are some critical-thinking strategies to use during a test.

Recall facts, procedures, rules, and formulas. You base your answers on the information you recall. Think carefully to make sure you recall it accurately.

Think about similarities. If you don't know how to attack a question or problem, consider any similar questions or problems that you have worked on in class or while studying.

Notice differences. Especially with objective questions, items that seem different from what you have studied may indicate answers you can eliminate.

Think through causes and effects. For a numerical problem, think through how you plan to solve it and see if the answer—the effect of your plan—makes sense. For an essay question that asks you to analyze a condition or situation, consider both what caused it and what effects it has.

Find the best idea to match the example or examples given. For a numerical problem, decide what formula (idea) best applies to the example or examples (the data of the problem). For an essay question, decide what idea applies to, or links, the examples given.

Support ideas with examples. When you put forth an idea in an answer to an essay question, be sure to back up your idea with as adequate number of appropriate examples.

Evaluate each test question. In your initial approach to any question, evaluate what kinds of thinking will best help you solve it. For example, essay questions often require cause-and-effect and idea-to-example thinking, while objective questions often call for thinking through similarities and differences.

Next, you will see how these general rules apply to specific types of questions.

HOW CAN YOU MASTER SPECIFIC TYPES OF TEST QUESTIONS?

Objective questions,
Short-answer questions that test your ability to recall, compare, and contrast information, and to link ideas to examples.

Subjective questions,
Essay questions that require you to express your answer in terms of your own personal knowledge and perspective.

Although the goal of all test questions is to discover how much you know about a subject, every type of question has a different way of asking you to show what you know. Answering different types of questions is part science and part art. First, the strategy changes dramatically according to whether the question is objective or subjective.

For **objective questions**, you choose or write a short answer you believe is correct, often making a selection from a limited number of choices. Multiple-choice, fill-in-the-blank, and true/false questions fall into this category. **Subjective questions** demand the same information recall as objective questions, but they also require that you plan, organize, draft, and refine a written response. They may also require more extensive critical thinking and evaluation of thinking processes. All essay questions are subjective. While there are some guidelines that will help you choose the right answers to both types of questions, you must also learn to "feel" your way to an answer that works. If you spend some study time writing from memory what you know, you will greatly improve your ability to correctly answer both objective and subjective questions.

Multiple-Choice Questions Require Recall, Not Recognition

Multiple-choice questions are the most popular type of question found on standardized or other machine-scored tests. Often professors give multiple-choice exams that are not machine-scored, because they can be graded quickly.

Multiple-choice items seem to require only recognition since the answers are provided on the test. In order to correctly answer college multiple-choice items, however, you must be able to do more than recognize a key word. Successful test takers study with the goal of unaided recall. This broadens their knowledge base and increases the likelihood of picking the correct answers. The following strategies can help you answer multiple-choice questions.

> **Recognition,**
> Knowing what the correct answer looks or sounds like.

> **Recall,**
> Knowing what the correct answer is, and why it fits.

Carefully read the directions.   In the rush to get to work on a question, it is easy to read directions too quickly or to skip them, assuming that the questions will be self-explanatory. Directions, however, can be tricky. For example, while most test items ask for a single correct answer, some give you the option of marking several choices that are correct. For some tests, you might be required to answer only a certain number of the test questions.

Read each question thoroughly before looking at the choices.   Then try to answer the question. This strategy will reduce the possibility that the choices will confuse you.

Underline key words and phrases in the question.   If the question is complicated, try to break it down into small sections that are easy to understand.

Pay special attention to words that could throw you off.   For example, it is easy to overlook negatives in a question ("Which of the following is *not . . .*").

Think of an acceptable answer in your mind before you look at the choice of answers.   This process helps trigger recall, which is more accurate than mere recognition.

If you don't know the answer, eliminate and cross out those answers that you know or suspect are wrong.   Your goal is to leave yourself with two possible answers, which would give you a fifty-fifty chance of making the right choice. The following are questions you can ask as you work to eliminate choices:

> ➤ Is the choice accurate in its own terms? If there's an error in the choice—for example, a term that is incorrectly defined—the answer is wrong.

> ➤ Is the choice relevant? An answer may be accurate, but it may not relate to the essence of the question.

> Are there any qualifiers? *Absolute* qualifiers like *always, never, all, none,* or *every* often signal an exception that makes a choice incorrect. For example, the statement, "Children always begin talking before the age of two" is an untrue statement; while most children begin talking before age two, some have a later start. Analysis has shown that choices containing *conservative* qualifiers *(often, most, rarely, may sometimes be, can occasionally result in)* are often correct.

> Do the choices give you any clues? Does a puzzling word remind you of a word you know? If you don't know a word, does any part of the word seem familiar to you?

As a last resort, look for patterns that may lead to the right answer, then use intelligent guessing. The ideal is to know the material so well that you don't have to guess, but that level of knowledge is not always possible. When you really aren't sure, use these hints to help you made an educated guess. Test-taking experts have found patterns in multiple-choice questions that may help you get a better grade. Here is their advice:

> Consider the possibility that a choice that is *more general* than the others is the right answer.

> Consider the possibility that a choice that is *longer* than the others is the right answer.

> Look for a choice that has a *middle value in a range* (the range can be from small to large, from old to recent). It is likely to be the right answer.

> Look for two choices that have *similar meanings*. One of these answers is probably correct.

> Look for *answers that agree grammatically with the question*. For example, a fill-in-the-blank question that has an *a* or *an* before the blank gives you a clue as to which answer is correct.

Make sure you read every word of every answer.   Instructors have been known to include answers that are almost right, except for a single word.

When questions are keyed to a long reading passage, read the questions first.   This will help you, when you read the passage, to focus on the information you need to answer the questions.

Here are some examples of the kinds of multiple-choice questions you might encounter in an Introduction to Psychology course.[2]

1. Arnold is at the company party and has had too much to drink. He releases all of his pent-up aggression by yelling at his boss, who promptly fires him. Arnold normally would not have yelled at his boss, but after drinking heavily he yelled because _____ .

   a. parties are places where employees are supposed to be able to "loosen up"

   b. alcohol is a stimulant

   c. alcohol makes people less concerned with the negative consequences of their behavior

   d. alcohol inhibits brain centers that control the perception of loudness

   (The correct answer is C.)

2. Which of the following has not been shown to be a probable cause of or influence in the development of alcoholism in our society?

   a. intelligence   c. personality

   b. culture   d. genetic vulnerability

   (The correct answer is A.)

3. Geraldine is a heavy coffee drinker who has become addicted to caffeine. If she completely ceases her intake of caffeine over the next few days, she is likely to experience each of the following EXCEPT _____ .

   a. depression   c. insomnia

   b. lethargy   d. headaches

   (The correct answer is C.)

True/False Questions Are Harder Than They Look

True/false questions test your recall of facts as well as your understanding of concepts, including minor details. Read them carefully to look for qualifiers that can turn a statement that would otherwise be true into one that is false. Similarly, a statement you think is false may also be turned around with a qualifier. Qualifiers to watch out for include: *all, only,* and *always* (the absolutes that often make a statement false), and *generally, often, usually,* and *sometimes* (the conservatives that often make a statement true).

   If you're truly stumped on a true/false question, underline each separate idea embedded in the statement and judge each part separately. College-level true/false questions are often harder than they look because each statement can be a combination of many separate ideas, each of which should be judged separately. Here are some examples of the kinds of true/false questions you might encounter in an Introduction to Psychology course. The correct answer follows each question:

Are the following questions true or false?

1. Alcohol use is clearly related to increases in hostility, aggression, violence, and abusive behavior. (True)
2. Marijuana is harmless. (False)
3. Simply expecting a drug to produce an effect is often enough to produce the effect. (True)
4. Alcohol is a stimulant. (False)

Short-Answer, Matching, and Fill-in-the-Blank Items

To answer these kinds of test questions correctly, study so that you can use and/or tell what you know from memory. As is the case with multiple choice, correct answers require recall, not just recognition (see p. 227). Therefore, the best study is writing to rehearse, followed by unaided writing to recall. The following are a few item-specific suggestions for preparing for and taking these kinds of test items:

> ➤ Work on correct spelling of terms for fill-in-the-blank. Instructors can be picky about spelling on these items.

> ➤ Mark matching items as you use the answers. This will help you keep track of which choices you have used and which you have left to choose from. You may wish to write notes in the margins next to matching items to reinforce the information you know about them.

> ➤ Do not pad short-answer items with irrelevant information. Get to the point.

Essay Questions Especially Require Prediction and Practice

It is a common myth among college students that essay tests are harder than multiple-choice tests because on multiple-choice tests, the answer is there—you just have to *find it*. This isn't necessarily the case. An essay question allows you the freedom to express your knowledge and views on a topic, in a much more extensive and personalized manner than any multiple-choice or short-answer question can provide. With the freedom to express your views, though, comes the challenge to both exhibit knowledge and show that you can organize and express that knowledge clearly.

Start by reading the essay questions. If you have a choice from among a group of questions—such as answering two out of three given possibilities—first decide which you are going to try. Then focus on what each question is asking, the mind actions you will need to use, and the writing directions. Read the questions carefully and do everything that you are asked to do. Some essay questions may contain more than one part.

Certain action verbs can help you figure out how to think, so watch for them and know exactly what they mean. Table 8-1 explains some words commonly used in essays. Underline these words as you read the essay question, and use them to guide your writing.

Next, budget your time and begin to plan. Outline, draw, or diagram the main points you want to make and indicate the examples you plan to cite to support these ideas. Let this outline be your guide as you begin to write.

You're under time pressure, so don't spend too much time on introductions or flowery prose. Start with a thesis statement or idea that states your

TABLE 8-1 COMMON ACTION VERBS ON ESSAY TESTS

Analyze—Break into parts and discuss each part separately.

Compare—Explain similarities and differences.

Contrast—Distinguish between items being compared by focusing on differences.

Criticize—Evaluate the positive and negative effects of what is being discussed.

Define—State the essential quality or meaning. Give the common idea.

Describe—Visualize and give information that paints a complete picture.

Discuss—Examine in a complete and detailed way, usually by connecting ideas to examples.

Enumerate/List/Identify—Recall and specify items in the form of a list.

Explain—Clarify the meaning of something, often by making analogies or giving examples.

Evaluate—Give your opinion about the value or worth of something, usually by weighing positive and negative effects, and justify your conclusion.

ILLUSTRATE—Supply examples.

Interpret—Explain your personal view of facts and ideas and how they relate to one another.

OUTLINE—Organize and present the sub-ideas or main examples of an idea.

PROVE—Use evidence and argument to show that something is true, usually by showing cause and effect or giving examples that fit the idea to be proven.

Review—Provide an overview of ideas and establish their merits and features.

State—Explain clearly, simply, and concisely, being sure that each word gives the image you want.

SUMMARIZE—Give the important ideas in brief.

Trace—Present a history of the way something developed, often by showing cause and effect.

position (you can turn around the wording of the question to begin your answer) and tells in a basic way what your essay will say (see Chapter 7 for a discussion of thesis statements). In the first paragraph, introduce the essay's key points. These may be sub-ideas, causes, effects, or even examples. Use clear, concise language in the body of the essay. Carefully establish your ideas and support them with examples, looking back at your outline to make sure you are covering everything. Wrap it up with a conclusion that is short and to the point.

Try to write legibly—if your instructor can't read your ideas, it doesn't matter how good they are. Instructors who have to read twenty or more essays for a single class may not have the energy to decipher messy handwriting. Try printing and skipping every other line if you know your handwriting is problematic. Avoid writing on both sides of the paper since it will make your handwriting even harder to read. You may even want to discuss the problem with the instructor.

Do your best to save time to reread and revise your essay after you finish getting your ideas down on paper. Look for ideas you may have left out, ideas you didn't support with enough examples, and poorly phrased sentences that might confuse the reader. If an idea seems incomplete, don't hesitate to add a clarifying sentence or two in the margin. An essay is a first-draft writing, so it's better to add than to leave out in the name of neatness! Finally, check for mistakes in grammar, spelling, punctuation, and usage. No matter what subject you are writing about, having a command of these factors will make your work all the more complete and impressive.

Here are some examples of essay questions you might encounter in an Introduction to Psychology course. In each case, notice the action verbs from Table 8-1.

---

1. Summarize the theories and research on the causes and effects of daydreaming. Discuss the possible uses for daydreaming in a healthy individual.
2. Describe the physical and psychological effects of alcohol and the problems associated with its use.
3. Explain what sleep terrors are, what appears to cause them, and who is most likely to suffer from them.

HOW CAN YOU LEARN FROM TEST MISTAKES AND MODIFY YOUR PREPARATION AND TEST-TAKING STRATEGIES FOR FUTURE SUCCESS?

The purpose of a test is to see how much you know, not merely what grade you can achieve. The knowledge that comes from attending class and studying should allow you to correctly answer test questions. Knowledge also comes, however, when you take the time to learn from your mistakes.

How Can I Prepare for exams?

Jeff Felardeau, Selkirk College—Nelson, BC, Adult Basic Education

I've been out of school for quite a long time, so when I returned and had to memorize material for exams, I just wasn't prepared. The labor work I was doing didn't require me to use my memorization skills. I had the most difficulty memorizing for classes like biology and any of the sciences where you have to memorize a lot of facts. I'd work hard by repeating the information over and over in my mind, but I'd only be able to recall it for a short time afterwards—long-term  learning wasn't there. Whenever I'd prepare for an exam, I'd find myself in a "cram" mode because I didn't remember any of the material from class. It was like learning the material all over again.

I took a class called College Success, which gave me some good study tips. There I learned things like mind-mapping, listening skills and note-taking styles. I also learned to use word associations and visualization to help remember the material. It's helped me improve a lot, but still I get stuck in old habits and patterns and forget to apply the methods that will really help me improve. I know that if I don't change these old study patterns and habits, I'll hit the wall sooner or later. I can't keep using methods that served me in the past but are no longer effective for where I am today. What do you suggest?

Miriam Kapner, New England Conservatory—Boston, MA, Junior in Oboe Performance

Even though you have a good understanding of what it takes to prepare for an exam, the key is to remain disciplined. If your mind is wandering in class and you find you're staring out the window looking at those clouds, remember that you have control of your mind. By staying focused in class you will not have to study so  much when exam time rolls around. Although we all fall victim to daydreaming, try to gain control of your mind by thinking of your goals or by using simple mind tricks. Even if the class has a very dry teacher, there are ways to keep focused. One day a friend and I sat down and figured out exactly how much each class was costing us. When we realized the amount of money we were spending for that hour, it was a real eye-opener. If I'm really having a hard time, I make sure I ask at least two questions per class. This forces me to pay attention.

In order to memorize, you need to be able to find some order. It helps if you have a reference point to begin with and then look for certain patterns or categories. I also use mnemonic devices to help me remember. In fact, I can still remember the ones I learned in elementary school: General Electric Lights Never Dim for the first five books of the Bible and of course, Every Good Boy Does Fine for the lines in the treble clef. But mainly, whatever steps you take to improve your preparation for exams, remember that you are in control of your mind—not the other way around.

> *"The only fence against the world is a thorough knowledge of it."*
>
> John Locke

If you don't examine what you get wrong on a test, you might repeat the same mistake again on another test and perhaps in life. Learn from test mistakes just as you learn from mistakes in your personal and business life. The following strategies will help.

Try to identify patterns in your mistakes. Look for:

> ➤ *Careless errors*—In your rush to complete the exam, did you misread the question or directions, blacken the wrong box on the answer sheet, inadvertently skip a question, or write illegibly?

> ➤ *Conceptual or factual errors*—Did you misunderstand a concept or never learn it in the first place? Did you fail to master certain facts? Did you skip part of the assigned text or miss important classes in which ideas were covered?

If you have time, try to rework the questions you got wrong. Based on the feedback from your instructor, try to rewrite an essay, recalculate a math problem starting from the original question, or redo the questions that follow a reading selection. Although revisiting avoidable mistakes can be frustrating, the process can help you know what to do differently next time. If you see patterns of careless errors, promise yourself that you'll be more careful in the future and that you'll save time to double check your work. If you pick up conceptual and factual errors, rededicate yourself to better preparation.

After reviewing your mistakes, fill in your knowledge gaps. If you made mistakes on questions because you didn't know or understand them, develop a plan to comprehensively learn the material. Solidifying your knowledge can help you in exams further down the road, as well as in life situations that involve the subject matter you're studying. You might even consider asking your instructor if you can retake the exam, if you have the time to do so. The score might not count, but you may find that focusing on learning rather than on grades can improve your knowledge and help you to build self-respect.

If you fail a test completely, don't throw it away. First, take comfort in the fact that many students have been in your shoes and that you are likely to improve your performance. Then recommit to the process by reviewing and analyzing your errors. Finally, be sure you understand *why* you failed. This is especially important for an essay test, because while most objective questions are fact-based and clearly right or wrong, subjective questions are in large part subject to the opinion of the grader. Respectfully ask the instructor who graded the test for an explanation. You may also want to ask what you could have done to earn a better grade.

sine qua non

Although the Latin language is no longer commonly used, it is one of the most dominant ancestors of modern English, and many Latin words and phrases have a place in the English language. The Latin phrase *sine qua non* (pronounced "sihn-ay kwa nahn") means, literally, "without which not." Translated into everyday language, a *sine qua non* is "an absolutely indispensable or essential thing."

Think of true learning as the *sine qua non* of test taking. When you have worked hard to learn ideas and information, taking it in and using different techniques to review and retain it, you will be more able to take tests successfully, confident that you have the knowledge necessary to answer the required questions. Focus on knowledge so that test taking becomes not an intimidating challenge, but an opportunity to show what you know.

Chapter 8: Applications

Name _____ Date _____

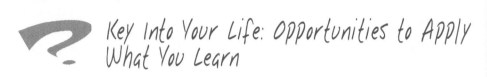 Key Into Your Life: Opportunities to Apply What You Learn

Exercise 1: Try This Test!

If you study for objective tests (especially for multiple-choice and true/false items) as though the test were short-answer instead, you'd have more to recall when approaching such items. Use your knowledge from previous reading and this chapter to answer the following items. Note that you must explain each answer in writing in the space provided as well as picking the correct option:

1. The least helpful information to know about a piece of text to be read and learned is:

    a. the purpose for reading

    b. the difficulty

    c. your familiarity

    d. the author

    Explain your choice: _____

    _____

2. One of the best solutions to reading problems is:

    a. looking up unfamiliar words in the dictionary

    b. to read more slowly

    c. writing summaries as you read

    d. answering questions at the end of the chapter

    Explain your choice: _____

    _____

3. The most efficient way to study for an objective test is to

    a. concentrate on the big ideas first

    b. concentrate on memorizing the details

    c. prepare as though you were preparing for an essay test

    d. do both a and c

    Explain your choice: _____

    _____

4. In order to take a test most efficiently, one should

   a. read all of the test first

   b. start on the easiest part first

   c. start on the beginning immediately

   d. question as one reads

   e. c and d

   f. a and c

   Explain your choice: ⎯⎯⎯⎯⎯⎯⎯⎯⎯⎯⎯⎯⎯⎯⎯⎯⎯⎯⎯

   ⎯⎯⎯⎯⎯⎯⎯⎯⎯⎯⎯⎯⎯⎯⎯⎯⎯⎯⎯⎯⎯⎯⎯⎯⎯⎯⎯⎯⎯⎯⎯⎯

5. The most efficient way(s) to study notes from classes include(s) all except

   a. framing questions from the notes

   b. recopying notes

   c. rereading notes

   d. consolidating book material with class notes

   e. all the above

   Explain your choice: ⎯⎯⎯⎯⎯⎯⎯⎯⎯⎯⎯⎯⎯⎯⎯⎯⎯⎯⎯

   ⎯⎯⎯⎯⎯⎯⎯⎯⎯⎯⎯⎯⎯⎯⎯⎯⎯⎯⎯⎯⎯⎯⎯⎯⎯⎯⎯⎯⎯⎯⎯⎯

<u>True or false</u> (Be sure to justify your answers.)

⎯⎯ 6. Graphic aids in textbooks are meant to help poor readers.

Reason: ⎯⎯⎯⎯⎯⎯⎯⎯⎯⎯⎯⎯⎯⎯⎯⎯⎯⎯⎯⎯⎯⎯⎯⎯⎯⎯⎯⎯

⎯⎯ 7. The ways you prepare for different tests are all really very different, depending on the kinds of tests.

Reason: ⎯⎯⎯⎯⎯⎯⎯⎯⎯⎯⎯⎯⎯⎯⎯⎯⎯⎯⎯⎯⎯⎯⎯⎯⎯⎯⎯⎯

⎯⎯ 8. One should always underline as one reads to highlight important information.

Reason: ⎯⎯⎯⎯⎯⎯⎯⎯⎯⎯⎯⎯⎯⎯⎯⎯⎯⎯⎯⎯⎯⎯⎯⎯⎯⎯⎯⎯

⎯⎯ 9. In taking a test, it is essential to answer the hardest questions first.

Reason: ⎯⎯⎯⎯⎯⎯⎯⎯⎯⎯⎯⎯⎯⎯⎯⎯⎯⎯⎯⎯⎯⎯⎯⎯⎯⎯⎯⎯

⎯⎯ 10. Time management is derived from deciding *how long* you should spend on studying.

Reason: ⎯⎯⎯⎯⎯⎯⎯⎯⎯⎯⎯⎯⎯⎯⎯⎯⎯⎯⎯⎯⎯⎯⎯⎯⎯⎯⎯⎯

   The ability to justify an answer is a key ability in test taking! You may wish to compare and contrast your answers, and the rationale for your answers, in small groups or with a partner.

Exercise 2: Analyze Study Questions

Use a textbook, a review book, or a study guide for a course you're now taking. Look at the sample study/test questions in the book and complete these exercises:

> ➤ In the space below, copy down two questions from your materials—if possible, one multiple-choice question and one true/false question. For each question, name a strategy or strategies from this chapter that will help you solve it and why.

Question 1: _____

_____

_____

_____

_____

Question 2: _____

_____

_____

_____

List two essay questions from your materials. For each, describe how a particular strategy or strategies from this chapter will help you answer the question.

Question 1: _____

_____

_____

_____

Question 2: _____

_____

_____

_____

Look back at Table 8-1, "Common Action Verbs on Essay Tests." List the verbs from the table that are found in sample essay questions in your book. Define any verbs from your book that do not appear in the table.

_____

_____

_____

Exercise 3: Exam-Error Post-Test Analysis

When you get back your next test (in any class), take a detailed look at your performance.

> ➤ Write what you think of your test performance and grade. Were you pleased or disappointed? If you made mistakes, were they careless errors or did you lack knowledge of facts and concepts?

_____

_____

_____

_____

> ➤ Next, list the test preparation activities that helped you do well on the exam and the activities you wish you had done—and intend to do for the next exam.

Positive things I did:

_____

_____

_____

Positive actions I intend to take next time:

_____

_____

_____

> ➤ Finally, list any choices/activities you are _not_ likely to repeat when studying for the next test.

_____

_____

_____

Exercise 4: Learning From Your Mistakes

For this exercise, use an exam on which you made one or more mistakes. Perhaps an instructor can help you with this analysis.

> ➤ Why do you think you answered the question(s) incorrectly?

_____

_____

> ➤ Did any qualifiers such as _always, sometimes, never, often, occasionally,_ or _only_ make the question(s) more difficult or

confusing? What steps could you have taken to clarify the meaning?

_____

_____

_____

> Did you try to guess the correct answer(s)? If so, why do you think you made the wrong choice?

_____

_____

_____

> Did you feel rushed? If you had had more time, do you think you would have gotten the right answer(s)? What could you have done to budget your time more effectively?

_____

_____

_____

> If an essay question was a problem, what do you think went wrong? What will you do differently the next time you face an essay question on a test?

_____

_____

_____

_____

KEY TO COOPERATIVE LEARNING: BUILDING TEAMWORK SKILLS

If possible, choose a study partner who is in one of your other classes as well as this one. Work together to learn the required material for a particular test. Use the following checklist to quiz each other and measure how well you have prepared:

———— I asked the instructor what will be covered on the exam and the format of the test questions.

———— I tried to learn as much as I could about the kinds of tests the instructor gives by talking to former students, looking at old exams, and talking with the instructor.

———— I used critical thinking to explore difficult concepts that might be on the test.

———— I took a pretest.

———— I tried to prepare my body and mind to perform at their best.

———— I used positive self-talk and other techniques to overcome negative thoughts that might affect my performance.

———— I have gotten my personal life (including my children) under control so I can focus on the exam.

———— I have a plan of action that I will follow when I see the test for the first time. I'll try to get an overview of the test, learn test ground rules, schedule my time, and evaluate questions and choices in case I have to guess at answers.

———— I reviewed strategies for handling multiple-choice, true/false, and essay questions; I feel comfortable with these strategies.

Go through the entire checklist before the exam. Talk together about which checklist items are a particular strength or concern for you, and why. Help each other overcome areas of weakness, and try to build each other's confidence and test-taking skills. After the exam, meet with your partner to evaluate the checklist. Improve it according to your needs, adding new questions that you think should be included or crossing out questions that didn't seem to be necessary. Your improved checklist will help you do even better on the next exam.

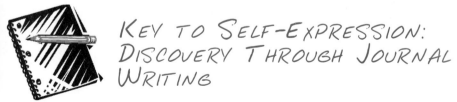

KEY TO SELF-EXPRESSION: DISCOVERY THROUGH JOURNAL WRITING

To record your thoughts, use the lined page preceding the next chapter or a separate journal.

Text Anxiety   Do you experience test anxiety? How do you feel as you walk into a testing room? Do you think your performance on tests accurately reflects what you know, or do your test scores fall short of your knowledge and capability? If there is a gap between your knowledge and your scores, why do you think this gap exists? Describe the steps you can take that will give you the confidence to do well on tests.

KEY TO YOUR PERSONAL PORTFOLIO: YOUR PAPER TRAIL TO SUCCESS

End-of-Chapter Cumulative Essay Question   As you prepare for tests, you have the opportunity to put into action many of the skills you have learned, including critical thinking, reading, studying, listening, memory, note-taking, and writing, as well as specific test-taking skills. By now, you have probably read all the chapters associated with these skills. Think back on what you learned (you can also refer to the chapters), and develop a plan that shows how you will apply your new knowledge about study skills as you prepare for your next exam. Here are some of the topics you can consider:

> ➤ The specific critical-thinking techniques that will help you master the material

> ➤ The memory techniques that work best for you

> ➤ The note-taking system that allows you to take comprehensive class notes

> ➤ How you like to use PQ3R when you study

> ➤ What techniques help you write your best

> ➤ The test-taking strategies that will help you prepare for and take your exams

Using separate sheets of paper, construct your plan, using an outline or a think link; then turn your preliminary plan into a well-thought-out, well-written essay.

This exercise asks you to apply what you learned in several different chapters. To successfully complete the exercise, you have to know yourself and the techniques that will work for you as you prepare for your exams. Not every suggestion in this book is right for you. Choose the skills that will work in your life and then use them to become a better student.

Journal Entry

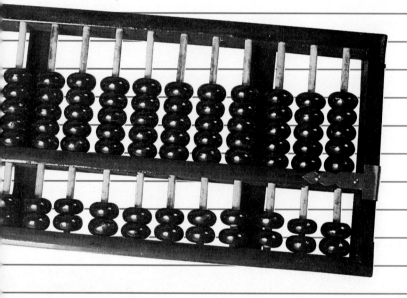

Prentice Hall

SOLVE

MATH, SCIENCE, AND COMPUTERS:

Becoming Comfortable With Numbers and Technology

In this chapter, you will explore answers to the following questions:

Why do you need math skills?

How can you master math basics?

How can you overcome math anxiety?

What techniques will help your performance on math exams?

What do learning math and learning science have in common?

What basics should you know about computers?

When asked about math and/or science, many students reply by saying—often with a sense of pride—"I hate math," or "I was never any good at math and science." In today's world, however, a basic knowledge of and ability in math, science, and computers are as necessary and critical as the abilities to read and write.

This chapter will look at the need for mathematics in today's highly competitive and technologically changing world. You will explore two of the most common problem areas in mathematics: word problems and math anxiety. You will also examine several problem-solving strategies and discover that learning to think "mathematically" is linked to doing well in other types of problem-solving courses, especially in the sciences. Finally, the chapter will briefly discuss the growing role of computers in your personal and academic life as well as in the business world.

WHY DO YOU NEED MATH SKILLS?

Math is much more than a course to be dealt with in school and then put aside. Math is an integral part of the modern world. Consider the following:

> ➤ You make $2000 per month in your job. How do you determine how you allocate your money to pay your bills?

> ➤ You want to carpet your house. However, many of the rooms and hallways are not regularly shaped. How do you determine the amount of carpet you need to buy?

> ➤ You are trying to schedule your classes for next semester. Each of your classes is only offered at certain times. How do you go about making the best possible schedule?

> ➤ In Canada, the rate at which the spruce budworm can defoliate balsam firs is a major problem. The budworm population is affected by its birth rate, its death rate, and predations by birds, while the balsam fir population is affected by such factors as seed pollination, weather, fire, and budworm defoliation. How would you study this problem, taking into account the growth of the budworm population and the growth of the balsam fir?[1]

These are just a few examples of problems involving mathematics that you might encounter in your personal life, school, and career.

Fill in your answers to the brief questionnaire in Figure 9-1—it will help you explore whether your beliefs about mathematics are based in reality.

Types of Math Skills You Might Need

Math skills are becoming more important in this world of increasingly complicated technology. Your level of math knowledge will affect all areas of your life. The level of competency you need will vary depending on your specific career goals and objectives, but everyone will need some minimum amount of skill. These skills can be broadly broken down into the following areas: thinking logically and reasoning, arithmetic, algebra, geometry, probability and statistics, calculus and differential equations, and higher math.

Thinking Logically and Reasoning

Inductive reasoning, Making a generalization based on several specific outcomes; example-to-idea thinking.

The single most important skill that math teaches you is the ability to think logically and critically. Math is, at heart, a problem-solving discipline. The ability to think logically and to solve problems is crucial to everyday life. You need to think logically in deciding how to plan your day, where to eat, what to eat, how you will drive your car, and so on. Logical thinking involves two types of reasoning: **inductive reasoning** and **deductive reasoning** . Although mathematics seems to develop skill primarily in deductive reasoning, it is actually created through a process of both deductive and inductive reasoning.

Deductive reasoning, Using a generalization to predict a specific outcome; idea-to-example thinking.

FIGURE 9-1   MATHEMATICAL BELIEFS AND MYTHS

The following statements are to be marked true (T) or false (F). Read them and mark each one according to your opinion about the validity of the statements.

_____ 1. Men are better at doing mathematics than women.

_____ 2. Mathematics completely relies on logic, disregarding intuition.

_____ 3. Mathematicians are more intelligent than other people.

_____ 4. People are born with an ability to do mathematics.

_____ 5. Mathematics is a rigid subject.

_____ 6. Mathematicians are able to solve problems quickly, in their heads.

_____ 7. Mathematicians rarely make mistakes.

_____ 8. Very few people are any good at mathematics.

_____ 9. Counting on your fingers is wrong.

_____ 10. Mathematics is not creative.

_____ 11. Mathematicians are eccentric.

_____ 12. There is a lot of memorization in mathematics.

_____ 13. Most people don't need to know mathematics for daily living.

_____ 14. It is always important to get the exact answer in mathematics.

_____ 15. There is always only one best way of solving a problem.

_____ 16. You must always know how you arrived at an answer.

_____ 17. Math can be fun.[2]

Here's the truth: Upon examination, _none_ of these statements are universally true—and the last one is true more often than you would expect. Surprisingly, mathematics _can_ be fun. You can only find out if you try.

Inductive reasoning, or induction, means determining a generalization from a list of specific events (example-to-idea thinking).   For example, if you see thirty men in a row wearing red shirts, you might conclude that all men wear red shirts. In mathematics, induction is often used in determining what a statement or theorem might be. However, it requires a proof of some sort before an induction is considered valid. In the instance above, you would need proof before concluding that all men wear red shirts.

Deductive reasoning means applying a general statement to a specific instance (idea-to-example thinking). For example, if you were told that all fish were goldfish, and you had a fish in a tank, you could conclude it must be a goldfish. Using deduction requires caution, however, because when applying any generalization you need to know whether the generalization is in fact true (which, in the above instance, it is not). This is especially necessary in such fields as sociology and psychology.

Another factor in reasoning is the ability to **estimate** . In 1989, the National Council of Teachers of Mathematics recognized the importance of estimation skills in their publication, *Curriculum and Evaluation Standards for School Mathematics.* In these standards, the NCTM notes the use of exploring estimation strategies, recognizing when estimation is important, using estimation to determine the reasonableness of results, and applying it in working with quantities, measurement, computation, and problem solving. Estimation involves both inductive and deductive processes. The ability to use estimation effectively will save you time and effort in solving many real-world problems.

Estimate,
To calculate the approximate amount of; to make a rough or preliminary calculation.

Arithmetic

Many of your everyday tasks require arithmetic. Arithmetic consists of numerical computations such as addition, subtraction, multiplication, and division. It also includes handling decimals, fractions, ratios, and proportions. Examples of where these skills are used are:

➤ Paying the correct amount on a bill and seeing that you received the correct change

➤ Calculating tips in restaurants

➤ Balancing your checkbook

➤ Comparison shopping at grocery stores and clothing stores

Algebra

Algebra,
A generalization of arithmetic in which letters representing numbers are combined, often with other numbers, into equations according to the rules of arithmetic.

A knowledge of **algebra** is needed almost as frequently as arithmetic. Many times you figure out problems without consciously realizing that you are using algebra. Some places where algebra shows up are:

➤ Computing interest on credit cards and loans

➤ Figuring your GPA

➤ Cutting or enlarging cooking recipes

> ➤ Solving problems in areas such as geology, biology, anthropology, chemistry, nursing, physics, and astronomy

> ➤ Determining efficient travel plans

Algebra involves determining an unknown value using known values. For example, if you wanted to make 100 cookies and had only enough flour for three batches, you might use algebra to figure out how many cookies would have to be in each batch: $3(X) = 100$, where 3 is the number of batches, X is how many cookies, and 100 is the number of cookies desired. Through algebra you can find that $X = 100$ divided by 3, or approximately 33. Therefore, you need a cookie recipe that makes about three dozen cookies.

Geometry

Along with algebra, geometry is the most-needed math skill in everyday life. The most important uses of geometry occur in determining areas and volumes. However, geometric ideas occur in many other forms. Examples of places geometry is found in your life are:

> ➤ Determining the amount of paint needed to paint a room or a house

> ➤ Determining what size heater or air conditioner is needed for a room or house

> ➤ Determining how much punch you should make for a party

> ➤ Determining how closely you can pass a car

> ➤ Buying and arranging furniture and appliances

> ➤ Packing luggage

For example, when you pack up a suitcase for a trip, in your head you are calculating the size of the different items you will put in the suitcase, adding them up, and determining whether they will fit inside the space determined by the size of the suitcase sides.

Probability and Statistics

A knowledge of basic probability and statistics is needed to understand the relevance and importance (or lack thereof) of the overwhelming amount of statistical information we are deluged with from the media. Without some knowledge in these areas, you are unable to evaluate the usefulness of such information. For example, if a woman reads breast cancer statistics, her statistical and probability knowledge can help her determine what her chances are of contracting breast cancer, and how certain precautions can improve those chances.

For some careers, such as actuarial or genetic science, a strong background in probability and statistics is crucial. Some areas of business, eco-

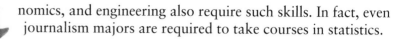

nomics, and engineering also require such skills. In fact, even journalism majors are required to take courses in statistics.

Calculus and Differential Equations

Calculus and differential equations are needed for most engineering fields, business and economics, physics, and astronomy. Any problem in which a rate of change is needed involves calculus and differential equations. Many problems that involve work, water pressure, areas, and volumes also use calculus.

Higher Math

There are some fields and careers in which a high level of mathematics is required. Linear algebra occurs in some business areas and industrial engineering. Abstract algebra appears in computer science and physics. Other careers that require even further mathematics are theoretical physics, economic research, and, of course, mathematics itself.

Certainly not every student will need to master calculus or linear algebra. The basics, however, will be of use to everyone.

HOW CAN YOU MASTER MATH BASICS?

Learning mathematics is essentially the same as learning any other skill. General learning strategies that apply to all subjects will be useful in learning math as well. Certain specific strategies, however, will help improve your math learning. Mastering math basics involves your approach to the classroom, the textbook, studying, homework, and word problems.

The Classroom

In taking a math class, as with any other class, attendance is the single most important factor in your performance. Nothing can replace the learning experience of your presence each day in class. Go to class alert and prepared. Be aware of the topic being covered that day. Be prepared to ask questions on the previous topic and homework. In taking notes, follow general note-taking guidelines: Note examples, focus on the central ideas, and connect supporting examples to those ideas. Pay special attention to things the instructor emphasizes.

The Textbook

Math textbooks seem to add an extra level of difficulty for many students. The ability to read a math textbook is a skill that must be developed. Do not expect to read mathematics in the same way that you would read literature, history, psychology, and so on.

Reading math is often a time-consuming process. When reading a math book, try keeping a pad of paper with you. As you read, slowly, take special note of the examples. If steps are left out, as they often are, work them out on your pad. Draw sketches to help visualize the material as you read. Do not move on until you understand the example and how it relates to the reading. The examples provide keys in working the homework.

Also, note what formulas are given. Consider whether these formulas are important; recall whether the instructor emphasized them. Be aware that in some classes you are responsible for all formulas, while in others, the instructors will provide them to you. Look over your lecture notes and see how they compare with the text. After you read the section(s), then you are ready to attempt the homework.

Studying and Homework

Following class, try to review your notes as quickly as possible. This is as crucial in mathematics as it is in other classes, if not more so. It's especially important to fill in missing steps in the instructor's examples before you forget them. In reviewing your notes, have the book alongside and match lecture information to the book. Then work on the homework.

Since math is a problem-solving course, doing a lot of problems is critical. Do not expect to just sit down and do every problem without effort. Often the effort required is quite challenging—and the realization of how much effort is needed often provokes students to quit. The frustration factor can be quite high. To fight frustration, stay flexible. If you are stuck on a problem, go on to another one. Sometimes you need to take a break to clear your head.

If you have done the assigned homework but still aren't sure about the method, do some of the other problems. Doing a lot of problems is the only way to really learn how the concepts and the formulas work. Try a few problems under test conditions—that is, in a time-constraint situation with no cues.

Math is an area where study groups can be extremely useful. Other people's perspectives can often break a thought logjam. Even if your math classes have smaller lab sessions, try to set up study groups outside of class. Plan to do as much of your homework as you can and then meet to discuss the homework and work through additional problems. Be open to other students' ways of thinking, and don't hesitate to ask them to explain their thought processes in detail.

Word Problems

In math, the single largest stumbling block is word problems. There is a famous *Far Side* cartoon titled "Hell's Library," which shows a shelf filled with books entitled *Story Problems, More Story Problems,* and so on. This highlights word problems as the number one fear of students of math. The bottom line is that word problems will be the most common way you will encounter mathematics throughout your life. Therefore, the ability to solve word problems is a necessary skill.

Why do people have so many difficulties with word problems? The reason lies with the fact that word problems force you to translate between two languages, English and mathematics. Math is a language in and of itself, and an extremely precise one. English and other living languages, however, are not precise. Although this lack of precision helps such languages achieve their richness in poetry and literature, it makes the process of translating more difficult.

Steps to Solving Word Problems

Translating from English or any other language to math takes a lot of practice. George Polya, in his 1945 classic, *How to Solve It,* devised a four-step method for attacking word problems. This procedure has been adopted in one form or another in nearly every math textbook.[3] The basic steps are as follows:

1. *Understand the problem.* This means reading the problem carefully. Understand what it is asking. Know what information you have. Know what information is missing. Draw a picture, if possible.

2. *Devise a plan.* Try to decide how you want to solve the problem. Think about similar problems. Try to relate the given information. This is the translation step, where you need to develop and use your problem-solving strategies.

3. *Carry out your plan.* Solve the problem. Check each of your steps.

4. *Review your result.* Check your answer, if possible. Make sure you've answered the question the problem is asking. Does your result makes sense in the context of the problem? Are there other ways to do the problem?

The best way to develop your skills in solving word problems is by doing a lot of them. Do extra problems. Practice a lot. The following section lays out several problem-solving strategies by working through different types of word problem examples.[4]

> *"The word impossible is not in my dictionary."*
> Napoleon

Problem-Solving Strategies

Strategy 1—Look for a pattern.   G. H. Hardy (1877–1947), an eminent British mathematician, described mathematicians as makers of patterns and ideas. The search for patterns is one of the best strategies in problem solving. This process is used in police work as well as in mathematics. *Example 1:* Find the next three entries in the following:

a. 1, 2, 4, ___ , ___ , ___

b. O, T, T, F, F, S, S, ___ , ___ , ___

c. 1, 1, 2, 3, 5, 8, 13, ___ , ___ , ___

Solutions to Example 1:

a. One important thing to remember about trying to identify patterns is that you may very well make connections and find a different pattern than someone else. This doesn't mean yours is wrong. In example 1a, there are actually several possible answers. Here are two:

1. First, you might recognize that each succeeding term of the sequence is twice the previous term. In that case, the next three values would be 8, 16, 32.

2. Another possibility is that you might notice the second term is 1 more than the first term and the third term is 2 more than the second. This might lead you to guess the fourth term is 3 more than the third term, the fifth term is 4 more than the fourth term, and so on. In that case, the next three terms are 7, 11, 16.

b. Example 1b is a famous pattern that often appears in puzzle magazines. The key to it is that O is the first letter of o̲ne, T is the first letter of t̲wo, and so on. Therefore, the next three terms would be E, N, and T for e̲ight, n̲ine, and t̲en.

c. Example 1c is another famous sequence called the Fibonacci sequence. It's named after Leonardo of Pisa (c.1170–1250), an Italian mathematician who was also called Fibonacci. In 1202, he wrote a book about algebra called *Liber Abaci* in which he introduced this sequence. You determine each succeeding term by adding the two immediately preceding terms together, so term three is $1 + 1 = 2$, term four is $1 + 2 = 3$, and so on. This means the next three terms are $21 = 8 + 13$, $34 = 13 + 21$, and $55 = 21 + 34$. The Fibonacci sequence occurs frequently in nature. The seeds of a sunflower spiral out from the center in a Fibonacci number of rows, for example, and the scales of a pineapple spiral in a Fibonacci number of rows as well.

Strategy 2—Make a table. A table can be used to help organize and summarize information. This then may enable you to see a pattern that lets you solve a problem.

Example 2: How many ways can you make change for a half dollar using only quarters, dimes, nickels, and pennies?

Solution to Example 2: To attack the half-dollar problem, you might construct several tables and go through every possible case. You could start by seeing how many ways you can make change for a half dollar without using a quarter, which would produce Tables A and B on the following page.

There are thirty-six ways to make change for a half dollar without using a quarter. Using one quarter results in Table C on the following page. Using one quarter, you get twelve different ways to make change for a half dollar. Lastly, using two quarters, there's only one way to make change for a half dollar. Therefore, the solution to the problem is that there are $36 + 12 + 1 = 49$ ways to make change for a half dollar using only quarters, dimes, nickels, and pennies.

Strategy 3—Examine a simpler case. Often patterns can be found to help solve a problem by looking at a simpler case.

Table A

Q	D	N	P
0	0	0	50
0	0	1	45
0	0	2	40
0	0	3	35
0	0	4	30
0	0	5	25
0	0	6	20
0	0	7	15
0	0	8	10
0	0	9	5
0	0	10	0
0	1	0	40
0	1	1	35
0	1	2	30
0	1	3	25
0	1	4	20
0	1	5	15
0	1	6	10

Table B

Q	D	N	P
0	1	7	5
0	1	8	0
0	2	0	30
0	2	1	25
0	2	2	20
0	2	3	15
0	2	4	10
0	2	5	5
0	2	6	0
0	3	0	20
0	3	1	15
0	3	2	10
0	3	3	5
0	3	4	0
0	4	0	10
0	4	1	5
0	4	2	0
0	5	0	0

Table C

Q	D	N	P
1	0	0	25
1	0	1	20
1	0	2	15
1	0	3	10
1	0	4	5
1	0	5	0
1	1	0	15
1	1	1	10
1	1	2	5
1	1	3	0
1	2	0	5
1	2	1	0

Example 3: In a portion of a city, the streets divide the city into square blocks of equal size, as seen in the following picture. Sam drives his bus daily from the bus terminal (B) to the train station (T). One day, he drove due west from the bus depot to the courthouse (C) along Ash Street, and then due south to the train depot on Seventh Street, covering a distance of eleven blocks in all. To relieve the monotony of the drive, Sam varies his route, but to conserve fuel, he doesn't travel any unnecessary distance. How many possible routes are there from the bus depot to the train station?

C

B

T

Solution to Example 3: By starting at the bus depot (B), you can look at simpler cases of this problem to attempt to determine a pattern. Looking at the following diagram, you are able to find the number of ways to get to each point from B.

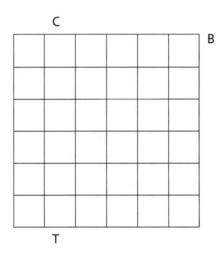

The numbers in the lower left corners of each cell represent the number of ways to go from the bus depot (B) to that corner. In looking at the pattern, notice, after checking the first few for yourself, that each corner number can be derived by adding the numbers in the corners directly north and east of the corner where you are. In other words, add the two numbers for the two corners closest to B that directly connect to your corner. In doing this, you will find there are 462 possible routes from the bus depot (B) to the train station (T).

Strategy 4—Identify a sub-goal.   Breaking the original problem into smaller and possibly easier problems may lead to a solution to the original problem. This is often the case in writing a computer program.
Example 4: Arrange the nine numbers 1, 2, 3, . . ., 9 into a square subdivided into nine sections in such a way that the sum of every row, column, and main diagonal is the same. This is what is called a *magic square.*

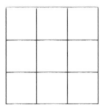

Solution to Example 4: Since each number will go into one of the squares, the sum of all the numbers will end up being three times the sum of any given row, column, or main diagonal. The sum of $1 + 2 + 3 + 4 + 5 + 6 + 7 + 8 + 9 = 45$. Therefore, each row, column, and main diagonal needs to sum to $45/3 = 15$. Now you need to see how many ways you can add three of the numbers from 1 to 9 and get 15. In doing this, you should get:

$9 + 1 + 5 = 15$	$8 + 3 + 4 = 15$
$9 + 2 + 4 = 15$	$7 + 2 + 6 = 15$
$8 + 1 + 6 = 15$	$7 + 3 + 5 = 15$
$8 + 2 + 5 = 15$	$6 + 4 + 5 = 15$

   Now, looking at your magic square, notice that the center position will be part of four sums (a row, a column, and the two main diagonals). Looking back at your sums, you see that 5 appears in four different sums; therefore 5 is in the center square.

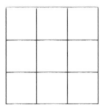

The number in each corner appears in 3 sums (row, column, and a diagonal). Looking through your sums, you find that 2, 4, 6, and 8 each appear in three sums. Now you need to place them in the corners in such a way that your diagonals add up to 15.

2		6
	5	
4		8

To finish, all you need to do is fill in the remaining squares to get the needed sum of 15 for each row, column, and main diagonal. The completed square is as follows:

2	7	6
9	5	1
4	3	8

Strategy 5—Examine a related problem.   Sometimes a problem you are working on is similar to a previous problem. In that case, it is often possible to use a similar approach to solve the new problem.

Example 5: Find a magic square using the numbers 3, 5, 7, 9, 11, 13, 15, 17, and 19.

Solution to Example 5: This problem is very similar to Example 4. Approaching it in the same fashion, you find that the needed row, column, and main diagonal sum is 33. Writing down all the possible sums of three numbers to get 33, you find that 11 is the number that appears four times, so it is in the center.

	11	

The numbers that appear three times in the sums and will go in the corners are 5, 9, 13, and 17. This now gives you:

13		17
	11	
5		9

Finally, completing the magic square gives you:

13	3	17
15	11	7
5	19	9

Strategy 6—Work backwards. With some problems, you may find it easier to start with the perceived final result and work backwards.
Example 6: In the game of "Life," Carol had to pay $1500 when she was married. Then she lost half the money she had left. Next she paid half the money she had for a house. Then the game ended and she had $3000 left. With how much money did she start?
Solution to Example 6: Carol ended up with $3000. Right before that she paid half her money to buy a house. Since her $3000 was half of what she had before her purchase, she had 2($3000) = $6000 before buying the house. Prior to buying the house, Carol lost half her money. This means that the $6000 is the half she didn't lose. So, before losing half her money, Carol had 2($6000) = $12,000. Prior to losing half her money, Carol had to pay $1500 to get married. This means she had $12,000 + $1500 = $13,500 before getting married. Since this was the start of the game, Carol began with $13,500.

Strategy 7—Draw a diagram. Drawing a picture is often an aid to solving problems. Pictures are especially useful in gaining insight into geometrical problems. However, the use of pictures and drawings can be helpful in many other types of problems.
Example 7: There were twenty people at a round table for dinner. Each person shook hands with the person to his or her immediate right and left. At the end of the dinner, each person got up and shook hands with every-body except the people who sat on his or her immediate right and left. How many handshakes took place after dinner?
Solution to Example 7: To solve this with a diagram, it might be a good idea to examine several simpler cases to see if you can determine a pattern of any kind that might help. Starting with two or three people, you can see there are no handshakes after dinner, since everyone is adjacent to everyone else.

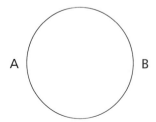

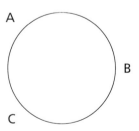

In the case of four people, we get the following diagram, connecting those people who shake hands after dinner:

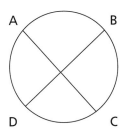

In this situation, you see there are two handshakes after dinner, AC and BD. In the case of five people, you get this picture:

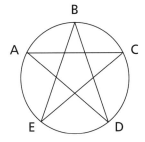

In this case, you have five after-dinner handshakes: AC, AD, BD, BE, and CE. Looking at one further case of six people seated around a circle gives the following diagram:

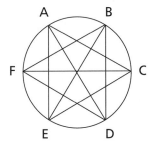

In this diagram, there are now a total of nine after-dinner handshakes: AC, AD, AE, BD, BE, BF, CE, CF, and DF. In noticing from the diagrams what is happening, you realize that if there are N people, each person would shake N − 3 people's hands after dinner (they don't shake their own hands or the hands of the two people adjacent to them). Since there are N people, that would lead to N(N − 3) after-dinner handshakes. However, this would double-count every handshake, since AD would also be counted as DA. Therefore, this is twice as many handshakes as actually took place. So, the correct number of handshakes is [N(N − 3)]/2. So finally, if there are twenty people, there would be 20(17)/2 = 170 after-dinner handshakes.

Strategy 8—Write an equation. This is the most often used strategy in algebra.

Example 8: A farmer needs to fence a rectangular piece of land. He wants the length of the field to be 80 feet longer than the width. If he has 1080 feet of fencing available, what should the length and width of the field be?

Solution to Example 8: The best way to start this problem is to draw a picture of the situation and label the sides.

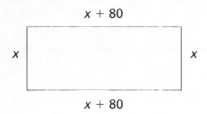

Let x represent the width of the field and $x + 80$ represent the length of the field. The farmer has 1080 feet of fencing and he will need $2x + 2(x + 80)$ feet of fencing to fence his field. This gives you the equation:

$$2x + 2(x + 80) = 1080$$

Multiplying out: $\qquad\qquad\qquad 2x + 2x + 160 = 1080$

Simplifying and subtracting 160: $\qquad\qquad 4x = 920$

Dividing by 4: $\qquad\qquad\qquad\qquad\qquad x = 230$

Therefore, $\qquad\qquad\qquad\qquad\qquad x + 80 = 310$

As a check, you find that $2(230) + 2(310) = 1080$.

Strategy 9—Guess and check. Once discouraged in favor of algebraic or other methods, it is now recognized that guess and check is an integral way many people solve everyday problems. The strategy involves making an initial guess, checking to see if it is correct, and then using that information to make another guess.

Example 9: Looking out in the backyard one day, Sue saw an assortment of cats and birds. Counting heads, she got a total of 22. Counting the feet, she got a total of 68. How many cats and birds were in the yard?

Solution to Example 9: Since Sue saw a total of 22 cats and birds (assuming none had more than one head), a good first guess might be that there are 11 cats and 11 birds. Checking the number of legs then gives:

$$11(4) + 11(2) = 44 + 22 = 66 \text{ legs.}$$

Since Sue counted 68 legs, this isn't quite correct, but it is close. Since you need more legs, and cats have more legs than birds, there need to be more cats and fewer birds. Suppose then there are 12 cats and 10 birds. This would give you

$$12(4) + 10(2) = 48 + 20 = 68 \text{ legs,}$$

which is exactly what you wanted. Therefore, Sue sees 12 cats and 10 birds in the backyard.

These sample problems are designed to help you understand some of the basic math strategies you will use in your classes. If they have made you feel anxious, however, you will benefit from some information about math anxiety.

HOW CAN YOU OVERCOME MATH ANXIETY?

Math anxiety is a term used to describe any of several high-stress, uncomfortable feelings that appear in relation to math. One of the most common—often caused by a failure on an exam or failure to learn a topic—is a student's belief that he or she can't do any math at all. As a result of this feeling, students sometimes just give up, feeling the subject is impossible. Additionally, students often won't ask for help because they don't want others to think that they're stupid. A sense of personal embarrassment often occurs.

This sensation of incompetence is very common. If a student has understood the subject up to that point, however, the immediate leap to "It's impossible" on the next topic is usually not a rational response, but an *emotional* one. For this reason, the student might be able to relieve this anxiety by taking the subject a little slower and not hesitating to ask questions. If a student feels uncomfortable asking questions in class, he or she should seek out an instructor during office hours, a fellow classmate, or a tutor. The key is to avoid letting your anxiety have power over you. Work hard not to let an anxiety attack paralyze you and prevent you from seeking the help you need.

> "Minds are like parachutes. They only function when they are open."
> Sir James Dewar

Gender Issues and Math Anxiety

In the United States, there is evidence that women, more than men, are afflicted with math anxiety. This has resulted in the inaccurate perception that women aren't as adept at math as men are. Recent research has sought to determine whether there are some key gender issues involved in learning and teaching mathematics and the sciences. Another misperception in the United States is that people are born with or without an ability to do mathematics. This misperception implies that if you can't do a math problem, then you will never be able to do mathematics. In contrast, in a similar study done in Asia, people indicated that what was needed to be good at mathematics was simply hard work.

Use the questionnaire in Figure 9-2 to get a basic idea of your math anxiety level.

Before and During Exams

Math anxiety occurs most often right before or during an exam. The sense of not knowing anything or of being a failure looms large as a person gets ready to take a test or suddenly happens in reading a problem on a test. At

FIGURE 9-2   EXPLORE YOUR MATH ANXIETY⁵

Answer the following statements by marking a number from 1 (Disagree) to 5 (Agree).

_____ 1. I don't like math classes, and haven't since high school.

_____ 2. I do okay at the beginning of a math class, but I always feel it will get to the point where it is impossible to understand.

_____ 3. I can't seem to concentrate in math classes. I try, but I get nervous and distracted and think about other things.

_____ 4. I don't like asking questions in math class. I'm afraid that the teachers and/or the other students will think I'm stupid.

_____ 5. I stress out when I'm called on in math class. I seem to forget even the easiest answers.

_____ 6. Math exams scare me far more than any of my other exams.

_____ 7. I can't wait to finish my math requirement so that I'll never have to do any math again.

_____ YOUR TOTAL

Scoring Key:
28–35: You suffer from full-blown math anxiety.
21–27: You are coping, but you're not happy about mathematics.
14–20: You're doing okay.
 7–13: So what's the big deal about math? You have very little problem with anxiety.

this point, a student often describes what happens next as completely "blanking out." This can happen also on exams for other subjects, but there seems to be an especially high incidence of it in math exams.

The best way to overcome test-time anxiety is through positive reinforcement. You must put yourself in the situation often enough to become comfortable with it. Keeping up with your homework is a major step. Understanding the concepts and preparing well in advance will help you feel confident. Taking timed practice exams will give you a sense of the time factor. Doing your homework or taking practice exams in the exam location will ease the sense of disorientation that occurs when you're in an unfamiliar environment. These are all strategies that will help you become more familiar, and especially more comfortable, with the subject and your surroundings. Figure 9-3 shows additional ways to reduce math anxiety.

Even though math anxiety is a real and potentially paralyzing problem, students need to realize that they must also take responsibility for their math anxiety. Personal responsibility is a key to becoming successful in

FIGURE 9-3 TEN WAYS TO REDUCE MATH ANXIETY[6]

1. Overcome your negative self-image about math.

2. Ask questions of your teachers and your friends, and seek outside assistance.

3. Math is a foreign language—you need to practice it often.

4. Don't study mathematics by trying to memorize information and formulas.

5. READ your math textbook.

6. Study math according to your personal learning style.

7. Get help the same day you don't understand something.

8. Be relaxed and comfortable while studying math.

9. "Talk" mathematics. Discuss it with people in your class. Form a study group.

10. Develop a sense of responsibility for your own successes and failures.

college and in life. Figure 9-4 lists responsibilities that students should be aware of and accept regarding mathematics and math anxiety.

Finally, along with being a responsible student, you also have rights regarding your mathematical learning. Sandra Davis has written a list of these rights, among which are the following:[8]

➤ The right to learn at your own pace.

➤ The right to ask any questions you have.

➤ The right to need, and seek, extra help.

➤ The right not to understand.

➤ The right to view yourself as capable of learning math.

➤ The right to be treated as a competent person.

➤ The right to dislike math.

➤ The right to define success in your own terms.

Beyond working to control your math anxiety, several other techniques will help you do your very best when you are tested on your math skills.

FIGURE 9-4   MATHEMATICS CODE OF RESPONSIBILITIES[7]

It is my responsibility to:

1. Attend all math classes and do all assigned homework.

2. Acknowledge the rights of others to learn at their own pace.

3. Seek extra help when I need it.

4. Visit the teacher during office hours or schedule an appointment for help.

5. Come to class prepared, with my homework done and any questions I have ready to ask.

6. Speak up in class when I don't understand.

7. Put forth at least the same effort for my math classes that I give to other subjects.

8. Begin my math study at my current skill level, and be honest with myself about what that level is.

9. Maintain a realistic attitude about my abilities.

10. Research instructors prior to registering for class.

11. Learn, and use, stress-reduction skills.

12. Act as a competent adult.

13. Approach math with an open mind rather than assuming it will be a nightmare.

14. Establish realistic goals and expectations.

15. Face failure if it happens, learn from it, pick myself up, and move ahead.

WHAT TECHNIQUES WILL HELP IMPROVE YOUR PERFORMANCE ON MATH TESTS?

In addition to the general strategies for test taking that you have explored, there are several other techniques that can help you achieve better results on math exams. These include reading through the exam first, doing "easy" problems first, using objective exam strategies, and checking answers.

Read Through the Exam First

It's important when you first get an exam to read through every problem quickly. As you read through the exam, make notes on how you might attempt to solve the problem, if something occurs to you immediately. If possible, categorize the problems according to what type of problem they are.

Do "Easy" Problems First

Doing "easy" problems first means that if you read a problem and know immediately how to do it without thinking too hard about the method, then do that problem. Go through the exam doing all of the problems that come most easily to you. In general, it is not a good idea to start with the first problem, then move to the second problem, and so forth, following the exam order exactly. Although some tests start with easier problems and increase in difficulty, this logic will not always apply—other tests may list problems in random order.

There are two major reasons for starting with the easiest problems. First, the goal of any exam is to achieve the highest score possible. On many math exams, all problems are worth the same number of points. You are much better off earning the points for the problems you know how to do than spending twenty minutes on a really hard problem, not getting it, and then having very little time to do the problems you know how to do. Even if the problems have different point values, you are still better off doing the problems you know how to do and ensuring that you earn those points.

The second reason is that as you do the "easy" problems, you begin to think more positively about the exam. This eases some of the tension and stress that cause math anxiety. As your anxiety eases, you gain in confidence. Suddenly, problems that you weren't sure how to solve when you first read them become easier. Even if you don't get through some of the harder problems, your confidence will help you earn as many points as possible. You are always better off missing points on problems you didn't know how to do than missing points on the problems you knew how to do.

Use Particular Objective Exam Strategies

If your math exams are objective in nature, there are several helpful strategies to use. First, if the questions are multiple choice or matching, hide the answer choices. Work out the problem without looking at the answers. Carefully check your work, making sure you've answered the question accurately and completely. Finally, look at the choices and see if your answer is one of them. If not, you may be able to immediately eliminate some of the choices. Mark out any eliminated choices so that you will not keep looking at them. Examine your work and the remaining choices. If possible, put the remaining answers into the problem and see if they work. If not, go to another problem and come back to this one later. See Chapter 8 for more details.

Check Answers

One of the most beneficial strategies, and one of the hardest to train yourself to do, is to check your work carefully. Once students have finished a problem, they tend to not want to look at it again. If you have finished an exam early, it is always a good idea to look back over your work, especially if you were unsure of some problems. This doesn't mean you should automatically begin changing answers, however. Keep track of which answers you change; see if changing them helped or hurt you. Be aware of your own tendencies. For example, if you often lose points for careless mistakes, checking your work can help you catch these. The more of this you can learn to do, the better you will do on the exam.

All the strategies you are learning aren't useful just in your math classes. Many science classes have a mathematical element that will require you to use your math knowledge.

WHAT DO LEARNING MATH AND LEARNING SCIENCE HAVE IN COMMON?

Many of the issues you face in mathematics occur also in science. Therefore, many of the strategies discussed for mathematics will also apply to the sciences. Sciences such as chemistry, physics, and astronomy are quite often problem-solving courses. There are also classes in geology, anthropology, and biology that fall into this category. The math strategies you have explored will be applicable to these sciences.

"The proper and immediate object of science is the acquirement, or communication, of truth."
Samuel Taylor Coleridge

For example, in beginning chemistry, you will usually have to balance chemical equations. This involves applying such strategies as writing an equation, drawing a diagram, perhaps working backwards, or even guess and check. In physics, the study of forces and electromagnetism involves applying problem-solving strategies developed from vector calculus. In fact, the most common strategy in working force problems involves drawing a diagram called a force diagram. The key to remember is that while these strategies are listed as mathematical strategies, the actual process of applying them is far more wide-ranging, helping you to develop into a critical thinker and problem solver. This is an ability you will need in every aspect of your life.

In addition to the need for new problem-solving skills, the change from high school science to college science is quite similar to the change in mathematics courses. Some of these common areas are:

> The pace of the courses will be faster in college than in a high school course. Quite often, what was done in a year in high school will be done in a semester or less in college.

> The assignments will be considered crucial in college. However, your instructor may not collect them often, if at all. You will be responsible for staying caught up.

REAL WORLD PERSPECTIVE

I'm not naturally comfortable with the sciences. What will help me succeed in my science courses?

Julie Wheeler, Junior at the University of Colorado at Denver, English Writing Major, Communications Minor

Even though writing term papers is like second nature to me, I am not predisposed to doing well in the sciences. I remember having to struggle through high school chemistry class, where I sat every day watching other students taking down notes and nodding their heads in the receipt of newfound knowledge. I never quite understood the information that the professor scribbled on the board.  The book was a little better, as I could read over it several times, but when tests came, it was obvious to me that I was missing the point. Unfortunately, my grades reflected my level of understanding, and I feel like the experience forever tainted my ability to comprehend science.

The university I attend requires me to take science classes to fulfill my general requirements, and I am dreading having to tackle these classes. When I look at my choices, I can only imagine what I will have to endure in each one. Biology and chemistry definitely seem over my head, and I don't know much about the others. The list spans from physics to geology, but I don't know how to decide which of these classes would be the lesser of the evils. How do I choose which science classes to take, and then make it through them so that I can graduate?

Jason Schierkolk, Arapahoe Community College, Emergency Medical Science Major

Doing well in the sciences can sometimes be difficult. Since my major is heavily weighted on science, I have become very adept in the area. However, for students who are not in scientific majors, most universities and colleges offer classes that will fulfill your requirements without forcing you into something that you feel destined to fail. Some of these courses include geology, environmental science, and astronomy. They are still "scientific" in terms of concrete  knowledge and even some formulas, but are not as technical as courses such as physics, chemistry, and biology. Also, there are sometimes courses that are offered specifically for non-scientific majors. They might be listed as "Biology for non-majors," and so on.

If you must take a science class without the slightest idea of how you will pass, stay organized. Most professors will give you several formulas and processes to solve most of the problems you will face. Be sure to keep them organized and clearly marked for quick reference. Also, using a tape recorder in class will help you go back to something you don't understand. Professors are almost always willing to help students who are having a hard time, especially if you show that you are willing to learn and are staying caught up in the reading. Come to them with specific problems or questions that they can help you to work through.

If you keep an open mind, you can likely do well in whatever you set your mind to, be it chemistry, physics, or any other wall you come up against. You will have to work hard—harder than you may have ever worked before—but you will find that the most helpful secret to these classes is giving them all you've got.

> ➤ The classes may be much more theory-oriented. Your class periods may devote more time to proving and deriving theorems, with less time spent on examples and problems.

> ➤ The class size might be considerably larger than in high school. You may be in classes taught in large auditoriums with several hundred people enrolled. Your classes may also be organized differently. You may have a lecture section, a recitation section or discussion section (often led by a teaching assistant), and possibly a lab section.

> ➤ The expectations of the instructors might be quite different from in high school. You may be expected to understand and be able to apply the concepts and principles. Skill in manipulating symbols or memorizing facts may be de-emphasized.

> ➤ You may be expected to be technologically proficient. This could mean using graphing calculators or sophisticated software packages such as Mathematica, Maple, Derive (mathematical packages), Minitab, SAS (statistical packages), or course-specific software.

Of course, your science courses will go beyond basic mathematical operations. Many of these courses, however, will hinge on mathematical principles. Thinking mathematically will help you both understand specific operations and apply them to the more general scientific knowledge you learn.

WHAT BASICS SHOULD YOU KNOW ABOUT COMPUTERS?

As the world continues to become more technologically complicated, the role of computers becomes increasingly prevalent. In almost every job, knowledge of basic computer use is a necessity. The use of computers in composing letters, desktop publishing, maintaining databases, keeping spreadsheets, working on the Internet, communicating by e-mail, and numerous other tasks will make computer literacy a requirement in the job market.

The basics in computer use fall into four general categories: word processing, databases and spreadsheets, the Internet, and e-mail.

Word Processing

The ability to use a computer to write letters, papers, briefs, and so on is now a requirement at most institutes of higher learning, as well as at many businesses. There are many word-processing software programs, and each has its own quirks. Two of the most commonly used are Microsoft Word and Word Perfect. Besides composing documents, features such as a spell check and a grammar checker are extremely useful.

Databases and Spreadsheets

The ability to organize and store large volumes of information and data has always been important in most businesses. The easiest way to do this is through the use of some type of computer software for managing databases and spreadsheets. Again, there are many software programs specifically designed to handle, organize, and analyze large volumes of information. Some of the more common programs are Lotus, Symphony, and Microsoft Excel. A knowledge of one or more of these is becoming increasingly beneficial. This is especially true for most careers in business and science, and increasingly so in your personal life, such as if you use a computer to manage your personal finances.

The Internet

The Internet, a worldwide network of connected businesses, universities, governments, and people, is expanding continually. The ability to use the Internet allows you to access the world and communicate with others almost instantaneously. You can now do extensive research on any topic as well as buy, sell, and market products on the Internet. It will be hard to be well prepared for the work force if you have no Internet experience. There are several Internet providers such as Netscape, Microsoft Explorer, America Online, and Prodigy that offer various Internet services and options.

Once on the Internet, use some type of search engine to locate information or web "sites" or "pages" (locations on the web established by businesses, organizations, or individuals). Some of the most common search engines and their locations, or web addresses, on the World Wide Web are:

> *Yahoo* (http://www.yahoo.com)

> *Excite* (http://www.excite.com)

> *Infoseek* (http://www.infoseek.com)

> *LookSmart* (http://www.LookSmart.com)

> *Lycos* (http://www.lycos.com)

> *SEARCH.COM* (http://www.search.com)

When you use your provider to access the World Wide Web, you can put any of these search engines to work for you. Go to your provider's web access field and type in the address of the search engine you want to use. Use the options provided by the search engine to search for your topic. Try to narrow it as much as possible to avoid being overwhelmed with too many possibilities or "hits." If you know the web address of a particular web site, you can type it in directly using a search engine. If you need help learning about the Internet, don't hesitate to ask a librarian, fellow student, or tutor to show you the ropes.

E-mail

The ability to communicate electronically is rapidly becoming a challenge to the post office. The major advantage is the speed at which electronic mail (e-mail) can be sent, received, and responded to. If your college has an e-mail system in place, you may be required to communicate with your instructor, submit homework, and even take exams via e-mail. Many schools offer some type of orientation to learn about e-mail. Every student who has access to e-mail should spend time becoming proficient in electronic communication.

al-Khowârizmî الخوارزمي

Mohammed ibn Musa al-Khowârizmî was an Arabic astronomer who lived around 825. An 1857 Latin translation of a book no longer existing in the original begins "Spoken has Algoritmi. . . ." Hence his name had become Algoritmi, from which was derived the present word *algorithm*. An algorithm is a series of steps used to solve a particular problem in mathematics or the sciences. Many computer software programs are simply strings of algorithms used to do certain functions. It is also interesting to note that the term *algebra* comes from the title of al-Khowârizmî's 830 book, *A-jabr w'al muqâ-balah*.

For those of you who don't know Arabic, this word may seem completely out of your realm of knowledge. Just as if you were to study Arabic or any other language, however, success in math boils down to steady work and focus. When you put your mind to it, you can become as fluent in math, science, and technology as you are in your native language.

Chapter 9: Applications

Name _____   Date _____

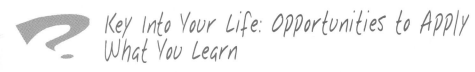 *Key Into Your Life: Opportunities to Apply What You Learn*

Exercise 1: Where Are You When It Comes to Math?

Math anxiety seems to afflict many people in today's world. As everyday life, society, and business become more technological, anxiety can become a serious problem. The severity of math anxiety is causing critical shortages of people who are qualified to handle this emerging technology. How do you deal with the challenges of mathematics? Respond to the following statements as accurately as possible in light of your own experiences and the information provided in the chapter.

1. When I make an error on a math problem, I _____

   _____

   _____

2. When I get embarrassed about doing math, I _____

   _____

   _____

3. When I'm unable to solve a particular problem, I _____

   _____

   _____

4. If I were able to do mathematics, I would _____

   _____

   _____

5. When I'm able to solve a problem that was difficult, I feel _____

   _____

   _____

6. One thing I enjoy about doing math is _____

   _____

   _____

7. Working on mathematics makes me feel _____

   _____

   _____

Exercise 2: The Math/Science Autobiography

For the following exercise, choose a math and/or science class you are taking (if you have none, choose one you took as recently as possible). With regard to that class, write an autobiography of your experiences in the subject. Examine both where you've come from and where you would like to go. Use the information from the chapter to help you.

1. My major reason for taking this class is _____
   _____
   _____

2. Before this class, the last math/science course I took was _____
   _____
   _____

3. An early experience I recall from a math/science class was _____
   _____
   _____

4. I remember one particular math/science teacher because _____
   _____
   _____

5. I feel _____ was the most difficult topic to learn,
   because _____

6. I feel _____ was the easiest topic to learn, because _____
   _____
   _____

7. I believe I learned my current attitudes about math/science when _____
   _____
   _____

8. To improve my attitudes about math/science, I expect to do the following for myself:
   _____
   _____

9. To improve my performance in math/science, I expect to do the
   following:
   _____
   _____

Exercise 3: Which Strategies Did You Use?

Using a math or science book, copy down three questions from the text. For each question, name a problem-solving strategy or strategies from this chapter that will help you solve the problem. Solve the problem on a separate piece of paper. Afterwards, state here why you chose the strategies you did. Are there other ways to solve the same problem?

Problem 1: _____

_____

_____

Strategies: _____

_____

_____

_____

Problem 2: _____

_____

_____

Strategies: _____

_____

_____

_____

_____

Problem 3: _____

_____

_____

Strategies: _____

_____

_____

_____

KEY TO COOPERATIVE LEARNING: BUILDING TEAMWORK SKILLS

Choose one or two people from one of your math/science classes—fellow students with whom you feel comfortable working. Use problems from your assigned text.

1. Choose one problem. Each of you work on the same problem separately. After finishing the problem, come together to share your methods of solution. Discuss how each of you approached

the problem. What steps did you each take in solving the problem? What strategies did you use? How did you check to see if your procedures were correct?

2. Now pick a different problem on which to work together. After solving this problem, discuss how you went through the problem-solving process. Did you learn more or less by working together as compared to working separately? Were you able to solve the problem faster by working together than you did with the problem you worked alone? Did you gain a better understanding of the problem by working together?

3. Generalize your experiences to discuss attitudes about math/science. What do each of you do to overcome challenges? What positive steps do you each take in problem solving?

KEY TO SELF-EXPRESSION: DISCOVERY THROUGH JOURNAL WRITING

Math Myths Reflect upon your experiences as a high school student in math and/or science. Look back over the myths listed at the beginning of the chapter. Were you influenced by any particular one or two of these negative myths concerning math and/or science? Explain which ones and how you were influenced by them. Also, write about what steps you can do to replace those myths with positive attitudes and actions.

KEY TO YOUR PERSONAL PORTFOLIO: YOUR PAPER TRAIL TO SUCCESS

End-of-Chapter Cumulative Essay Consider your possible choice of a major or career. What mathematics and/or science will you need to achieve your goals? Did your feelings and experiences in math and/or science affect your choice of major or career? If so, in what ways?

Interview several people, including an instructor, who work in your choice of major/career. Ask them how much math and science are needed for this major/career. Did they choose it based on the level of math or science necessary? Now that they are in this field, is the amount of math/science and problem-solving skills more or less than expected? What types of problem-solving skills are needed? In addition, investigate this major/career by looking at the course catalog to see what math and science are needed; if you have access, search out information about your major/career choice on the Internet.

After completing your investigation, write an essay reflecting on the roles math, science, and problem solving have in your choice of a major/career.

Journal Entry

ENDNOTES

CHAPTER 1
....

[1]Barbara Soloman, North Carolina State University.

[2]Howard Gardner, *Multiple Intelligences: The Theory in Practice* (New York: HarperCollins, 1993), pp. 5–49.

[3]Joyce Bishop, Ph.D., Psychology faculty, Golden West College, Huntington Beach, CA.

CHAPTER 2
....

[1]Paul R. Timm, Ph.D., *Successful Self-Management: A Psychologically Sound Approach to Personal Effectiveness* (Los Altos, California: Crisp Publications, Inc., 1987), pp. 22–41.

CHAPTER 3
....

[1]Frank T. Lyman, Jr. "Think-Pair-Share, Thinktrix, Thinklinks, and Weird Facts: An Interactive System for Cooperative Thinking." From *Enhancing Thinking Through Cooperative Learning*, Neil Davidson and Toni Worsham, eds. (Columbia, NY: Teachers College Press, 1992), pp. 169–181.

[2]Dennis Coon. *Introduction to Psychology: Exploration and Application,* 6th ed. (St. Paul: West Publishing, 1992), p. 295.

[3]Sylvan Barnet and Hugo Bedau. *Critical Thinking, Reading, and Writing: A Brief Guide to Argument,* 2nd ed. (Boston: Bedford Books of St. Martin's Press, 1996), p. 43.

CHAPTER 4
....

[1]U.S. Department of Education. National Center for Education Statistics. *The Condition of Education 1996,* NCES 96-304, by Thomas M. Smith (Washington, D.C.: U.S. Government Printing Office, 1996), p. 84.

[2]Sherwood Harris, *The New York Public Library Book of How and Where to Look It Up* (New York: Prentice Hall, 1991), p. 13.

[3]Steve Moidel, *Speed Reading* (Hauppauge, NY: Barron's Educational Series, 1994), p. 18.

[4]Francis P. Robinson, *Effective Behavior* (New York: Harper & Row, 1941).

[5]Sylvan Barnet and Hugo Bedau, *Critical Thinking, Reading, and Writing: A Brief Guide to Argument,* 2nd ed. (Boston: Bedford Books of St. Martin's Press, 1996), pp. 15–21.

[6]Adapted from Robert A. Carman and W. Royce Adams, Jr., *Study Skills: A Student's Guide for Survival,* 2nd ed. (New York: John Wiley & Sons, 1984), pp. 131–132.

[7]Ibid., p. 141.

[8]John J. Macionis, *Sociology,* 6th ed. (Upper Saddle River, NJ: Prentice Hall, 1997), p. 174.

CHAPTER 5
....

[1]Louis E. Boone and David L. Kurtz, *Contemporary Business Communication* (Upper Saddle River, NJ: Prentice Hall, 1994), p. 39.

[2]Ralph G. Nichols, "Do We Know How to Listen? Practical Helps in a Modern Age," *Speech Teacher,* March 1961, pp. 118–124.

[3]Herman Ebbinghaus. *Memory: A Contribution to Experimental Psychology.* Trans. by H. A. Ruger and C. E. Bussenius. (New York: New York Teacher's College, Columbia University, 1885).

[4]Based on experiment conducted by R. S. Nickerson and M. J. Adams, "Long-Term Memory for a Common Object," *Cognitive Psychology,* 1979 (11), pp. 287–307.

[5]Philip Kotler and Gary Armstrong, *Marketing: An Introduction,* 4th ed. (Upper Saddle River, NJ: Prentice Hall, 1997), p. 201.

CHAPTER 6
....

[1]Walter Pauk, *How to Study in College,* 5th ed. (Boston: Houghton Mifflin Co., 1993), pp. 110–114.

CHAPTER 7
....

[1]Information for Figure 7-2 and for freewriting sample from Louis E. Boone, David L. Kurtz, and Judy R. Block. *Contemporary Business Communication,* 2nd ed. (Upper Saddle River, NJ: Prentice Hall, 1997), pp. 508–509.

[2]Analysis based on Lynn Quitman Troyka, *Simon & Schuster Handbook for Writers* (Upper Saddle River, NJ: Prentice Hall, 1996), pp. 530–531.

[3]Philip R. Harris and Robert T. Moran, *Managing Cultural Differences,* 3rd ed. (Houston: Gulf Publishing Co., 1991), p. 59.

CHAPTER 8
....

[1]Steven Frank, *The Everything Study Book* (Holbrook, MA: Adams Media Corporation, 1996), p. 208.

[2]Many of the examples of objective questions used in this chapter are from Gary W. Piggrem, Test Item File for Charles G. Morris, *Understanding Psychology,* 3rd ed. (Upper Saddle River, NJ: Prentice Hall, 1996).

CHAPTER 9
....

[1]Adapted from J. D. Murray, *Mathematical Biology* (Berlin: Springer-Verlag, 1989), pp. 4–8.

[2]Adapted from "Do You Believe?" by Ashley DuLac and Kathryn Brooks, as reprinted in *Overcoming Math Anxiety* by Sheila Tobias (New York: W.W. Norton & Company, 1993), p. 237.

[3]George Polya, *How to Solve It* (London: Penguin, 1990).

[4]Rick Billstein, Shlomo Libeskind, and Johnny W. Lott, *A Problem Solving Approach to Mathematics for Elementary School Teachers* (Reading MA: Addison-Wesley Longman, 1993), pp. 5–36.

[5]Adapted from Ellen Freedman (March 1997). Test Your Math Anxiety [online]. Available: http://fc.whyy.org/CCC/alg1/anxtest.htm (March 1998).

[6]Ellen Freedman (March 1997). Ten Ways to Reduce Math Anxiety [online]. Available: http://fc.whyy.org/CCC/alg1/reduce.htm (March 1998).

[7]Adapted from Kathy Acker (March 1997). Math Anxiety Code of Responsibilities [online]. Available: http://fc.whyy.org/CCC/alg1/code.htm (March 1998).

[8]Sheila Tobias, *Overcoming Math Anxiety* (New York: W. W. Norton & Company, 1993), pp. 226–227.

BIBLIOGRAPHY

There is certainly more to know about the subjects in this book than we can present here. Following are some additional resources you may want to consult. Both the subject areas and the author names are listed in alphabetical order. Some of these subject areas, such as writing and time management, are covered in the text. Other subject areas, such as financial aid and stress management, are not covered but often play crucial roles on your path toward study success.

COLLEGE SURVIVAL

Baker, Sunny, and Kim Baker. *College After 30: It's Never Too Late to Get the Degree You Need!* Holbrook, MA: Bob Adams, Inc., 1992.

Jeffers, Susan, Ph.D. *Feel the Fear and Do It Anyway.* New York: Fawcett Columbine, 1987.

Shields, Charles J. *Back in School: A Guide for Adult Learners.* Hawthorne, NJ: Career Press, 1994.

Weinberg, Carol. *The Complete Handbook for College Women: Making the Most of Your College Experience.* New York: New York University Press, 1994.

CRITICAL THINKING

Noon, Donald J., Ph.D. *Creative Problem Solving.* New York: Barron's, 1993.

von Oech, Roger. *A Whack on the Side of the Head.* New York: Warner Books, 1992.

von Oech, Roger. *A Kick in the Seat of the Pants.* New York: Harper & Row Publishers, 1986.

ENGLISH AS A SECOND LANGUAGE

Blosser, Betsy J. *Living in English: Basic Skills for the Adult Learner.* Lincolnwood, IL: National Textbook Co., 1989.

Hornby, A.A., and C.A. Ruse. *Oxford ESL Dictionary for Students of American English.* New York: Oxford University Press, 1986.

FINANCIAL AID

ARCO. *College Scholarships and Financial Aid,* with ARCO's Scholarship Search Software. New York: Simon & Schuster, 1995.

Beckham, Barry, ed. *The Black Student's Guide to Scholarships: 600 Private Money Sources for Black and Minority Students,* 4th ed. Lanham, MD: Madison Books, 1996.

Black, Richard. *The Complete Family Guide to College Financial Aid.* New York: The Berkley Publishing Group, 1995.

Cassidy, Daniel J. *The Scholarship Book: The Complete Guide to Private-Sector Scholarships, Grants, and Loans for Undergraduates,* 5th ed. Englewood Cliffs, NJ: Prentice Hall, 1996.

McKee, Cynthia Ruiz, and Phillip C. McKee, Jr. *Cash for College: The Ultimate Guide to College Scholarships.* New York: Hearst Books, 1994.

Oldman, Mark, and Samer Hamadek. *The Princeton Review Student Advantage Guide to America's Top Scholarships.* New York: Random House, 1996.

LEARNING AND WORKING STYLES

Barger, Nancy J., Linda K. Kirby, and Jean M. Kummerow. *Work Types: Understand Your Work Personality—How It Helps You and Holds You Back, and What You Can Do to Understand It.* New York: Warner Books, 1997.

Gardner, Howard. *Multiple Intelligences: The Theory in Practice.* New York: HarperCollins Publishers, Inc., 1993.

LISTENING

Robbins, Harvey A. *How to Speak and Listen Effectively.* New York: AMACOM, 1992.

MATH

Hart, Lynn, and Deborah Najee-Ullich. *Studying for Mathematics.* New York: HarperCollins College Publishers, 1995.
Lerner, Marcia. *Math Smart: Essential Math for These Numeric Times.* New York: Villard Books, 1995.
Tobias, Sheila. *Overcoming Math Anxiety.* New York: W.W. Norton & Company, 1993.

MEMORY

Lorayne, Harry. *Super Memory—Super Student: How to Raise Your Grades in 30 Days.* Boston: Little, Brown & Company, 1990.

READING AND STUDYING

Armstrong, William H., and M. Willard Lampe II. *Barron's Pocket Guide to Study Tips: How to Study Effectively and Get Better Grades.* New York: Barron's Educational Series, 1990.
Frank, Steven. *The Everything Study Book.* Holbrook, MA: The Adams Media Corp., 1996.
Silver, Theodore, M.D., J.D. *The Princeton Review Study Smart: Hands-on, Nuts and Bolts Techniques for Earning Higher Grades.* New York: Villard Books, 1996.

SELF-IMPROVEMENT

Covey, Stephen. *The Seven Habits of Highly Effective People.* New York: Simon & Schuster, 1989.

STRESS MANAGEMENT

Boenisch, Ed, Ph.D., and C. Michele Haney, Ph.D. *The Stress Owner's Manual: Meaning, Balance, and Health in Your Life.* San Luis Obispo, CA: Impact Publishers, 1996.
McMahon, Susanna, Ph.D. *The Portable Problem Solver: Coping With Life's Stressors.* New York: Dell Publishing, 1996.
Radcliffe, Rebecca Ruggles. *Dance Naked in Your Living Room: Handling Stress and Finding Joy!* Minneapolis, MN: EASE, 1997.

TEST TAKING

Browning, William G., Ph.D. *Cliffs Memory Power for Exams.* Lincoln, NE: Cliffs Notes Inc., 1983.
Fry, Ron. *"Ace" Any Test,* 3rd ed. Franklin Lakes, NJ: Career Press, 1996.

TIME MANAGEMENT

Fry, Ron. *Managing Your Time,* 2nd ed. Hawthorne, NJ: Career Press, 1994.
McGee-Cooper, Ann, with Duane Trammell. *Time Management for Unmanageable People.* New York: Bantam Books, 1994.
Timm, Paul R., Ph.D. *Successful Self-Management: A Psychologically Sound Approach to Personal Effectiveness.* Los Altos, CA: Crisp Publications, Inc., 1987.

WRITING

Andersen, Richard. *Powerful Writing Skills.* Hawthorne, NJ: Career Press, 1994.
Delton, Judy. *The 29 Most Common Writing Mistakes (And How to Avoid Them).* Cincinnati, OH: Writer's Digest Books, 1985.
Friedman, Bonnie. *Writing Past Dark: Envy, Fear, Distractions, and Other Dilemmas in the Writer's Life.* New York: HarperCollins, 1993.
Frueling, Rosemary and N.B. Oldham. *Write to the Point! Letters, Memos, and Reports That Get Results.* New York: McGraw-Hill, 1988.

Gibaldi, Joseph. *MLA Handbook for Writers of Research Papers,* 4th ed. New York: The Modern Language Association of America, 1995.

Goldberg, Natalie. *Writing Down the Bones: Freeing the Writer Within.* Boston: Shambhala, 1986.

Markman, Peter T., and Markman, Roberta H., Ph.D. *10 Steps in Writing the Research Paper,* 5th ed. New York: Barron's Educational Series, 1994.

Staff of the Research and Education Association. *REA's Handbook of English Grammar, Style, and Writing.* Piscataway, NJ: Research and Education Association, 1995.

Strunk, William Jr., and E.B. White. *The Elements of Style.* New York: Macmillan, 1979.

Troyka, Lynn Quitman. *Handbook for Writers,* 2nd ed. Englewood Cliffs: Prentice Hall, 1990.

INDEX